The Modern Language Teacher's Handbook
Revised Edition

Alan Smalley
Principal Lecturer in French, Leeds Polytechnic

David Morris
Advisory Division, Leeds Education Authority

Stanley Thornes (Publishers) Ltd

First published in 1985 by Hutchinson Educational as The MLA Modern Language Teacher's Handbook
ISBN 0-09-161-220-9

Revised edition first published in 1992 by:
Stanley Thornes (Publishers) Ltd
Ellenborough House
Wellington Street
CHELTENHAM GL50 1YW
England

96 97 98 99 00 / 10 9 8 7 6 5 4

British Library Cataloguing in Publication Data
Smalley, Alan
    The modern language teacher's handbook.
    – Revised ed.
    I. Title   II. Morris, David
    407

    ISBN 0-7487-1247-X

Typeset by Northern Phototypesetting Co. Ltd
Printed and bound in Great Britain

Contents

PART TWO: Running a modern language department

PART THREE: Beyond the school

PART FOUR: Reference section

Introduction

The first edition of this book appeared in 1985 and immediately sold very well so that, within a fairly short time, it had become out of print. The question of producing a reprint was considered but in the meantime there had been such rapid strides made in modern language teaching that it was decided to produce a new edition, completely rewritten, in order to offer a really up-to-date reference work for all users of the book.

As a result, we can say that this new edition takes into account the GCSE examinations which rely on a communicative syllabus and, in addition, it reflects the spirit and the letter of the National Curriculum which will have great influence on the teaching of modern and community languages for many years to come.

With those two major influences in mind, we have taken what we believe to be the best of the first edition and blended it with what is of greatest importance in the National Curriculum and GCSE syllabuses of the different examination bodies.

Also, in the past few years, there has been an influx of new technologies into the classroom – computers, satellite TV and the like. Teaching approaches have responded to these innovations as well as to new ideas on the way languages are learnt. In particular, there is a new emphasis on pupil-centred learning, on autonomy and on the world outside the classroom.

We consider that we have produced a work which will have a wide-ranging appeal with important issues for students in training, for probationary teachers and for the experienced head of department whose responsibility it is to see that the majority of the recommendations in this book are effectively carried out in his or her department.

The first edition was described as 'an indispensable reference book' (*BALT Journal*, October 1986) and we have every intention that this new edition should be viewed similarly. We have tried to avoid anything that will date rapidly and included instead ideas which will be adapted easily as times change. One major innovation is the inclusion of sections of classroom ideas based on topics and skills that are to be exploited in the new National Curriculum. These sections are based on many years of practical classroom experience and are ideas which really work.

A reference book it will remain, to be browsed through or turned to for a quick idea to use with a difficult class. It advances no single theory of language teaching but seeks to reflect the general trend, as teachers approach and implement the National Curriculum. It holds no brief for any particular language but it does seek to lay down general principles as they may affect all the 19 languages recognised by the National Curriculum. With these points in mind we hope that all who make use of this book will benefit from the increased confidence and competence it is intended to foster.

PART ONE

Survival in the classroom

1 First days in school

The first few days in a new school are well known to be difficult ones for any teacher. For the new and inexperienced teacher they can be particularly traumatic, and though the purpose of this book is to help *all* teachers of modern languages, this opening section is particularly relevant for new entrants to the profession.

Of course, if they are joining a well-run school, the first morning of the new term will certainly not be the first time they have visited the school; but unfortunately this can happen, as more and more local education authorities and individual schools are reduced to making temporary appointments at short notice.

We hope that the suggestions made in this book will equip all teachers of modern languages to face the challenges of the profession and to tackle the problems which, in the nature of things, confront every teacher from time to time. If the obvious is stated, it is important to remember that it may not be obvious to the less experienced. If the seemingly impossible is counselled, we ask that it should not be condemned without trial.

This book is equally concerned with the new (and experienced) head of department who faces unprecedented challenges as schools approach the turn of the century. It offers advice therefore to the head of department and to those who aspire in their career to take on such responsibility. Readers will find in the pages which follow advice of many kinds, all of which is based on real situations observed in schools over many years.

To all new staff: school policy in general

School policy which transcends any single department needs to be clearly known from the start. It is useful to go to the school with a checklist to ensure that all the main points are covered, namely:

- School hours
- Dates of terms
- Dates of examinations for all years of pupils
- Important deadlines in the school year
- Dates of parents' evenings for various year groups
- Dates for completion of reports
- Basic facts about the school – size, pupil intake, pupil background, etc.

New staff need to get to know the colleagues they will be working with as soon as possible. Not only *who*, but who does *what* has to be found out at once.

Figure 1: Challenges facing the new teacher

- ☐ What is the role of the deputy heads, the year tutors, the form tutors?
- ☐ How is contact made with parents?
- ☐ What steps have to be taken to ensure that personal details are known in the school and the LEA in order to ensure payment of salary?
- ☐ For many teachers and for all new heads of department finance is an important issue. How is money allocated to and within the department? What amounts are available to be spent in the current year? Is there any contingency fund for emergencies?
- ☐ Examination policy is crucial to the effective running of the school. Which examination board and, more importantly, which syllabuses are used? Is it possible to enter pupils for examinations run by other boards?
- ☐ Equipment, especially audio-visual equipment, is precious. What is the school's attitude to such equipment? Is it owned by departments or are certain items owned in common?
- ☐ Governing bodies are now more significant. What is the attitude of the governors to particular subjects and to particular teaching methods? Who are the teacher representatives? Where are the reports of the meetings they have attended?
- ☐ Who is the staff tutor? What help can they give to help the settling-in period and also, just as importantly, to help new teachers build up their careers?

All the above are matters of vital concern to any new member of staff taking up a post in a school. Many other vital and arguably more immediate questions are dealt with next.

The school and the department _____

As new arrivals approach the department, they should refer again to the checklist. It is safe to assume in most schools that the department works as a team with a common policy to govern its working methods. An approach to this ideal is the main theme of Part Two of this book. In a modern comprehensive school the structure of the courses and examinations is so complex that there can be little scope for individuals who prefer to do things their own way. An agreed policy is understood which individuals have had a share in forming.

Agreed working methods and a common philosophy usually arise from discussion at departmental meetings. This will certainly be so with regard to acceptance of methods and materials within the department. On the other hand, any matter bringing languages into contact with other subject areas will probably have been decided by an academic board, senior management team or council of heads of departments.

5

On first entering the school, however, teachers will be more concerned with *what* than *how* and we suggest the following checklist will be helpful:

☐ *Marking* Is there a departmental policy both as regards the system of grading (marks out of 10 or 20 or A to E or a range of comments) and an agreed method of correction? Do pupils always do corrections after a written exercise and, most importantly, are they checked?

☐ *Assessment* How are term/formative marks processed and stored? Do all term marks count towards a termly grade and how do formative assessments relate to the summative document? Is there any system of end of topic or unit assessment? Are all results communicated in detail to pupils and to parents?

☐ *Syllabus* Has a full copy of the departmental handbook and syllabus been handed on? Does it cover all aspects of the work in modern languages? Part Two of this book suggests what should be in the document.

☐ *Departmental stock* Content and location of textbooks, visual aids, tapes, worksheets, projectors, computer software, OHP slides, duplicating facilities, photocopiers etc. Is there a staff reference section containing the latest books on teaching aims and methods, publishers' catalogues, specimen copies, details of INSET courses, sets of past examination papers.

☐ *Departmental systems* Central records of pupils' progress, loans recording system, procedure for recording breakages and malfunction of departmental equipment and, very important, a petty cash account to cover minor replacements urgently required, for example, the projector lamp, replacement cassettes, one or two extra course books. Do all or any of these exist?

☐ *Language policy* Which pupils take which language? Who decides which language? Do pupils choose? If not what selection procedure is used for allocating pupils to the different languages offered? Of special concern to the new head of department should be the question of whether there are any members of the department whose skills are underused or ineffectively deployed. How many teachers are teaching French when their first language is German or Russian? In future could this expertise be more effectively deployed?

☐ *Public examinations* How are pupils selected for the different public examinations on offer? Are graded tests used in school? Who is responsible for the coordination of graded tests? Which members of staff have public examination experience? Who serves on examination boards? What about examination results? How do they compare with other subjects in the school? What reasons can explain any discrepancies? Staff changes? Changes of policy?

☐ *Cooperation* What examples are there of cooperation from department to department? A European Dimension involving history, geography and environmental studies? What is the liaison between the school and the feeder schools?

☐ *Overseas links* Are correspondence, visits and exchanges actively encouraged by the department? Who is responsible for such activities and how are they organised? How are pupils selected to take part in foreign visits? Is there any financial help available for children from underprivileged homes? Is there a thriving town-twinning scheme? How is it exploited? Is the school directly linked to a named school abroad?

☐ *Out-of-school activities*   Is there a language club? Is there any possibility of showing foreign films? Are parents able to join in with events concerned with languages and visits abroad? Is there any involvement in language festivals or competitions?

☐ *Support for staff*   Does the LEA employ an adviser whose specific brief is to foster language development within the authority? Do they visit the school and when can they be seen? Does the teachers' centre provide support for teachers of modern languages? If so, what?

The points to watch for, listed above, are those which any conscientious members of staff will almost automatically include in a survey of their new school. Indeed, for many new staff, they are points which will have been considered seriously before accepting the post. All the more reason for listing them here, for they may serve as useful points of reference for the teacher at present on the interview circuit. With all these points in mind no applicant need be stumped by that final interview question 'And now do you have any questions you wish to ask *us*?'

The probationary teacher _____

For the probationary teacher, the first few days in school may be even more exacting than they are for the experienced colleague simply moving into a new post. For this reason we pass on this advice to the beginner:

1   It is important to take the first available opportunity to talk with the member of staff who last taught the groups which the new teacher has this year. If the former teacher has left, an attempt should be made to contact that teacher at the end of the previous term, or to try to talk with someone who had a group more or less similar last year. (If they have *all* left, maybe this is the wrong job!) In such a conversation it is wise for beginners to establish in their mind what the general spirit of the group is. Is there an obvious leader? How is he or she best dealt with? One should listen carefully to opinion and keep in mind at all times that it *is* opinion being received and that everyone is biased in their attitudes occasionally. At the same time, in this discussion careful note should be taken as to where the pupils and the class are, in progressing through the programmes of study. It will probably mean starting a little before where they are, so as to revise and build up a new confidence with the new teacher.

2   The technique of keeping one ear open in the staffroom for remarks made by colleagues on pupils who are in your groups is a skill to be acquired. Much useful information can be gleaned in this way, though it is wise to learn to

distinguish staffroom information from staffroom gossip. There is doubtless in the school a formal way of passing on information about pupils and their families. General information about background, home conditions and school history may become part of school folklore which someone forgets to pass on to new arrivals. In the early days it is worthwhile formalising this knowledge by asking the year tutor or form tutor whether there is any information a teacher should have about particular pupils. In the post-Warnock era this becomes increasingly important, for it is a reminder that one child in five will need remedial or special education at some time in their school career. Special help will not always mean that the child is 'statemented' (though the new teacher will be well advised to read carefully the contents of any 'statement'). Special help may also be needed for the gifted child. However, teachers should beware of letting any negative comments prevent them from giving any child a fair chance.

3 In the first few days, the head of modern languages is bound to be the one the new teacher seeks to turn to most frequently for guidance. Any beginner will be wise to take every opportunity of talking to the head of department. It is through the HoD that a teacher will become aware of the aims of the department and precise help will be forthcoming about how to define one's objectives and how to go about achieving them. It is important in this respect to obtain a personal copy of the departmental handbook and scheme of work (see pp. 199–214). It should also be borne in mind that heads of department need to get to know the staff and that, only through contact with a colleague, can they decide the strengths of the newcomers and how best to deploy them in the department. Finally, the head of department is the person most likely to pass on to the head teacher impressions that are made in the early days. In a large school, with all the goodwill in the world, the head has to be dependent on what the heads of department pass on.

4 'Qui se ressemble s'assemble' says the French proverb and its truth is often demonstrated in the staffroom. It is quite remarkable (but perhaps natural) how teachers from the same department join together at break times to discuss progress and exchange ideas for putting across particular teaching points. The new teacher benefits enormously from this kind of contact which may lay the foundations for professional friendships destined to last for many years.

5 In every school one member of staff is designated to look after the interests and the progress of the probationary teachers – someone they have confidence in, we hope. It is important that they establish early contact with this colleague for he or she will want to know about work in progress fairly regularly and will expect to see a lesson taught on a regular basis. The more the beginner feels at ease with this colleague, the better they will perform on such occasions.

6   It goes without saying that lesson preparation is the most vital of all tasks in the early days. It may be galling to see an experienced teacher dashing off to a class without any *obvious* evidence of preparation but it is easy to be deceived. Certainly as one's skills as a teacher improve, preparation time becomes shorter and what is prepared for one year may, with minor adaptations, be perfectly adequate for the next year. For the beginner there is no such possibility. Every lesson is *ab initio* and much time has to be devoted to the making of materials as well as the actual planning of the lessons. Much sound advice will come from more experienced colleagues and it is well worth the beginner indicating to them what their future plans are. Some will lend apparatus, others will pass on worksheets, all will give advice. Lesson planning is dealt with in detail in Chapter 3.

7   It will pay to be fully familiar with the school routine as soon as possible. The best advice which can be given is to make notes and, if in doubt, to ask a colleague rather than a pupil who will consider the beginner a 'real wally' if he or she does not know what time the lesson ends or if it is 'homework night'.

8   A good knowledge of the geography of the campus is vital to efficient operation. It pays to have a good walk around in the early days to learn not only the locations of classrooms and subject areas but also, for example, the areas allocated for breaktimes to various year groups.

9   Other areas to become familiar with early in the new teacher's career are the library (What system of loans is there? Who is the librarian? Is it possible to borrow books for class use?), the technician's room (Does he or she maintain equipment for the modern language department?), the staff rooms (Which is for quiet work and which for conversation?) and the school office (make a friend of the school secretary).

10 The modern photocopier seemed like the final solution to so many teachers' problems but they quickly learnt that the copyright law prevents most copying of other people's work. It may seem a boon for producing multiple copies of original work but it must not be used to copy others' literary, dramatic, musical or artistic productions. It is important to remember that these four words are interpreted very broadly and may include tables, lists, even football results. The message is simple: **no appliance can be used for making unlicensed multiple copies** and any teacher who does runs the risk of severe penalty. Of course if permission is obtained or copies made under the regulations of the Copyright Licensing Agency, then that is another story. Note that some foreign news magazine publishers have given permission for multiple copying for class use. A list of the French publishers who have granted this right can be obtained from the Attaché Culturel of the French Embassy (see 'Organisations useful to the language teacher' in Part Four).

11   The early days in the classroom are crucial for establishing a good working relationship with pupils. To start with, the teacher should avoid seeking to prove that he or she is a great teacher. Friendliness is all very well, but it can be mistaken for weakness. Instead, beginners need to seek to establish a good reputation for sound work, energy, activity and encouragement to do well. Any experienced teacher will confirm that it is easier to move from a firm position to a more relaxed one. It is almost impossible to move the other way.

12   When meeting new pupils for the first time, it is a good idea to take a while in the first lesson to explain the methods the teacher intends to adopt for the group. Consult the head of department to see if the following points are covered in departmental policy. (If they are, then expect pupils to conform for it is unwise to introduce a totally different system and so cause confusion and perhaps even discipline problems as pupils seek to challenge the new authority.)

   a) Details of homework: when and where to hand in; incidence, quantity and type.
   b) Oral work: how it will be conducted; what is the purpose and the importance of always trying to say something.
   c) Written work: guidance on setting out headings, dates, etc. Perhaps each pupil can be given a model sheet to help with this.
   d) Group work: rules for moving into groups to facilitate this kind of learning.
   e) Expected standards of behaviour towards other pupils and the teacher.

   If pupils are given clear guidelines in these and other matters, it is easier to get their cooperation and provide a positive learning experience.

13   Some teachers like to give all pupils a name from the language they teach. The idea of giving French, German, or Spanish names certainly appeals to younger pupils, but it is doubtful whether it will make much of an impression with anyone above year 9; it is probably best to put up with whatever name the pupils are blessed with in real life.

   Learning names at the start is always a problem and until the teacher knows all the names he or she is not really in charge. Pupils resent the teacher who does not quickly learn to recognise every individual and they are right. Until one can put a name to every individual in the class, it can hardly be said that there is personal contact. Any methods which speed up the process are to be welcomed. Two easy ways are: a) have an individual seating plan and a pre-ordained place for everyone until such time as the names are known; or b) have a name card for display, as they do at international conferences, in front of each member of the class.

   The final reason for learning names quickly is that it enables the teacher to cut out masses of useless English verbiage when trying to identify 'the girl with the fair hair at the back, no, the one next to the boy in the blue pullover who's looking out of the window'.

14　It is vital to establish a reputation for being in the classroom on time to ensure a prompt start to the lesson. In many schools a lesson lasts 40 minutes and 5 minutes late each time soon hinders progress. When pupils arrive late it is essential to establish why. A common reason given involves playing one member of staff against another. If Mr X is blamed for finishing the previous lesson late it will be wise to check and let him know what the pupils are saying. If they are right, an enquiry will help. Occasionally a small group may arrive late from a far-flung annex. It is still important to check the story even if it involves timing movement. Punctuality also means returning work on time. If a promise is made that 'I'll return this work on Monday', every effort should be made to do so. The motto should be 'Make deadlines that can be kept'!

With the above points in mind, the teacher should be able to enter the classroom with confidence and, most importantly, feel that he or she has the confidence of the class. With mutual confidence real work can begin. Without it, little will be achieved.

The student on school practice _____

The school practice usually falls into two sections: the preliminary visit and the practice proper, which is either 'block' or 'serial'.

The preliminary visit

First impressions count on both sides. Students should make every effort to present themselves in as favourable a way as possible, neatly dressed and well equipped. In return he or she should be able to expect a courteous reception from the school staff who, knowing in advance of the visit, are able to find time to talk about the school, the classes and the materials available.

At this stage the most discouraging thing for the student is to hear the regular teacher say 'Do anything you want', since it implies that the student's contribution will have a negligible effect anyway. Much more helpful is for teachers to take the student into their confidence, explain what they are hoping to achieve over the next month and imply that the student will be required to make a valuable contribution to this programme. This does not restrict the students' scope. On the contrary it enables them to concentrate on specific and important aims and, within these, there is freedom to use methods recommended by both college and school advisers. Another unhelpful comment sometimes heard by students is 'Why on earth do you want to come into this profession?'. However much that may echo some staff's opinions, it has no place in conversations with trainee teachers unless it is to lead in to a genuine discussion on motivation and rewards.

On the first visit the student can reasonably expect to acquire the following information:

- Classes to be taught (with names of pupils and regular staff)
- Timetable with rooms
- Copy of relevant syllabus
- Precise details of present class work
- Precise details of where the student will take over
- Copies of all necessary text books
- List of materials and apparatus he or she can use.

Full details of the administration of this and other points is given in chapter 15.

The practice

For the first few days of a block practice the student should come to school with the intention of getting to know the future classes as well as possible by observing the regular teacher and the way he/she works with the children. This is not to say that the student will copy slavishly all that the regular teacher does, but it does mean that to be properly prepared he or she needs to be fully aware of how the class is used to working, since too many changes cause distractions, even upset, and complicate the period of settling in that all students have to go through.

Observation

This does not mean sitting at the back doing nothing. The student should be equipped with a substantial notebook and should be making structured notes on what is observed to be going on. At this stage the notes should be factual and not critical and they should cover matters such as the following:

- Teacher's method of starting the lesson
- Teacher's attitude to latecomers
- Use of foreign language for administration/classroom management
- Teacher's attitude to pronunciation accuracy
- Teacher's attitude to pupil error – method of correction
- Use of praise and reward (what sort?)
- Teacher's sympathy with class – warmth and friendliness
- Attitudes of pupils to teacher – polite, aggressive, truculent?
- Clarity of teacher's explanations – nonverbal clues
- Use of materials – how varied, confidence in use
- Activities – how varied?
- Teacher's handling of behaviour problems
- Extent of involvement of whole group
- Extent to which pupils volunteer answers
- Extent to which teacher appears to achieve the aims of the lesson
- Sense of achievement and enjoyment amongst pupils
- Content of lesson – vocabulary, structures etc.
- General comments on class age, experience etc.

With such a list, students will appreciate that there is much to be done before they begin their own teaching.

Teaching

There is little chance, other than in infants' schools, that the class will be naïve enough to think that they have just acquired a new, fully-qualified teacher. Whilst they are not likely to enquire about the class of your degree, nor ask for your views on the editorial in last week's *TES*, they know a student when they see one. Nevertheless, it pays to preserve some element of mystery, so students should introduce themselves, if the class teacher has not done so, and say what will be done with the class 'over the next few weeks' (avoid being too definite about when the practice ends). Students should not put up with inquisitive questions about their background but should get straight down to work (see notes for the probationary teacher pp. 7–11).

Classroom visitors

A number of people have the right and the duty to see a student teaching. In addition to the college supervisor, there is the teacher whose class is being taught, the head of department, the teacher in school with overall responsibility for students and the head. Consequently, the sooner the student gets used to the presence of visitors in the room, the more smoothly lessons will run. The following points should be noted:

1   It is a mistake to have a 'dress rehearsal' with the class for an expected visitor unless it is the same lesson with a different group of children.

2   When the visitor arrives, it is important for the student to indicate who is in charge, and it should be made clear by showing the new arrival to a seat and then continuing with the lesson.

3   Some visitors like to be involved in the lesson, other wish to fade into the background. Students should keep an eye open for the species attracted and play the game accordingly. Those who like to be involved usually prefer to play the part of a pupil and not to engage in a conversation on pedagogical techniques.

4   Visitors usually want to see lesson notes, not just to ensure that they exist but to get an idea of the student's aim in order to estimate its success. No great fuss need be made. As students go around the room they should simply hand over the notes as they pass by.

5   If anything goes wrong, it is important to continue as anyone would whether there was a visitor or not. Ability to cope with the unexpected is part of the teacher's overall competence. This does not mean that one should ignore a pupil bleeding to death. It means dealing promptly and efficiently with the incident, even sending for assistance if necessary, and then getting back to the lesson as quickly as possible.

6   After the visit comes the post mortem. The visitor may be unfamiliar with particular school problems and in this case the situation should be made clear. Or again the visitor may be a nonlinguist and unclear as to what the student hoped to achieve. Here also an explanation is called for. The discussion afterwards can be the most valuable part of the process and there is no need to feel obliged to defend everything done. There will have been mistakes. All learners make them, and throughout teachers' careers they will continue to receive criticism of one sort or another. All the better to learn to take it gracefully. Finally, it should be noted that any such discussion is best carried on away from the classroom and even away from other colleagues.

The end of the practice

This usually means that *the student* can go away having made mistakes – and the school can forget them. *The student*, however, should not forget; after carefully looking over classroom notes and comments on the lesson, decide what has been learnt and determine to apply the lessons on the next practice.

What follows in the the rest of this book will at least ensure that the probationary teacher is alerted to the demands of his or her chosen career.

2   Class organisation

Effective teaching begins when the teacher has 'got things organised'. Generations of pupils have recognised this simple fact. Precisely what organisation is, will depend on many factors, some of them constants, some variables as the following table illustrates:

Table 1: Factors affecting class organisation

Constants	Variables
Class size	Time of lesson
Age group	Location of lesson
Ability range	Mood of class
Aims	Teacher energy
Teacher preferences	Specific activity
	Materials available

With all the above factors in mind, teachers have to plan to organise a series of activities which together will enable them to achieve their ultimate aim. Obviously some activities will suit the constants and the variables better than others. Some variables, with experience, will become semi-variables i.e. the teacher can predict with some certainty what the mood of the class will be when a lesson occurs at a particular time or in a particular room or after any other lesson. Taking all these factors into consideration the teacher then has to ensure that appropriate programmes are offered. Such programmes may be broadly grouped under the following headings:

1   Oral work
2   Reading
3   Listening
4   Written work
5   Class work/group work.

Oral work

Ideally, the use of the foreign language should dominate all activities in the modern language classroom. Understandably, some teachers doubt the possibility of using the target language as the means of teaching a foreign language – yet countless teachers are quite convinced and in fact do it as a matter of course. In some respects it is a matter of confidence, not so much in one's ability to speak the language, but rather in the belief that pupils will understand and benefit. If it is started at the very first lesson and is practised sympathetically and systematically, it can be done successfully. There are various devices which can be used to reinforce understanding:

● using copious repetition, substitutions and synonyms
● using mime and gesture to reinforce what is said (nonverbal clues)
● giving a short list of classroom expressions for pupils to refer to in the early stages
● giving pupils plenty of opportunity to use the language rather than just hearing it
● copious encouragement
● writing on the blackboard or OHP to reinforce the spoken word
● being predictable, especially in the early stages, about the language used
● using explanations where difficult words are encountered (even in English)
● using pictorial aids e.g. pin men drawings on blackboard.

However, teachers must be aware that this way of learning a language is a slow business, an incremental process which does not guarantee pupil response in the language very quickly. They must be patient and expect pupil silence in the early stages.

The sooner the classroom routine is conducted in the foreign language, the more effective will all lessons become. In other words, one of the teacher's main aims will be to use the language for classroom instruction. It must be remembered also that when teachers give an instruction in the language, they are not necessarily calling for a verbal response. This helps and it is also good to remember that teachers can

15

reinforce with nonverbal clues. Thus '*Veux-tu bien ouvrir la fenêtre s'il te plaît*' accompanied by a gesture implying 'too hot', followed by a simple mime of opening a window, is often sufficient. Communication has begun and the pupil is already realising that communication in French is about real things.

At times, in the early stages it may be necessary for a teacher to clarify a situation once and for all. 'When you hear me say: "*Levez le doigt avant de répondre*", what am I asking?' (with appropriate gesture) will usually result in immediate clarification and the phrase has become part of the pupils' passive vocabulary, the exact meaning of each word dawning little by little as knowledge of the language increases.

But the aim of oral work is to help the learner move from the receptive to the productive skills and so, when such phrases as above are used as classroom commands, the skilful teacher quickly devises ways of ensuring that they are used both by the class in chorus and by individuals. A useful way of doing this is to allow individuals in the class to take the teacher's part and to have opportunities for group work (see below).

There will be a time, as acquisition moves on from listening to production, when teachers notice a silent period when pupils are not too willing to take part. It may be frustrating for the teacher and call for patience and understanding, but it is a frequently observed stage in the learning cycle. Frequent, structured opportunities to hear will pay off in the end. 'Comprehension precedes production' is a truism teachers sometimes forget. It is also true that the willingness to speak is influenced by affective factors within pupils and the giving of confidence is a vital part of the teacher's methods.

Correction of oral work

It is striking how very much more tolerant the native speaker is of errors made by foreigners trying to express themselves. Perhaps the image of the Englishman trying to say something which makes sense in a foreign tongue is similar to Dr Johnson's dog which walked on its hind legs (the wonder being not that it did it well, but that it did it at all!) But this cannot be the true explanation since English mother-tongue speakers are equally kind to foreign speakers of English. What we are probably saying is that the amateur linguist shows more common sense than generations of teachers have shown when they over-react to error in the spoken language. The effect is obvious: people who are afraid of being jumped on as soon as they open their mouths tend to want to keep their mouths tight shut.

All this is not to say that teachers should not correct error when they hear it, but that they should apply common sense. They should let the speaker finish what he has begun and, as in real life, prompt gently if necessary, in order to help the conversation along. Having taken in what the speaker is saying the teacher concludes by saying 'Yes, what you mean is ...' Then the pupil is given a model and can repeat it.

In the early stages of language learning pupils need to be aware of two grades of language error.

1   The incomprehensible, where the error is linguistic and maybe so gross that the listener cannot even fathom what the speaker is trying to say. This *structural* error may be the focus for correction which can be achieved by repeating a correct form in the same way as when correcting offspring: 'Daddy, I *goed* to the park last night.' 'Oh you went to the park?' It may call for explanations on the blackboard, the stopping of the flow of the lesson to provide feedback and so on.

2   The comprehensible but communicatively inaccurate error. In this case the focus is on meaning and the teacher may have to accept answers he or she did not expect, but which are linguistically correct. Here the tolerance of the teacher is important.

It may also be the case in a communicative activity, where the flow of the utterance is of utmost importance, that the teacher does not correct at all. To many, this might conflict with the traditional role of pedagogy where there has been an insistence on 100 per cent accuracy, but it is something the teacher must come to terms with in a communicative classroom. Unnoticed and uncorrected errors are an inevitable price to pay for more intensive personal involvement of pupils in group/pair work but it is not too high a price to pay if it unlocks tongues.

The explanation for the traditional schoolteacher's demand for accuracy lies in the nature of language itself. Of all school subjects, only language is set before pupils with perfection as an attainable goal. The native speaker is the criterion against which all performances are measured. On the other hand, historians do not say 'This 15-year-old's essay is not as good as the one A J P Taylor might have written on the same subject', and it is assessed accordingly. The wise (and successful) teacher takes a similar attitude to oral performance. Lots of encouragement, tolerance of some error and gentle correction when necessary, seen if at all possible through the eyes of the sympathetic native speaker.

> As a general rule in the early stages:
>
> The class should **say** only what they have **heard**
> The class should **read** only what they have **said**
> The class should **write** only what they have **read**
>
> **Hear** *before* **say** before **read** before **write**.

If the rule above is applied, it follows that pupils will be asked to say what they have heard either from the teacher, the assistant or a recording. It makes sense to give pupils practice in saying what they hear before asking them to recast material in order to answer questions.

Another rule of thumb in the early stages is:

Present   Clarify   Repeat   Exploit

Presentation of the new material orally, using visual aids, mime, gesture, video etc. At this stage it is a good idea for the teacher to warn the class that the material is new, and to give them something specific to watch out for. 'Listen carefully and at the end tell me who arrives, who comes late, what does he bring and why does Frau X tell him to go away?'

This kind of approach ensures listening to some purpose and stresses that the very first reason for learning a language is to acquire information. With a more advanced or high ability class, the introduction can be presented in the language. For weaker groups, it makes much more sense to do it in English at first.

Clarification   Here the teacher's skill is fully tested. The aim is to ensure that all the class comes to understand what they have been listening to. As far as possible (bearing in mind the constants and the variables) this section is implemented in the language but with recourse to English when necessary. Overuse of the foreign language at this stage may *mystify* when teachers are seeking to *clarify*. If it does have this effect it will exasperate and may be counterproductive. Far better to use a little English and be certain that everyone is with the teacher. Gradually over the year, the teacher's professionalism will wean the class from too much English.

It is at this stage that some teachers will feel that vocabulary notes should appear on the board or on the overhead projector. In many ways this is good planning and helps to reinforce the learning of new words and phrases. However, it seems sensible at this stage to keep the writing as merely a reading exercise since the fuss and commotion caused by switching to writing in order to copy down vocabulary becomes a major distraction from oral work. It is better to keep the copying for the final section: *Exploitation*.

Another useful idea is to imitate good practice in a primary school classroom. As the basic linguistic skills are being mastered, it can be useful to have on the wall a frieze with days of the week, numbers, colours etc., since it helps make a bright atmosphere. The help and support provided by such a display can be gradually withdrawn as the class masters the material, and replaced by more material when the work progresses.

Repetition   Despite the revolution in classroom teaching aids since the 1950s, examiners' reports do not suggest there has been a corresponding improvement in pronunciation. All the more reason for treating this section of the language lesson in a very business-like manner. First, the teacher should analyse the text being studied and isolate a few points of pronunciation that need particular emphasis. To ensure concentration it is helpful to put such phrases on the blackboard or on the

OHP and to spend a few minutes on these. Note that it was a strongly held opinion at one time that placing the written form in front of the pupil to stress the spoken form was simply compounding the difficulty. Now opinion has changed as teachers have come to recognise that from the age of five every single pupil has been trained to depend on the eyes for learning. So there seems little point in blindfolding the pupil in the language class.

In introducing the new vocabulary and structures, the teacher and the assistant are the models. It is vital to enunciate clearly, in order to establish correct vowel and consonant pronunciation. Once correct pronunciation has been established attention can be given to pace and intonation.

In practising the pronunciation of new material the following should be borne in mind.

1   The whole class should practise before any individual is called upon to perform publicly. In this way every pupil has an opportunity to engage in some anonymous practice within the group.

2   The teacher should move around the room all the time since that ensures that every single child has the chance to hear the correct pronunciation from close at hand. (Classroom acoustics may well distort speech from the front just sufficiently to make the language into nonsense.) At the same time the teacher who moves around has a better chance of hearing wrong pronunciations or careless or inattentive attempts at merely humouring the teacher by pretending serious work is going on.

3   When sloppy or inaccurate pronunciation is located it is a mistake to isolate the culprit and make him or her practise in public what has been done inefficiently in private. Such a tactic will simply alienate the pupil(s) in question. It is fair to assume that normally pupils will not deliberately distort what they hear. If what they say is in fact distorted they need to hear it again so the best practice is to make it a class point and practise as a group a few more times.

4   Before going to individuals, it is best to have small group practice and in any class there are plenty of ready-made groups:

    a) all the boys
    b) all the girls
    c) all this row
    d) all the back row.

    Some teachers like to have ready-made teams for all sorts of work:

    a) the Blues, the Reds; or
    b) the Lions, the Tigers; or
    c) les Lyonnais, les Lillois, les Parisiens.

5   To be effective, the pronunciation/repetition section needs to be *brief* and *brisk*. Any longer and concentration will be lost and the lesson killed stone dead. Far better to have two sessions separated by other activities.

6   When the class is practising a long or difficult phrase such as '*Il fait du brouillard*', break it into manageable portions and have them repeat it in *reverse* order, i.e. '*brouillard*', '*du brouillard*', '*fait du brouillard*', '*il fait du brouillard*'. Thus the new sound is repeated first and does not overtax the memory.

7   Lavish praise for good pronunciation does wonders for any pupil's ego. It also impresses the rest of the class that what the teacher is after is not unattainable. If a pupil is very successful at imitating the model, there is no reason why he or she should not become the model for group practice (see p. 36).

8   It is vital to maintain a constant standard of pronunciation from one lesson to another or things will begin to slip. On the other hand, language teachers have to recognise that not every pupil will reach the same standard and with some they have to be satisfied with less than perfection, as are the violin teacher and the games coach.

Exploitation   This section of the lesson makes the biggest demands of all on the teacher's inventiveness, enthusiasm, flexibility and vigilance. The more expert the teacher becomes, the more important this section becomes in the lesson scheme, for it is here more than anywhere else that the teacher's creativity has full rein.

By exploitation we mean providing the class with as many opportunities to *use* the material which, until this point, has been largely a passive acquisition. Pupils move from the receptive to the productive and from the imitative to the creative. This is not to disparage the foregoing stages which are an essential, *pre-communicative* stage of language acquisition. (This is witnessed by the extensive use of imitative language amongst children still in the early stages of mother-tongue learning.) Yet the sudden move on to this section of the lesson does not imply a sudden change in strategy. The skilful teacher still ensures that there is a gradual transition from the *imitative* to the *creative* and that the pupils are helped to the final stage by frequent references back to the stages in which they have already reached a fair degree of competence.

It is worth pointing out the great difference between oral work in language learning and oral work in other areas of the curriculum. In all other subjects the teacher puts questions to the class to find out who knows the answer and what the answer is. To the question 'In what year did Charles VIII of France invade Italy?' there is only one acceptable answer. The answers 1394, 1594 and 1694 are totally wrong. Equally inappropriate would be comments from the pupil such as 'I have no idea', 'Ask my neighbour', or 'I'm not sure'. In the foreign language class, however, the teacher welcomes any response in the language, for the purpose of the question is to provide the pupil with an opportunity to use the language he has acquired. Teachers would do well to stress this difference to their classes since there is no doubt that many pupils faced with questions could say something but hesitate to do so because they imagine the same rules apply in the language class as elsewhere, *i.e. they think the facts matter*. What in effect we are saying is that much of the question and answer work that goes on in the modern language class is the equivalent of the musician's scale practice. Within its limited context it is meaningful, improving agility and confidence – but it is only a step to the performance in the real world.

Summary

1   Pupils must be able to attain as high a degree of linguistic competence as possible.

2   They must be able to use the forms to express a communicative need.

3   They must be helped to use language to communicate personal meanings.

4   They must as far as possible become aware of the social meaning of the language they are learning. This is the creative process.

The pupil will only have the opportunity to develop communicative skills if there is motivation and the opportunity to express his or her own personality. Thus as teachers we need to respect individuals and their attempts to express themselves – however falteringly – in a supportive atmosphere. Teachers should cultivate the opportunity to develop interpersonal skills and relationships. Hence our belief in the value of group work in the language classroom (see pp. 34–42).

As Eric Hawkins says in *Modern Languages in the Curriculum*, the real key to language learning is allowing pupils to get things done *in* the language together with an awareness of structure. This means that however inventive the teacher is in using all the aids at his disposal, however favoured the school is in providing equipment, the real ingredient is the personal involvement of the pupils. The teacher should therefore strive in oral work and in all other activities and classroom arrangements to involve the pupil actively and fully.

Reading _____

Reading may be regarded as an extension of the 'exploitation' section referred to above since the reading which will be done in the first instance will be the text that has already been listened to, repeated and talked about in the earlier sections.

Reading is an activity which should be encouraged with collections of suitable material in the classroom. In an effort to encourage individual reading after the initial stages have been mastered, teachers could encourage pupils to keep a personal reading diary where they can record their progress through the reading scheme designed by the teacher. It is expensive to set up but well worthwhile with the well structured schemes such as *Bibliobus*. Other ideas are the magazines produced for foreign language learners by a number of publishers.

Slower learners may of course need extra help and this can be provided in a number of ways:

- using a nonteaching assistant or support teacher
- using the foreign language assistant
- reading to pupils as they follow the text
- letting pupils read together in pairs
- asking pupils to retell the story – maybe in English
- providing taped versions of books and reading material that pupils can take home on the 'talking books' principle (the FLA could help here)
- for some pupils using foreign texts of their English books with which they are familiar.

In view of the GCSE and the National Curriculum what are the characteristics of reading and the strategies needed by pupils to become fluent readers?

Authenticity of texts

The word authenticity should refer to both material and to task. The reading material presented to pupils should be designed as far as possible (bearing in mind the age and sophistication of the pupils) to reflect real usage for native speakers in the foreign country or in this country. For the latter consideration, teachers may make use of materials, for example, designed to help the foreign visitor or business person, or, in the case of Community Languages they may use, for example, newspapers and other publications in the target language produced for consumption here in the United Kingdom.

In respect of task, teachers should present the pupils with activities suggested by the material itself. To this end, they should ask themselves what was the purpose of the written materials, why were they written? If teachers examine these ideas, they will be more likely to devise realistic tasks to interest and stretch the pupils.

What is reading comprehension?

Reading with understanding means extracting from the text whatever is appropriate. Within the classroom or the examination, the carrying out of the *task* should demonstrate that the pupil has understood. It is important to understand that the skill of reading needs teaching; it cannot be left to chance for the pupil to pick up on the way. Reading, properly taught, can increase the pupil's independence and contribute to skills of analysis, dissection and forecasting.

What to read

The following is a selection of text types teachers may consider for different levels of attainment:

- novels, short stories, tales, plays, poems
- letters, telegrams, postcards, notes
- newspapers and magazines – headlines, articles, letters to the editor, sports results, adverts, weather forecasts, TV/cinema/radio lists
- leaflets and brochures
- handbooks, textbooks, guidebooks
- recipes and advice to get out of difficulties (Tante Marie)
- puzzles, jokes, problems, rules, comics, cartoons
- instructions, directions, notices, posters, road signs, graffiti, menus, price lists, tickets
- timetables, statistics, diagrams, telephone directories, dictionaries, phrase books, maps.

The list should be amended in the light of the suggested criteria for the particular examination board. However, it is possible and sometimes desirable to use other material in the light of the pupils' interests.

Why read?

Reading is not only for a purpose. It is not simply to extract information or to understand. It is also an activity indulged in for *pleasure*. This should therefore be a feature in the classroom, especially if it engages the pupils' imagination.

How to read

The main ways of reading are as follows:

- skimming – quickly reading text to get the main gist
- scanning – reading the text quickly to get a particular piece of information
- extensive reading – reading longer texts for global understanding
- intensive reading – shorter texts for getting particular details.

Research has revealed that it is better to introduce pupils to good reading skills if they are taught in this order:

Skimming → Scanning → Extensive → Intensive

This will enable teachers to give the pupils confidence, particularly when approaching authentic texts where there may be a large number of unknown elements. Faced with a difficult text teachers may ask what function a text fulfils (from a given list). This will enable pupils to latch onto an area which they can explore. If teachers also present the texts as far as possible in context, with the original typography and illustrations, for example, pupils can be encouraged to anticipate what they will find in the texts. This is essential to develop their skills of inference, anticipation and deduction.

Getting pupils to read authentic texts from the very beginning does not necessarily mean a more difficult *task* on their part. It is relatively easy to grade the task to suit the level of the learners.

Integrating reading with other skills

Reading should not be separated from other skills. There are few cases in real life when people do not talk or write about what they have read or act upon the information gleaned.

Teachers can therefore make links across the skill areas.

1   Reading and writing: e.g. summarising, note-making.

2   Reading and listening: e.g. comparing a newspaper article and a radio news bulletin.

3   Reading and speaking: e.g. giving a summary to other pupils in a group or a class.

Reading is an active skill

Reading must not be relegated to the last few moments of the lesson as a sort of time filler or as a way of keeping pupils quiet. It is a part of the communicative classroom and exercises should be meaningful and correspond as often as possible to what the text suggests. Exercises in themselves are neither good nor bad – they only become so when related to a given text. Reading activities should be suited to the text and the reasons for reading it.

Guidelines for the use of authentic material

1   It is important to use only material which was designed to be read.

2   The teacher should use original, not translated, material.

3   It is worthwhile using a guideline for selection – devices such as a settings and topics grid.

4   If possible, original typeface, layout, etc. should be retained as clues to help the reader.

5   The activities should be made as meaningful as possible.

6 Real situations are not always possible in the classroom. Teachers may have to accept a written answer where some other activities are appropriate in real life. But if points 1–5 are accepted then the focus will be correct.

Teaching learners to cope with the unknown

There will always be situations where the learner or reader has to cope with the unknown. Indeed teachers are specifically asked to bring pupils to this stage in the guidelines for the National Curriculum. They should therefore in their teaching programme give pupils access to such strategies so that gradually they will become more independent and be able to cope and react positively when they meet something that is beyond their experience. These strategies are not for testing in an examination scheme but are there to allow readers to cope.

Below is a list of general strategies, followed by some specific to reading. The teacher should:

Look for key words   Pupils should be helped to use these clues as to the general meaning of a reading item.

Use visual and other clues   This is a positive benefit from using authentic material with the layout, titles, photographs, etc. to help in decoding.

Use inference   It is important to teach pupils to use their own previous knowledge to predict what will come next.

Use grammatical markers   Pupils should be taught to recognise in context which word is a verb, which is an adjective, etc. by application of some basic rules of grammar and by the use of analogy.

Use the cultural context   Pupils will be helped in their search for meaning if they have some acquaintance with the culture of the target countries.

Encourage positive learning of vocabulary   Vocabulary should be learnt and noted in context together with patterns such as how to recognise, for example, diminutives such as 'ette' in English, French and Italian or suffixes indicating repetition such as 're' in English. A similar set of examples should be drawn up in the target language.

Strategies specific to reading comprehension

Use of cognates   Where possible, links can be made between words in English and the target language that have similar meaning – but beware of *faux amis*.

Use of near cognates   Links can also be made when there is a near identity in the two languages.

Being aware of common traps   Pupils should be aware of making assumptions when there is a clear difference between the two languages.

Examples of strategies that can be employed to exploit reading material other than by written answers

Here are some ideas to make reading comprehension more *active*, by asking pupils to *do* something to indicate their comprehension:

- tracing a map on a route
- drawing a diagram
- answering a letter
- reading a letter with accompanying photos, then putting the photos in the correct order as indicated by the story line
- reading a letter or biography and selecting the appropriate family tree
- matching descriptions, e.g. of a house and a picture
- matching articles and jumbled headlines
- preparing a meal following a recipe
- following rules and playing a game
- jigsaw reading: putting words or phrases in the correct order
- reading a text and filling in a table as a result
- comparing a guidebook and a letter received after a holiday
- reading a letter of complaint (e.g. to a hotel) and then filling in a complaints card such as one issued to hotel guests
- giving advice in the form of an answer to a problem.

Listening

Listening is an active skill which must be taught just as positively as other aspects of language learning. There will be the initial stages of listening to the teacher, as explained above, and then, as time goes by, the pupils must be given the chance to listen to material in a range of voices and registers. This is where the assistant comes into play and also where the cassette recording really comes into its own. The ultimate aim is to enable the pupil to cope with real listening tasks in real situations.

The first implication of this aim is that the material should be designed to be heard and not simply to be read by the pupil. It is very rare that one listens to written material being spoken – except in such circumstances as listening to a weather forecast or news bulletin on the radio.

This implies that the material should contain all the extra features normally heard in the spoken language – hesitations, *faux départs*, redundant phrases, remakes of items and a distinctive intonation. Pupils must be allowed to experience this.

There will be intermediate stages in the learning process, but the ultimate test will be to understand material which contains all the features of natural (and often unscripted) material. However, it is of the utmost importance that there should be a gradual progression for the pupil, who should be led from short excerpts to longer ones, from simple information gathering to more complex puzzling out of themes, attitudes, etc. which is required at higher levels.

Where there is only one teacher in the classroom (and this will normally be the case), there will be a need to use a tape recorder to bring into the classroom authentic examples of speech and dialogues. Most of the speaking people engage in is in the form of a dialogue and less often in the form of a monologue of rehearsed speech. Exceptions to this are such items as tannoy announcements, etc. – but even here, to re-create the authentic atmosphere, a recording is a good idea.

Making recordings

Good conditions for recording will help the pupil understand the final product. If it is not possible to obtain such conditions in school and recordings are needed to supplement what is available commercially, the LEA may very well have some suitable recording facilities available for use by teachers.

For further information on using the tape recorder as a resource see Chapter 7.

As far as possible ensure the listening material is in context. Thus, if dealing with bus travel as the lesson theme, the listening comprehension should fit into the broad theme. It is disconcerting and less productive to have a lesson based on one topic area, and to produce, out of the blue, listening material on another topic. Ideally, the whole lesson sequence will fit together, with listening as one activity in a carousel of activities. It is always possible (if a cassette recorder with headphones is available) for one pupil (or one group) to be listening while others are engaged in other skill areas.

Problems of listening comprehension

There are several problems peculiar to listening material which the teacher should be aware of. For example, the text is not under the control of the pupil. In the case of reading comprehension, the pupil can go at any speed and can re-read the text at will, and this may help him understand. In the case of listening, the speed of delivery is not always under the control of the listener. In real life one may be able to ask the speaker to repeat the passage (and it is important to teach the pupil how to ask for this). Another problem is related to speed of understanding. Pupils often think that foreigners speak quickly. This is an illusion, in so far as the listener is concerned, for in fact the speaker does not speak with undue speed though it appears so to the pupil. Why? Because of the process of understanding. The pupil has to put in action several processes. First of all, he or she has to decode sounds which are different, then has to understand the meaning and apply the question being asked by the teacher or the examiner. This implies that in the early stages in particular it will be important to allow the pupil plenty of time to understand and react to small pieces of language rather than slow up the delivery. Over time the gaps can be shortened and longer passages for understanding presented.

A further difficulty is that language listened to without the support of the written script is more difficult and pupils must be given time to be able to cope with this task.

Teachers will have to be aware of these extra problems as seen by the pupil and try and structure their listening tasks so as to give the pupil confidence.

Contextualisation

A great help in this respect is the context. In real life, people use all sorts of clues to help them understand. When at the railway station, they expect a certain kind of vocabulary and register, and this helps their understanding. Expectation is an integral part of the process. Therefore in the clinical atmosphere of the classroom, when teachers may be simulating all kinds of scenarios, the pupils should be given a clue as to what they are to expect. Before asking them to listen, the teacher could say, for example, that they are in the doctor's surgery. If the questions are written, the scene could be described at the head of the questions. As mentioned above, the theme of the lesson will also be a great help. This will draw the attention to the sort of vocabulary that will be appropriate.

What to listen to

The following list will give ideas as to the areas teachers can exploit in language learning. The list is in random order. Not all examples are purely listening activities, but all involve listening in the communicative situation. This is not an exhaustive list:

- listening to news/weather forecasts/sports reports, etc. on the radio
- discussing work and problems in a family
- making arrangements/exchanging news and gossip with family and friends
- chatting at parties and social events
- listening to announcements, for example, at the railway station or in a public place such as a shop
- receiving instructions, for example, how to get to a place or how to do something
- being interviewed
- watching film or TV
- listening to a speech
- attending a formal occasion such as a wedding, prize giving
- getting advice, e.g. from a doctor
- fly-on-the-wall techniques, for example, listening to a conversation and then transmitting the meaning to a third party who doesn't have a command of the foreign language, etc.; this can be used in many contexts, for example, when abroad or even in this country when with a foreign visitor.

Suggestions for listening strategies within GCSE/National Curriculum topic areas

This is a sample list only. Topic areas from the syllabus should be listed fully to determine all the possibilities for listening within each area.

Personal identification

People talking about themselves: identifying them from photographs by physical characteristics, clothing, age, etc.

Giving telephone numbers in various contexts.

Arranging to meet someone over the telephone; giving descriptions so that pupils can recognise each other.

Describing jobs and activities: pupils identify job or activity.

Family

Families described and recognised by photographs: using a family photo album.

House and home

Description of houses: pupils recognise the photos from supposed estate agents' brochure.

Pupils being shown round a partner's house; marking items on house plan.

Geography/weather

Guided tours: pupils follow on map or pictures.

Pretending to be on a bus tour of a town and listening to the guide.

Listening to weather forecasts (in context, for example, of deciding what to do that day while on holiday).

Travel and transport

Listening to directions: pupils trace route on town plan and map.

Listening to broadcast about accidents, etc.(e.g. local radio traffic report); pupils mark diversions etc on map.

Announcements on loudspeakers, for example, at stations.

Announcements on boats and aircraft.

Announcements on underground train about breakdowns, etc.

Accommodation

Listening in to telephone call to book rooms and accommodation in hotels, camp sites and youth hostels (can be done for a third party).

Food and drink

Matching up what a waiter says with the information on a bill or menu; there may be errors to spot. NB This technique of using a mismatch between the spoken and written information is a useful technique to apply to a number of contexts.

Health

Interviews with a doctor or at hospital: interpreting for a friend who is ill and who doesn't understand. This technique can be used to good effect for a number of scenarios.

Free time

Listening to a 'what's on' slot on radio or TV; deciding times of broadcasts, etc.

Football (or other sports) results: – filling in grid of results.

Giving list of pupils in the school who want penfriends; noting brief details on hobbies, likes, dislikes, etc., then matching them up with a cassette recording of similar details sent from the link school.

Relationships

Listening to telephone calls to enable pupil to make arrangements to go out.

School/career

Listening to cassette sent from link school requesting information.

General ideas not specific to a topic area

Listening to winning numbers in a lottery.

Listening to speaking clock.

Listening to road report to travel, for example, to a ski resort where there may be problems of weather or road conditions.

Looking at a visiting card or a card from a hotel: changing the telephone number according to what is heard.

Airline arrivals and departures: how do they concern pupils on their particular flight? (Give pupils details on their destinations, etc. beforehand.)

Giving the first part of a situation, for example, in a restaurant, at a bank. What is the pupil to do next, according to the recording?

Allowing pupils to listen to people speaking: they should find out what the attitude expressed and/or implied is. Or what the emotion is. The teachers should have a checklist of possible attitudes/emotions for them to tick. (Is the speaker happy, angry, enthusiastic, grateful, undecided, critical, etc.) This is a higher level activity only.

Setting the scene as for a well known scenario. Listening to an unexpected answer. For example, the train has been cancelled; the room the pupil booked has been let to someone else. Pupils must state what the unexpected reply is.

Matching headlines from a newspaper to the announcements heard on the radio. For higher levels this could be extended to finding out differences in details in the two accounts.

General tips on drawing up questions

Much of this advice refers to a testing situation, but can equally be applied to the normal classroom routine.

1   Make sure that the context for the questions is set. Do not let the pupils answer questions with no clues. There are always clues in real life.

2   In setting questions on a scene decide what the purpose of the speech was. If, for example, it is a weather forecast, why would one listen to the radio? It is likely that it would be to decide on what to wear or to know if it will be fine enough to swim. Questions should reflect the purpose of the speech. It is rare to listen just for the sake of listening.

3   Grade the questions. It is quite possible to use apparently hard listening material if simple tasks are asked of the pupils. A long passage may provide detailed listening practice for some pupils and for others the question may be simply to find a number, date or address. In this way one can differentiate by task rather than by outcome.

4   Ask clear questions with clear instructions. What? When? How? Why? How many? At what time? etc. If necessary ask for two or three points but make it clear how much the pupil needs to reproduce, e.g. What was he wearing? (3 items). Note that 'Why' is probably the most difficult question to answer.

5   Keep questions simple. If more complicated answers are required, add more questions, rather than make questions complex.

6   Answers, if written, will probably be in English (though this is debatable). However, consider having answers in other forms, e.g. by drawing, filling in columns, marking with a cross, drawing lines on a map, etc. (But the type of answer must be authentic and suggested by the text.)

7   In a long test situation, have a variety of answer techniques – it adds to the interest of the activity.

Writing

The point has been made several times that written work comes last in the skills the teacher seeks to pass on to his or her pupils. For some of them, written work may not go very far and teachers should be happy enough if reading comprehension is well established without expecting pupils to write creatively. But for a sizeable portion of learners the written skills are perfectly manageable if introduced gradually. Unfortunately, it is at the introduction of writing that teachers meet their first disenchanted pupils. The reasons are worth considering:

1   Teachers tend to demand 100 per cent accuracy.

2   A pupil with a good ear may have no gift for written work, even in English.

3   Writing seems less relevant to many pupils.

4   The complexities of the less phonetic languages (e.g. French) appear to be overwhelming.

5   Teachers and examiners make little distinction between spellings which change the pronunciation and/or meaning and those which have no effect.

6   Correct spelling implies an understanding of sometimes complex grammatical concepts (e.g. the agreements of past participles in French).

7   If translation is done the pupil can even lose marks for bad English!

It is of course hoped that translation does not loom large in any work below the sixth form, certainly not in any written work.

The introduction of writing

The copying of vocabulary into a vocabulary book is probably the first written exercise undertaken. Here the teacher must stress accuracy since this is to be the reference book to which the pupil will have to turn to frequently. At the same time as stressing the importance of accuracy, teachers will do well to underline the fact that the vocabulary book has to be neat and attractive, otherwise the learner will have no inclination to turn to it to do essential revision.

Copywriting involving cloze tests[1] ensures that the learner becomes familiar with the written form. For lower ability classes it pays to give the missing words for gap-filling exercises either in a box, in jumbled order at the foot of the exercise or, possibly, a series of three or four words at the end of each sentence from which the correct word may be chosen.

Sentence completion is an extension of the above. Again the variety of possible endings may be supplied and the learner picks the one which makes sense in the context. Such exercises are useful as homework since they are not likely to lead the

---

[1] These are in essence gap-filling exercises. Cloze is a test, formed from the word 'closure', in which pupils are required to supply words or phrases which the teacher has deleted from a text often previously studied.

pupil wildly astray and they can be done without supervision but with a good chance of success.

Substitution drills are also useful for homework for they fix a pattern in the pupil's mind and, provided that the preparatory work has been well done in class, they can be done at home without running the risk of forcing the learner to acquire wrong forms. Many basic grammatical forms lend themselves to this kind of reinforcement – pronouns for nouns, changes of tense, use of negatives, word order, etc.

Dictation is not the popular exercise it once was (though it *is* popular in France and even claims prime TV time for the national dictation competition). It may be available as an assessment procedure, but this does not mean that dictation is invalidated as a useful teaching tool. A particularly useful form of dictation is one in which the pupil is given a passage from which key words have been removed. The exercise then involves gap-filling by dictation. Occasionally, as a revision exercise it does no harm to dictate a complete passage from a text that has been studied in class. This is quite a different proposition from the traditional examination *dictée*.

The above ideas are basically pre-communicative exercises and drills. It will be as well to consult the examination syllabus to ascertain the type of communicative writing task that is needed by the pupils – writing letters, postcards, notes, filling in forms, telling stories and accounts, making summaries, etc. There will be three essential features to take into account:

- the purpose of the piece written
- the intended reader
- the context.

The importance of the link between writing and the reading skill cannot be underestimated. Considerable reading experience of the variety of text types the teacher hopes the pupils will produce is essential. Even writing a simple postcard can be fraught with difficulties and should follow on from a wide experience of reading authentic postcards from the foreign country. This can be done, for example, when there is an exchange class in school. Ask all the foreign visitors to write a postcard on the same topic, perhaps to their home after arriving in the UK. The teacher then has an enormous variety of real stimulus material to use in class. Other types of writing can have the same treatment.

One of the real problems with children's early attempts at writing is the fear engendered by committing themselves to paper. Some of this hesitation can be lessened by the use of the word processor for drafting.

Group work _____

The philosophy of language teaching over the past few years has been frequently summed up by the phrase *communicative teaching*. By this it is implied perhaps that the priorities lie with conveying meaning rather than with acquiring language forms which might or might not be used in later life to communicate with. This has been implicit in what has been said so far though it must also be acknowledged that there has to be proper recognition of the more traditional, formal aspects of language learning to ensure that communication does take place.

The *Final Report* of the National Curriculum working party acknowledges this and urges teachers to take note of linguistic structure in the planning of their courses. 'The inculcation of a good sense of linguistic structure . . .' (para. 3.21) is seen as important. One of the reasons is to 'enable pupils to use their current stock of language to cope with the unfamiliar and to learn how to find out what they do not know . . .' (para. 3.22). The members of the working party issued a word of warning in paragraph 3.20: '. . . the importance of the immediate goal of communication has led to some neglect of awareness of structure as an aid to language learning. However, such awareness not only contributes to pupils' general linguistic knowledge but also plays an essential role in ensuring progress in the longer term and as a basis for continued study at higher levels.'

Group work therefore needs to be put into perspective. It is NOT the panacea, the cure-all that will produce competent linguists. It is a tool, a device to ensure practice at the maximum intensity with the possibility of a varied diet for pupils in the language-learning process. Another consideration to be taken into account is the ability to arrange classroom activities so that pupil involvement is maximised. It should be a question of teaching and learning styles rather than teaching methods. Activities which involve the whole class, controlled by the teacher, are vital: vital for the introduction, reinforcement and clarification of structures, etc. However, it is unlikely to be the best method in all situations. The American psychologist Jerome Bruner has argued the importance of language in cognitive development when he states 'Language is not only the medium of exchange but the instrument the learner can use himself in bringing order to the environment'. We maintain that when pupils are allowed to experiment with language, and are allowed to function in a creative way, making language their own, then they move forward in their mastery. It is in group work that this is most easily allowed for.

Of course, group work is not an easy option, where the teacher can sit at the front of the class, dreaming of the summer holidays. It takes careful planning if it is to work. Many teachers find it difficult to manage; the art of letting go and giving some autonomy to pupils is not easy. There is the fear of chaos and ill-discipline. Group work should not be seen as the only method employed in the class – rather it is one weapon in a battery of skills to be used when appropriate by the teacher.

The pupils have to be encouraged to take responsibility for some of their learning

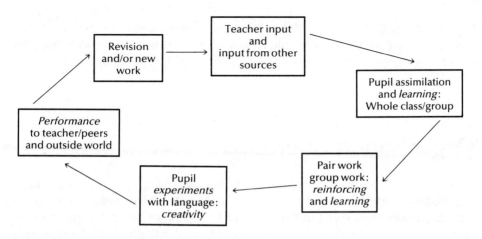

Figure 2: Rationale for group work

and to work with increasing independence. Group work then becomes an ingredient of the methodology – not an exclusive one but an important one.

We are not advocating a *laissez-faire* approach, but a carefully structured and well-managed framework in which to learn. (Note that we use the word *learn* and not just *teach*.)

What advantages are there in introducing group work as one part of the teacher's strategies?

1 Shyer pupils are usually more willing to participate than in large class groups.

2 There is more decision-making for individuals; in the full class approach the teacher is usually the decision maker.

3 Practice (in theory) is more intensive.

4 Non-linguistic skills such as responsibility-taking are more easily exercised.

5 The teacher can pay attention to individuals while others work.

Perceived disadvantages

1 Anarchy and noise!

2 The temptation to talk about last night's TV programmes.

3 Inability of teacher to monitor all pupils.

Let it be said that these can be real fears, but at the same time if teachers are to give their pupils the maximum possible chance to master, in a meaningful way, the target language, then some form of group activity will be essential.

Organisation of groups ────────────────

Some teachers find that a permanent arrangement of groups makes for good organisation within the classroom. Certainly, if teachers always work within their own classroom then this can even extend to a permanent arrangement of the furniture, so that the commands '*Et maintenant à vos groupes*'/'*Geht in eure Gruppen*'/*A vuestros grupos*' produce an immediate, known response with the minimum of fuss and commotion, since every pupil knows where to sit and who to join.

How does the teacher form groups?
In the early stages it will probably be best for the teacher to arrange the composition of the groups. Later it may be advisable to change this, but one should always be sensitive to friendship groups while at the same time avoiding groups made up of the shy and/or the socially 'outcast'.

What is the optimum group size?
In a class of 30 it is probably best to operate groups of five or six.

What about pupil accuracy?
This can be a problem. If the pupils are used to this from the first lesson, then trust can be built up and a balance can be struck between total teacher-monitoring on the one hand and the increased linguistic activity of pupils allowed by the method.

How does the teacher arrange the furniture?
As has been mentioned, if the teacher operates in one room all the time, then a permanent arrangement is fine, provided that all pupils can see the teacher and the blackboard without turning their backs when a whole-class activity is the order of the day (see Figure 3).

1 Desks and chairs in formal rows are ideal for formal classes where only the teacher needs to see everyone's face. Such an arrangement inhibits group work since any speaker can address only the teacher. All pupils sitting behind the speaker invariably complain that they cannot hear the speaker. Group work would involve a noisy furniture moving operation which would be time wasting and disruptive.

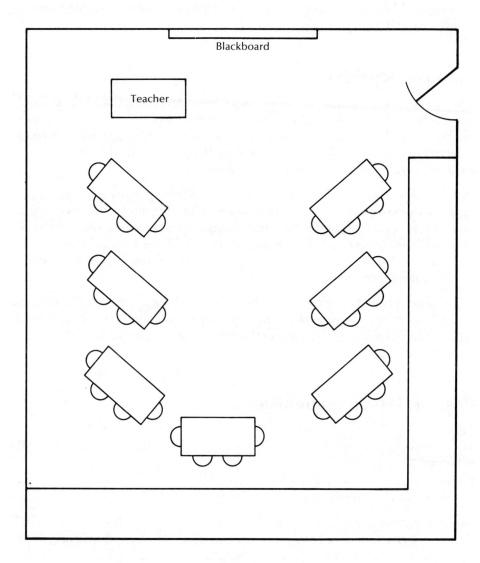

Figure 3: Arranging the classroom for group work: with this arrangement, pupils are mostly facing the blackboard and can form groups without too much furniture-moving in the middle of the lesson. It also allows a circulation area for the presentation of role-plays, etc.

2   Desks and chairs in two semi-circles allow for the formal lesson to take place with the teacher still able to see every pupil. In addition, one half of the class can see the other half. This facilitates team games and group discussions.

3 Desks and chairs in open circles round the room will allow pupils to be part of a group and at the same time be part of a full class for other activities. By adopting the plan in Figure 3 there is also the possibility of pair work giving even more flexibility.

Carousel activities

Having group activities as part of the stock-in-trade does not imply that pupils will always be in lock step with each other for their work. A variety of arrangements is possible, and such a variety can be a positive advantage in planning for differentiated activities. What is planned for the groups will also dictate (or be dictated by) the equipment and resources available.

In an ideal world, each classroom would have listening posts (or even two or three). These are essentially cassette recorders with branching headsets to allow, for example, up to six pupils to listen privately to a recording while the other groups do something else. It may be that all pupils will engage in the same activity in group work-time and equally it may be profitable to arrange a variety of activities around the theme of the lesson.

If the school plans its work sequence on a topic-web basis (see p. 214), then the carousel approach will be particularly appropriate as it allows pupils to work at differing speeds and it also minimises the need to have large numbers of copies of the materials used.

Possible lesson sequences

Lesson 1
Presentation by teacher
Whole class reinforcement
Reinforcement by variety of skills activities
Teacher closes lesson with 'altogether' activity

(*Advantages:* total teacher control.
Disadvantages: assumes all pupils learn at same rate; not all pupils will necessarily be involved; pupils do not 'own' the language.)

Lesson 2
Presentation by teacher
Whole class reinforcement
Group work with all groups doing same thing
Teacher closes lesson with 'altogether' activity

(*Advantages:* large amount of teacher control; some pupil control; ability to monitor individuals increased.
Disadvantages: assumes lock step rate of learning.)

Lesson 3
Presentation by teacher
Whole class reinforcement
Carousel activities
Whole group activity to close

(*Advantages:* some teacher control; individual responsibility for learning; acknowledgement that pupils learn at different paces; teacher can monitor individuals.
Disadvantages: need for careful pre-planning.)

An example of differentiated group work – Topic: housing

Input by teacher on the topic with appropriate concern for structures and language to enable pupils to operate independently.

This can be followed by:

Group 1 Reading material with estate agent's brochures (reading comprehension).
Group 2 Working with assistant talking about houses in UK and abroad.
Group 3 Using listening post for comprehension activities on house descriptions.
Group 4 Working on computer database, sifting material on houses to let within a given scenario.
Group 5 Group writing (with word processor perhaps) a house-for-sale description.
Group 6 Perhaps in pairs with imagined telephone conversation to rent a house.

If this arrangement lasts several lessons, then the pupils can have experience of all skill areas and end up with an experience which will be very valuable. Those who find writing difficult may have more or less time on that activity and in addition the teacher has been able to monitor a number of pupils while the others work. In the case of the reading activity, the burden of marking can be lessened by the use of self-correcting materials.

Basic organisational concerns

Before setting up group work there are several considerations:
● define the learning outcomes carefully
● set attainable aims
● set target times for the various activities and ring the changes
● ensure there is appropriate feedback to pupils on they way they performed
● set out the parameters, for example, on the use of the target language
● ensure all materials are to hand
● determine not to dominate the groups – allow experimentation.

Group activities

Work in pairs

The traditional form of group work requires no class movement and immediate contact. Set against this is the considerable disadvantage that the teacher cannot possibly get round all the pairs in the time allowed for this type of activity. Nevertheless, grouping of this kind allows one-to-one conversations, dialogue practice, learning and testing together, reading and listening, word-creation games, work on worksheets, and half dialogues, where one pupil has only half the information and the other pupil has the missing links (i.e. information-gap activities).

Work in teams

In this situation, the two teams face each other and the teacher is in the middle. This arrangement is ideal for team competition of the tennis variety i.e. question to one side, question to the other. Against this arrangement must be that it is just as inhibiting as the formal classroom arrangement with the added disadvantage that the weaker pupils have the strain of knowing that failure to give a correct answer involves personal humiliation and a let-down for the team. Guessing games of the '20 Questions' variety are most appropriate for this kind of organisation.

Open circle groups

These are probably the most productive arrangements and such work need not be competitive as in the teams above, although a spirit of competition could be introduced if necessary. With a maximum of five or six such groups to a class, there is a good chance that the teacher will be able to make a contribution to each group and keep a general eye on progress or lack of it. Where a class can be split with the help of an assistant or support teacher, then very valuable work can be done.

The open-circle group is sufficiently flexible to cope with fluctuation in numbers because of absence or withdrawal, yet it remains sufficiently dynamic for good role playing and other work to be developed.

Information-gap activities

Essentially this type of activity allows pupils to find out an item or piece of information unknown to them but known to someone else. In this way it is a genuinely communicative activity. In many classrooms it is the teacher who has the information and the pupils who need to find it out. This is deficient as a method in that the creator of the situation is always the teacher who is both the controller of the information and the source of the language activity. In the communicative activity involving group and pair work the pupils are more easily led into being suppliers of information, controllers also able to *create*, and thus we invoke a fundamental reason for communication – a personal involvement in the process. Space does not permit a long description of all the possible techniques – a few will give some flavour of the idea.

1 Questionnaire type work involving genuine questions, e.g. to the assistant.

2 Common denominator activities where pupils question each other until they find common interests, likes, activities, etc.

3 Pupils questioning each other on a picture they cannot see ('battleship game' rules). They reconstruct their own version of the picture of the partner from the answers.

An interesting addition to this technique is to involve the pupils *creatively* in constructing the situation. If they are practising the direction-giving role-play by using pair work and two different cards to build up questions/answers about finding their way, the teacher usually provides the stimulus cards. Here, it is the teacher's imagination in play. However, an interesting variation can involve the pupils' imagination.

The pupil pairs are given the basic sketch map of the town they are 'operating' in. They are not provided with the buildings other than, for example, by indicating the location by numbers. The pupils have to place the various buildings on their own map (without the partner seeing), as their individual whim takes them, and then ask the information-seeking questions on this basis. In this way it is not only the teacher's imagination that comes into play – it is a first step towards involving the pupil's imagination and this first step is a vital ingredient in personalising language acquisition and positively engaging the pupils.

Streaming and mixed ability

There are almost as many methods of pupil grouping as there are schools.

There is *streaming*, where pupils stay in the same ability group for a range of subjects, though in most schools such a rigid system has now been abandoned.

There is *banding*, where pupils are in broad ability groups and departments are free to regroup within the band. This is a particularly popular method for lower classes.

There is *setting*, where pupils can be put into ability groups to suit a particular department.

There is *mixed ability*, which, as the name indicates, groups pupils irrespective of their ability in the subject.

It may not always be in the gift of the language department to decide on the grouping method in isolation from other areas of the school. However, it will be vital that departments discuss the merits of different systems as the decision will certainly affect teaching and learning styles.

The arguments in favour of mixed ability language teaching are:

1   It prevents setting according to false criteria (e.g. ability in English or any other subject) or on flimsy evidence (e.g. a short, incomplete aptitude test).

2   Since language is a form of social expression, teaching the language socially should be the natural thing to do.

3   In the early stages of language learning which concentrate on oral rather than written expression, the gap between the most and least able is less apparent.

4   At the later stages (when reading and writing *are* introduced) mixed ability classes permit useful group work with the more able helping the less able.

Against mixed-ability teaching the following may be set:

1   In the whole class there is no doubt that the less able benefit, but it is not certain the more able do. Work needs to be targeted.

2   Many teachers instinctively, if not on purpose, aim at the middle ability and neglect the extremes.

3   The demands on the teacher increase enormously as he or she strives to produce satisfying work for the wide ability range.

4   Increased disciplinary problems stem from the failure to cope with the demands of a wide ability gap.

5   Different objectives need to be defined and this is magnified in a completely mixed-ability group, particularly for public examinations.

6   Better use of resources is achieved in more uniform groups.

3 Lesson preparation

Lesson preparation, whether short-term (one lesson or a group of lessons) or long-term (one term or one year), implies a philosophy, for without it how can one know what to prepare for? The syllabus normally expresses this philosophy and defines it in terms of aims and objectives, the aims being the ultimate achievement and the objectives being the means by which the final achievement is reached. (A fuller discussion on syllabus design and departmental policy is in Chapter 18.) In planning a lesson scheme, therefore, teachers have to keep in mind the distant goal and define the objectives within the lesson which will enable them to achieve the aims.

In the present day view of language teaching, teachers generally wish their pupils to reach that level of linguistic skill which will allow them to communicate competently orally and (for some) in writing with native speakers of the language they study.

There is, however, no need to state this aim except in the syllabus. On the other hand, teachers do need to define their objectives for any particular module, piece of work, week's lessons, or whatever pattern they work to in the department. If the objectives are precise and clear this will ensure that the lesson has a point.

> A lesson plan is a list of objectives together with notes on the materials and methods which will be used to reach these objectives.

In addition, one might reasonably expect to see an indication why a particular objective has been selected at this time, e.g it might arise from a previous pupil error or might be serving as an introduction to a new concept. It might be a *centre d'intérêt* and a structure involved in a topic area. What the learning aim is will be noted.

The conclusion will state how the threads of the lesson will be drawn together and what precisely pupils will be told they must remember for the next lesson.

In planning a series of lessons with the aims, objectives and stages outlined above, the teacher has to have in mind a whole series of questions which may be summed up as:

1   Factors which influence behaviour and learning ability (e.g. time of day, location of lesson, material available, known attitude, ability and experience of class, previous history, etc.).

2   Language activities the teacher hopes to use (group work, pair work, written work, use of FLA, etc.).

As a rough and ready guide it is no bad thing to recall the mnemonic which states that in every lesson there must be the following four elements.

> **Something old** (i.e. revision of past work)
> **Something new** (i.e. presentation of new work)
> **Something for fun** (i.e. song, game, role-play)
> **Something to do** (e.g. written work, pair work, oral presentation)

In working to the above formula it is helpful also to try to incorporate the four stages referred to in Chapter 2

> **Present   Clarify   Repeat   Exploit**

Having defined the objective of each lesson in general terms it is then no bad thing to jot down in note form how the various stages will be represented.

Present   What? How much material can the class take?

Clarify   What will need care? What can be clarified with objects in the room, by acting, by flashcards or by English translation even? Are there any confusions likely to arise? Are the tasks differentiated and suitable for all pupils?

Repeat   The teacher should consider pronunciation, new sounds, new combinations of sounds. How can the repetition be varied and interesting?

Exploit   What activities will be used?

Question and answer; role play; repetition; written work; vocabulary noting; use of questionnaires; use of IT

What materials will be exploited?

OHP; blackboard, worksheets; flashcards; slides; books; summary charts; cassettes; video, computers.

Before going ahead it is worthwhile checking that all material is to hand. Is the OHP available in the room? Is the room equipped with a screen, TV, etc.?

It is important to check the apparatus being used. Is there a spare bulb for the OHP? Can the teacher load the cassette correctly? Is the right disk available for the computer? On a reel-to-reel tape recorder is there a piece of paper at the right place to enable the teacher to find the exact spot quickly or has a note been made of the counter reference?

Before every lesson it pays to ensure that there is a 'fall-back'. The cassette player may not work. Is the script available to read from? (It is a waste of *everyone's* time looking for technicians to mend the fuse – it's bound to be their day at the dentist!). What if the teacher gets through the lesson more quickly than planned? Is there a 'five-minute filler' to call upon? It is also useful to have a written exercise up one's sleeve, for occasionally an over-excited class may be in the wrong mood for extended oral work, but may settle down to appropriate written work.

Conclusion

Far too many lessons fade away as the class hears the bell and they begin to pack. This is an unacceptable state of affairs which every teacher can contend with by ensuring in the lesson plan that there is a proper conclusion. So, except when the hoax fire alarm sends the class off as the teacher is in mid-sentence, it is important to draw the strings of the lesson together and to state plainly what the class is expected to retain. Finally it is often a good lead into the next lesson if the class are told what to expect next time.

A good diary is an essential piece of equipment, and on those blank pages generously provided by printers for doodles it is very useful to have the following checklists:

Check before the lesson: Are the following items available?

- ☐ Lesson notes with clear objectives
- ☐ Class register/mark book
- ☐ Class exercise books to return
- ☐ Seating plan or name cards
- ☐ Brief notes on question forms to be used
- ☐ Visual aids: slides, films, pictures, flashcards, figurines, OHP transparencies, video tapes, etc.
- ☐ Hardware: tape recorder/cassette recorder, video recorder, computer, OHP, etc.
- ☐ Chalk, felt tips, pens, rubbers, scrap paper, etc.
- ☐ Script, teachers' books, etc.
- ☐ Homework details
- ☐ Fallback work for emergency (OHP transparency or photocopied exercise).

Check the following as the class leaves:

- ☐ What does the class know now that they didn't know 40 minutes ago?
- ☐ What can the class do now that they couldn't do 40 minutes ago?
- ☐ What can the class do *better* now than 40 minutes ago?
- ☐ Did I attempt too much/too little?
- ☐ Did I do too much and the class too little?
- ☐ Did I use pupils' errors positively?
- ☐ Did any individual need special attention? Why?
- ☐ Did I do enough in the language?
- ☐ Did I allow time-wasting? A red herring?
- ☐ Did I set homework appropriate to the class?
- ☐ Where shall I pick up the next lesson?
- ☐ What should I note now?
- ☐ Have I made any enemies?
- ☐ What have *I* learnt?

4 Homework and marking

Homework

Of all school activities, homework often appears to be the least well planned. This is a pity since, properly thought out, homework can be considered to be an essential part of the lesson because it is in fact an extension of the lesson.

So often it is not so and pupils go home with something to do simply because it is 'homework night'. Perhaps the worst kind of homework that is set is the sort of activity which involves the pupil in the early stages in meeting new linguistic material – new vocabulary or new structures. What teaching skill is involved here? What care is taken over pronunciation when new words have to be looked up at the back of the book or even in a pocket dictionary? In some other school subjects it is probably easy to justify sending pupils home to enquire into unfamiliar areas. Many teachers rightly want their class to read around the subject and come up against problems they have to solve for themselves. The linguists generally do not belong to that group.

For the linguist, homework is to reinforce work done in class. Typical homeworks will involve the learning of vocabulary and structures already met in class. Written homeworks will require pupils to use recently acquired language in new combinations. Comprehension passages are perfectly possible and creative writing based on models is also useful. Learning homeworks are a positive tactic provided they are tested in some way. As many pupils have their own personal stereos it is perfectly possible to set listening homeworks or even ask them to record a passage or response on their own tape. All this adds a new dimension to homework.

General points

1   The teacher should aim to have one written and one learning homework per week.

2   It is important to prepare the written homework carefully in class.

3   To be sure that everyone is doing the right thing it pays to let pupils start homework in the last five minutes of the lesson. At the same time the teacher can supervise the dates, layouts and headings as well as iron out any unforeseen problems.

4   All written homework should be marked by the teacher if there is any element of assessment towards a grade. Swapping books to correct answers called out from the front will *not* do since it leads to very slapdash work, carelessness, etc.

5   All homework should be handed in. It is a mistake to adopt the attitude 'It's his loss, not mine'.

6   In addition to any number mark, grade or assessment, it is useful to add a written comment, however brief (but positive).

7   A mistake occurring in a number of exercise books indicates a need for further classwork in that area. Some teachers mark such an item in the pupils' book 'class' to indicate that it will be dealt with again, or 'ask' to remind the pupil to enquire further.

8   When the weekly learning homework is set it must be tested next lesson. This is the sort of marking for which pupils *can* exchange papers. It is always wise to collect in papers at the end and, periodically, check them carefully.

9   Not all learning homeworks need be followed by a written test. An oral review can be just as revealing and just as effective.

10   All schools give pupils and parents an idea of the amount of time to be spent on homework. Some teachers like pupils to indicate at the foot of the exercise how long they have spent on it.

11   It is sometimes a good idea to involve parents in homework by asking for a parent's signature against the time taken.

12   Above all it must be stressed that homework should be an integrated part of the teaching and learning sequence and not a bolt-on addition.

Marking

1   It is important to mark clearly, promptly and regularly both classwork and homework. As a general rule every exercise book should be seen once a week.

2   Before beginning to mark new work it is sensible to ensure that corrections for the previous work have been done and that the pupil has seen where he or she went wrong. It is still helpful to have corrections done in full underneath the work that is being corrected.

3   Generally it is better to add the correct version over or under a word that is wrong. However, with exercises that can be gone over in class an underlining will do. With such work as, for example, essays where each one is unique, mere underlining will not do. To leave plenty of room for corrections, pupils should be asked to write on alternate lines. (This should really apply to all language exercises.)

4   The teacher should always insist on presentable work, especially from examination forms. Scruffy presentation should be penalised to bring home the point.

5   When giving back work it is often helpful to a class to show examples of work which have received high marks. It sets standards and also points out that the standards set by the teacher are attainable. (But the teacher should avoid always using the same pupil's work and be sensitive to those pupils who, though not reaching the highest marks, have nevertheless reached good levels within their capabilities – this sensitivity should be part of every teacher's considerations.)

6   Comments on work *are* appreciated. *Fair* is virtually meaningless and not worth writing. Positive praise should be given whenever possible and, if necessary, a diagnostic comment, e.g. 'Vocabulary is good but you are still careless with past tenses. Ask if unsure'.

7   When marking it helps to place books in piles according to the marks awarded. It is then a relatively simple matter to do a quick check on the marking standards.

8   It pays to enter all marks in the mark book as marking proceeds. It then avoids the time-wasting and possibly embarrassing practice of calling out marks in class.

9   It is best not to enter into arguments about marks in class. Take the book for a check. If an error has been made it can then easily be corrected with the minimum of fuss. If there has been an error, it is best to admit it at once for pupils like fair dealing.

10   Examination classes will appreciate being told what the official marking scheme is. It gives them a good idea where they stand and all boards now make this information generally available. In any case, all classes will benefit from clearly articulated targets and criteria for assessment so openness is a good thing with all groups (see Chapter 20).

11   The teacher should have a *positive* as well as a negative marking scheme which gives rewards as well as points out error.

12   It is important that the mark book gives a picture of pupil progress in all four skill areas. A full discussion of this is to be found in Chapter 20.

13   At least some of the written work can be marked in class. The teacher goes round from desk to desk to do this most effectively.

14 Although onerous, marking should never be neglected. It helps the pupil and is equally important for the teacher since it helps him to monitor his effectiveness.

5 Question techniques

The technique of questioning is one that has to be carefully developed by the teacher of modern languages since its purpose and function is somewhat different from that required for the world outside the classroom. In real life you do not usually go about questioning people about what you have just told them, nor do you ask the same question three times using different words or put the same question to three different people. You certainly never ask for a reply in chorus when you have obtained a perfectly satisfactory answer from one or two individuals – except perhaps at the pantomime where the convention of repetition is readily accepted.

It is important to recognise, however, that even in communicative classrooms, there will be the need for pre-communicative techniques to enable the pupil to operate eventually in the communicative situation.

The repetition convention can easily be established in the classroom and, indeed, it has to be, to ensure that all pupils get adequate practice in speaking the language. Unreal as it may be, pupils soon come to accept the process as a necessary one just as the musician accepts scale practice. True, one does have slightly lunatic conversations in the language classroom, as Ionesco enjoys pointing out, but teachers have come a long way since the days when, in linguists' folklore as perpetuated in grammar book methods, postillions were struck by lightning.

Progress in techniques has lately been put into focus by the increase in group work in the language classroom. The possible boredom of whole class repetition is lessened by the use of a variety of group formations. A full discussion on this topic is on pp. 34 – 41.

And it is not just a matter of establishing the fact that questioning must take place for it is equally important that pupils understand how questioning operates and what are exactly the rules of the game.

Rule 1, which every teacher new to a class should clearly establish, is that *facts are negotiable*. The important thing is to talk. If the substance of the answer is wrong it can soon be put right. If the pupil fails to speak there is little the teacher can do other than obtain the answer from another pupil and then return to the one unable to reply the first time round.

Rule 2 for younger classes is that if they listen carefully to the question they will often have at least the form of the answer from the question. In the earliest days this may sound ridiculous but is necessary: '*Nous sommes aujourd'hui mardi. Quel jour sommes-nous?*'/'*Heute ist Dienstag? Welcher Tag ist heute?*'

So the routine:

> Give the answer
> Put the question
> Get the answer

can become a natural part of the conversational give and take in the classroom. (It is a frequently observed fact that this technique is instinctively employed by many parents involved in first language acquisition with their child.)

Rule 3 is that a natural conversational answer may be adequate but sometimes, for the sake of practice, a slightly longer answer is the best one to give. Thus the natural answer to the question 'Where are you going?' is simply 'To school'. But the language teacher likes to hear more than this occasionally.

Richard Johnstone, in his book *Communicative Interaction: a Guide for Language Teachers*, talks about two types of strategies: problem-reducing strategies and problem-creating strategies. It is a useful distinction and the teacher should be aware of both approaches.

In the former (problem-reducing) strategies, the teacher takes care to nurture, with the help of props and support, the embryonic pupil reply. This is facilitated by the use of familiar topics, structures and vocabulary, by the use of careful, clear talk, by the recycling of information, by structurally simplified language, by simple tasks notified in advance, by dominant teacher talk in the language, by modelling on a teacher version and recycling. Perhaps this is similar to what has been called the pre-communicative phase.

The wise teacher hopes that the vast majority of his pupils will be able to operate at least for some time in another way: 'problem creating'. In this area Johnstone cites several features: the target language is normal; context-reduced language is introduced; the cognitive level is raised; expression of personal feelings is encouraged; tasks are more precise, forcing learners to use particular areas of vocabulary, for example; there is less support by teachers.

These distinctions need to be born in mind when tackling the problem of questioning. The ultimate aim is to go from the state of utter dependency on the teacher to a state of autonomy for the learner. The art of teaching is to allow the pupil to progress from one state to another in safety.

50

Some other general questioning points are:

1   In the early stages, questions expressed in the affirmative with interrogative inflexion in the voice are most easily understood. This fact is noticeable even amongst native speakers in France: '*C'est Monsieur Givry qui achète encore une bouteille?*'

2   The teacher should *always* put the question to the class first, and give pupils time to think, instead of naming an individual.

3   It is important to look around. If a pupil is avoiding the teacher's gaze it indicates not wishing to be asked. Perhaps the pupil needs to hear the question again, so it should be repeated quickly.

4   The teacher should select the pupil to answer or call for a volunteer. If the pupil clearly can't answer, it is better not to wait. It causes embarrassment and is unlikely to produce an adequate reply. Instead they should pass on to someone who can.

5   Then the teacher should go back to the one(s) who have failed to answer or who gave an inadequate answer. They should put the same question again and be lavish with praise.

6   Finally, before leaving the question, it is often a good check and an interest reviver to put the same question to the class and get it back in chorus.

7   It is vital to judge the pace and rhythm of the lesson. Briskness is essential but balanced by a mature judgement as to the state of understanding shown by the pupils.

8   It is important to build on pupil error and very helpful if occasionally the teacher goes back to an error made and clarifies for the whole class why it was wrong. It is important though to beware of too many interruptions of this kind when communication is the focus.

9   Body language, mime, gesture, intonation, facial expression, etc. all contribute to the understanding of a question and are all part of the language teacher's stock-in-trade.

10   No teacher, however experienced, can ask effective questions without pre-planning.

11   The coverage of the questions around the class is important. Observation has shown that boys get more attention than girls in mixed classes and that pupils sitting on the edge of the teacher's field of vision get less attention than those

within the normal triangle of sight. It is important therefore to move around the class to vary the angle of vision.

Types of question

1   Direct questions to the class expressed affirmatively or in an interrogative form – often in the early stages with the answer before the question. The teacher should be aware that this is a necessary 'drill' stage and is not a proper communicative activity.

2   Questions in the negative, inviting contradition.

3   Questions offering an alternative. Very useful since the substance of the answer is provided in the question e.g. '*Ce jour-là, est-ce qu'il faisait beau ou est-ce qu'il pleuvait?*'/'*War das Wetter an den Tag schön oder hat es geregnet?*'/'*¿Aquel día, hacía buen tiempo o llovía?*' There is no reason why a third choice cannot be added.

4   Questions in the third person are easiest to answer since no change of person is involved in the reply.

5   Questions in the second person require a change to first person and this bothers many beginners.

6   The teacher should put a question in the third person, get an answer then put the same question in the second person to the individual concerned.

7   The same question can be put in a number of different ways so that pupils become familiar with the context, the subject matter and the answer. Such a technique also avoids mere repetition of an answer as it is passed on:

   a) '*Ist Berlin größer als Bonn?*' Answer: '*Ja, es ist größer.*' '*Ja, es ist größer als Bonn.*' (Teacher can work towards the full answer though the first is an adequate response.)
   b) '*Ist Berlin größer als Bonn oder London?*' (Here a yes answer is impossible because a choice is offered.)
   c) '*Welche ist die größte Stadt, Berlin, London oder Bonn?*' (Here a simple deduction has to be made and the text is not simply regurgitated.)

8   Factual questions are the simplest to deal with and should always be at the start of the questioning sequence but pupils will soon become bored if they do nothing but repeat what the text tells them.

9   Inference questions are then called for. Questions beginning 'Do you think that . . . ?' go well into this sort of work.

10   Pupils *must* have the opportunity to formulate questions. One early way is to put a question to the class, elicit the answer and then ask a pupil to put that question or a similar one to a friend. Pupils making up questionnaires for group/pair work is useful.

11   The teacher can ask pupils to note down questions as they occur because someone will play the part of the teacher later on when the same questions are then asked.

12   Formulating questions to known answers is a positive technique. The OHP can be used to reveal questions as they are needed or elicited.

13   One pupil can put a number of questions or 'question relay' is sometimes preferred. A puts question to B who answers and then questions C, etc. The Chinese whisper game is a possibility.

14   Whenever possible the teacher should try to bring the questions round to the pupils' own lives and experiences before leaving the topic. After factual questions on Madrid based on a text studied in class it is a good thing to ask '*¿Has estado una vez en Madrid? ¿Te gusta Madrid?   ¿Prefieres Londres o Madrid?*' this kind of work ensures further practice in the language and increases personal involvement – an important motivating factor. Where a story is studied, rather than a factual account, pupils can still be invited to give their own views and opinions. After eliciting the facts of the story the teacher can continue with '*¿Qué harías si . . .?*'

15   A further method of arousing personal participation and at the same time offering practice with other tenses is to invite pupils to guess what *will* happen in the story.

An important point about all questioning in the language class is that the questions can offer something for everybody. The alert teacher watches pupil behaviour and gives out questions appropriate to the ability of different individuals. Progress can, however, be quite marked and because of the intensive nature of the question practice a pupil who was quite unable to answer in the early part of the lesson may very well cope adequately later on. In this case a real sense of achievement is experienced by the learner.

6 Discipline in the classroom

Basic considerations and technique _____

In recent years the word 'discipline' appears to have taken on unfortunate overtones which the teacher would do well to ignore. Modern linguists should remember instead that the origin of the word lies in the Latin *discipulus*, a pupil, one who learns, from *disco, discere* – to learn. There is no suggestion of a punitive element being involved and there is no need for such an idea. For the good teacher, discipline means quite simply the art of creating the best learning conditions possible in the circumstances. Without good learning conditions, no effective learning can take place, and every conscientious teacher gives thought as to how good conditions can be created and maintained.

Even amongst successful teachers, it is seldom that two can be found to agree on exactly what produces good discipline. It is certainly true that physical conditions seem to have something to do with it. Time of day and the time of the lesson have some significance and any teacher who finds that he or she is invariably with the same class for the last lesson of the day may justifiably protest vigorously. But even this factor is not the main one. This is why Mrs Jones has a perfectly orderly class at 3.30 while her colleague next door is desperately praying for either the end of the lesson or the end of the world.

Whatever the secret ingredient may be, it is generally agreed that before any worthwhile learning can take place good order has to be established in the language classroom.

Children will not learn French or German grammar when there is a din in the room. They need a well-ordered, purposeful and caring atmosphere. What then does the modern language teacher need in his or her knapsack to ensure that learning takes place?

Preliminary considerations

Before we look at the qualities of the teacher, there are one or two other points to be made. Too often classrooms may be dull, untidy and not conducive to good work. It is our experience that there is likely to be less vandalism, and more respect for the fixtures and the furniture if the teacher takes care and encourages the pupils to do likewise.

So:

1   Before the start of term teachers should see that the room carries a good display of posters, *realia* and above all pupils' work.

If pupils enter a well-cared for room, there is less likelihood of vandalism. Once graffiti are allowed to appear and remain, there will soon be an epidemic.

2   Polite requests before the lesson and at the close for litter to be put in the wastepaper basket discourages untidy behaviour.

3   A well-ventilated room, with some fresh air, helps a great deal. How often do teachers come into a room following a previous lesson with its unmistakable lingering school smell? It is not good for the health and disturbances are created when dealing with the opening of windows during the lesson.

5   Blackboards should be clean before the lesson and a routine to clean it at the end ready for the next lesson or the next teacher in the room will be much appreciated.

6   Professional pride in the physical surroundings can be a positive help.

All the above are necessary preliminaries that go a long way to forestalling trouble. Making sure it is nipped in the bud is sound advice, as will be seen later when discipline is discussed.

In *Modern Language Teachers in Action*, the report for the language teaching research project organised at the University of York, the researchers considered what qualities make up a language teacher's general proficiency.[1] The following were enumerated *in order of importance*:

1 Discipline, firmness, control; 2 Humour; 3 Patience; 4 Enthusiasm.; 5 Liking for, interest in, sympathy for pupils; 6 Consistency, fairness.; 7 Understanding problems; 8 Planning; 9 Confidence.

It will not pass unnoticed that top of the list comes *discipline* and in a sense the other eight qualities might be seen as those elements essential to securing discipline. There are, however, other qualities of professionalism which can be usefully indicated.

Discipline is not something we can teach. It cannot really be caught. It usually comes with experience which means in fact that the teacher has become sensitive to atmosphere, pupil involvement and has acquired a sense of timing such as that developed by an actor. With the image of the good actor in mind (for the teacher often is a performer), the following considerations will go a long way to help to create the right conditions for good discipline.

---

[1] D Sanderson *Modern Language Teachers in Action*. University of York, 1982, p. 87

Voice

The importance of the voice for any teacher needs no justification here. A flat, monotonous tone will kill a lesson stone-dead and then behaviour problems will quickly follow. If the teacher fails to do anything about the voice then it is the end of the lesson and, frankly, probably the end of a career.

To be successful, teachers should really, from the beginning, cultivate a voice which can be varied in *pitch, pace* and *volume*. For the actor such control is seen as normal and teacher expectation must be the same. Every teacher of languages should develop the art of mimicry to represent the different characters in any anecdote he or she is called upon to recount. Suggesting that teachers can vary the voice in pitch is not to imply that they should make complete fools of themselves by reading female parts in a high falsetto, and male roles as if they were Daddy Bear. But between these two extremes there is a whole range of voices that can be 'put on' without undue strain on either the teacher's vocal chords or the pupils' credulity or self-restraint.

It should not be forgotten, however, that the teacher's voice is under considerable strain and the modern language teacher's more than most. To minimise strain he or she should rely as little as possible on *volume*. Shouting seldom helps to convey advice, information, emphasis and encouragement. Starting by shouting means that there is nothing to work up to if the need really does arise. On the other hand shouting does arouse bad feeling and it is certainly fatiguing. One only has to go to the school disco with its loud music to prove the point about the difficulty of trying to communicate in a noisy atmosphere. Moral: reserve the *fortissimo* for desperate circumstances and moments of high drama in your narration. For more mundane events it will be found that an equally good if not better effect is created by varying the *pace* of one's utterances and by *reducing volume*. If muttering begins, it pays to drop the voice rather than to yell. If what the teacher is saying has any importance at all the talking at the back will subside quickly.

Voice *projection* is an important ability to develop. Again we stress, projection does not mean shouting. It means clarity of diction achieved by taking advantage of the mouth as a resonance chamber. This ability to project the voice is vital for any successful teacher since it not only means that the teacher can be heard without difficulty but, in some strange way, it conveys to the listener the confidence and the authority of the speaker. Whatever the reason it somehow guarantees a hearing.

Speaking in the classroom to a group audience also requires the teacher to adopt a certain formality of usage. It is important not to be casual, using throwaway remarks no one beyond the front row can ever catch. Good clear speech is not the trademark of someone seeking to dominate the situation. It is simply a mark of respect shown to the people addressed. In the case of any teacher, the voice serves as a model. For the language class, a good clear model is essential for pupils to attain any kind of authentic foreign accent. As for English usage, which every teacher of modern languages has recourse to on occasions, it is important to ensure that speech is fairly standard, not characterised by so many regionalisms that pupils from another part of the country treat his or her speech as a joke.

Hands should be kept away from the mouth and every effort should be made to avoid the 'gerrit' and 'gorrit' type of language heard in school playgrounds. There is of course, a school of thought which argues that teachers increase in stature in the eyes of pupils if they speak in their classroom vernacular. There is however little proof of this and, if anything, probably the reverse is true.

The *tone* of voice adopted for addressing the multitude, or what seems like the multitude when meeting the 9th form on a wet Friday afternoon, is not appropriate for speaking to individuals. Queen Victoria, it will be remembered, disliked Gladstone because he addressed her 'like a public meeting'. He was not unique. Teachers, however, meet with more blunt critics than perhaps a nineteenth-century prime minister ever did and pupils will soon show their resentment if they are individually pinned to the wall by the teacher's every utterance.

Manner

The ideal attitude to adopt with classes is one of firmness tinged with pleasantness. If the teacher is offended by the pupils' behaviour (over-familiarity, cheek or even downright abuse) the class should be left in no doubt about the effect of such behaviour. Teachers are like any other human beings and the method of turning a deaf ear to offensive remarks is not one that should be frequently applied.

Equally important in the manner adopted towards pupils is one's consistency. This again is a quality mentioned in the York Report. It simply means that what is rebuked today must be rebuked tomorrow, and what is praised in one pupil must merit praise in another. Pupils respect staff they can rely on. They do not cause problems for the teacher known to be fair in his dealings. To be fair it is important not to get boxed into a corner, by making generalisations that later may be regretted. The teacher who says 'I will keep you all in if ...' has to do just that; if he says 'I always give double homework for those who forget their homework' is riding for a fall for there are occasionally extenuating circumstances in everyone's life.

Presentation

Whilst it is well known that the teacher cannot afford a new outfit each term and may perhaps, not wish to appear ultra smart, there is no denying that a neat, clean appearance suggests efficiency and a concern for personal appearance which is transmitted to pupils immediately. Any parent will confirm that their children do come home and express their opinions on the appearance of the teachers in the school. Dirty finger nails, dirty clothes, messy hair, general untidiness are not just noticed but criticised by pupils.

The same applies to teachers' handwriting, treatment of books and writing on the blackboard. Everything matters and those teachers who leave themselves open to criticism also leave themselves open to disciplinary problems which arise naturally from lack of respect.

Credibility

Every successful teacher has this quality though precisely what it is for any individual teacher may be difficult to define. It implies that pupils have confidence in him or her, trust the teacher's opinion and accept the standards of work that are set. It is fairly easy to destroy or, at any rate, to lose this credibility by being 'caught out'. Frequent confessions of ignorance about the language taught, unfamiliarity with the country whose language is being taught, failure to be well prepared for the lesson, inability to cope with the various mechanical aids in the classroom, forgetfulness about homework and promised tests will all reduce the teacher's credibility rating in the eyes of the pupil.

Once credibility begins to disappear (or fails ever to appear) the class will almost instinctively resort to a 'try-on'. Discipline problems have begun. The teacher's inability to tell the difference between a 'try-on' and a genuine request for information confirms the class's diagnosis. 'Please Sir, what is the French for "Bra"?' is almost certainly a 'try-on'. Any doubt can be dispelled by observing the pupil's behaviour. Having put the question loudly, the pupil looks round to see what effect he or she is having on the others. If not spotted and nipped in the bud, the problem may soon get out of hand.

Knowing your stuff

This is the positive side of credibility. For most pupils (and parents), 'knowing their stuff' is the teacher's first virtue. Certainly among the more academic pupils this is highly respected at any level. For the less academic, language teachers still 'know their stuff' if they reveal familiarity with the country they teach about, if they talk about events they have witnessed. If, in addition, they prove in front of the class that they are fluent in the language, possibly by doing a duet with the assistant, the problem is resolved.

Position and posture

For pedagogical and strategic reasons it is important to move around the room. Even speaking from the back of the room is a positive move since:

1　It alters the voice quality, resulting in variety.

2　It gives the teacher a different viewpoint.

3　It gives teachers an opportunity to check the quality of their visuals. (Is the writing neat and clear? Are the OHP slides properly displayed?)

4   It keeps the class on its toes.

5   It allows the teacher to hear the pupils' speech more clearly.

6   During writing sessions it allows the teacher to have individual conversations.

With a full class of 30 it is hardly ever possible to sit down at the front and to do so invites inattention and distractions. With a smaller group, say half a class, sitting at the front or even perched on the edge of the desk becomes possible but it is important to remember that a change implies a change in atmosphere. This is not to imply that there is hostility afoot in a room of 30 pupils but simply to accept the fact that, to make an impact on 30 people at once, is no easy task, and to sit down so that half the group cannot see the teacher is to invite trouble.

As for posture and body language, teachers need to keep in mind that the way they move, the way they sit, the way they get up again all convey a message to the class. If staff wipe their shoes over the chairs someone else has to sit on, do they really care? If the teacher sprawls over the desk, is he really ready to give a good lesson? All too quickly the 'couldn't care less' attitude rubs off on the class.

Finally, in this section, it is important to remember that it is not only teachers who choose their places in the classroom. Pupils also make a choice, particularly in schools which have a mass migration at the end of each lesson to permit the use of specialist rooms. In this kind of situation, the teacher will be wise to allocate places from the start of the school year and insist that pupils keep to the allocated places. There are many advantages in this system and few disadvantages. In the worst of all possible worlds, nonspecialist rooms are filled up as pupils arrive. In this sort of uncontrolled situation it will be noticed how the front row is avoided as long as possible. The class are sorting themselves out and teachers will be wise to watch who goes where. They will be wiser still if they quickly take a hand in helping pupils to find places! Making for the back row is a sure sign of opting out of a lesson.

Style

Having style means appearing relaxed and self-confident even when this is not so. Such self-confidence is transmitted to the class. A tense, overwrought teacher tends to have a frothy, unsettled class, and a vicious circle has begun which may not necessarily be reduced by the bell at the end of the lesson.

Self-confidence also implies confidence in the pupils, which arises from knowing them well. The illusion of knowing them reasonably well can be sustained by, at the very least, knowing them all by name (hence the importance of a seating plan or name cards). Pupils immediately react much better to their names than to a hit-and-miss description which can easily be used for deliberate misunderstanding.

Finally, good style means adopting the right tone and posture for any situation. It involves developing a tone, which, although perfectly pleasant, suggests that no one will do anything other than what the teacher has asked for. Surprisingly it works, though in the early days of teaching it may just be bluff.

Humour

This is a highly rated quality in the York Report but it needs to be handled with care. Provided the humour is not barbed, provided it does not trade in sarcasm (a quality hated by pupils) it is fine. If humour means simply having a sense of fun, having the capacity to create funny situations for role-playing instead of the eternal dreary station booking-office, then this is indeed a desirable quality and one to be envied if not copied by those who lack it. Teachers should remember too that pupils have a sense of humour and if they show that they appreciate that, they are well on the way to a good class relationship.

Patience

Like humour, this is a two-edged weapon. It is the first quality every aspirant to the teaching profession names as an essential. In the eyes of the pupils it means a teacher who 'does not go mad with you' when you get it wrong. The teacher who 'flies off the handle' at every mistake should not be a language teacher, and possibly not a teacher at all. In all language work so much depends on pupil confidence and their willingness to participate, that anything which inhibits such contributions is obviously counterproductive.

Enthusiasm

This is part of the credibility referred to above. If the teacher does not convey excitement and interest in what he or she teaches, this is bound to be picked up by the class. The enthusiast may occasionally be seen as an eccentric by some pupils but they are still affected by him or her. Enthusiasm is transmitted in so many little ways: greetings in the corridor in French, German or Spanish, displays around the room, invitations to foreign visitors to meet the pupils, anecdotes about visits abroad, organisation of foreign visits, obvious delight at holding a conversation in the language, interest and concern about the pupils' own foreign contacts (letters from penfriends, visits, etc.).

Dealing with classroom disturbances _____

Firstly, it is important to be sure what the school policy is and to stick to that. Idiosyncratic punishments invented by the teacher will almost certainly bounce back and may cause considerable embarrassment to all concerned. Any teacher who is forced into a position of having to withdraw and apologise has lost his credibility and hence the respect of the pupils.

If detention is a recognised school system, then teachers must be sure to use it exactly as laid down. Most schools insist rightly on a minimum of 24 hours' notice being given in writing to parents. Such punishments should be used sparingly as they rapidly become ineffectual and can become a joke if half the class ends up in detention – in the 'overtime club'.

If the school policy is to set extra written work or lines, beware of building up resentment against languages by setting dreary exercises. Nor should the teacher set an essay in English on useless titles such as 'Why I was late to class three times'. Such methods undermine colleagues, for example those in the English department who are striving to prove that writing is exciting and creative.

If there can be such a thing as a best punishment it must be the one which produces something worthwhile and which does not imply a complete waste of time for the pupil. Socially useful work is the answer and in the modern languages department it means the manufacture or renewal of visual aids – posters, flashcards and reading cards. Other ideas include the repair of wall displays and text-books.

Before deciding on the punishment it is vital to be sure that the real culprit has been apprehended. Even when sure, it pays to deal with the offender *after* the lesson because:

1   It keeps everyone wondering.

2   Teacher and pupil have time to cool off.

3   A ringside seat is not offered free to spectators who will delight in confrontation.

4   The offender is denied an audience to play to and, since this may have been part of the reason for the original offence, a refusal to allow him to call further attention to himself is a sound punishment.

For all these reasons the teacher's best way of putting an end to a minor disturbance is to say 'See me at the end'. Teachers should make sure that they *do* see the offender and not allow him or her to slip away.

Some schools operate a system of help from the head of department, year tutor, etc. If this is the case it is best to use the system appropriately.

Some schools operate a system which permits the less experienced staff to send the offender to the head of department or other senior member of staff. Generally it is better to resolve the difficulty oneself, but this other system at least gets the offender out of the room to 'cool off'. On the other hand, the senior colleague should have a true account of the offence as soon as possible otherwise the complaining teacher may be presented as the guilty party by the clever pupil.

If, on occasions, the offence is serious, the following advice should prove helpful:

1   The teacher should never reply in kind by resorting to foul language or, worse, to violence.

2   If attacked, it is important to tell the assailant that there are witnesses in the class and that the consequences will be serious.

3   The teacher should report the attack in full to the school authorities and complete the written report, giving essential details (date, time and place of attack, cause, previous warnings, action taken).

4   When things have calmed down, the event should be discussed with colleagues. What should have been known by the staff about the pupil and his background? Have any mistakes been made and can the teacher do anything to avoid a repetition?

In all classroom disturbances it is important to ascertain *why* the incident occurred. Investigation often reveals the following:
- boredom
- a dare
- testing the teacher
- pupil thinks he has been unfairly treated (picked on)
- sarcasm on the part of the teacher
- things going wrong at home or in another class.

If boredom is the cause, and this is common, the teacher should look at the structure of the lesson. Any of the following may apply:
- too much of the same thing
- not enough to do
- too much to do
- wrong sort of work for either the pupil or the time of day.

One of the main rules for the teacher who wishes to keep control is to avoid trouble by giving satisfying work, involving the pupils in purposeful activities and setting realistic targets which pupils can attain.

When there has been a confrontation, it is wise to give offenders an opportunity to rehabilitate themselves by recovering their self-respect during what remains of the lesson.

Most teachers will also agree that on occasions it is best *not* to see or hear something unless it threatens to become overwhelming, disturbing or offensive to all the others in the class.

If there is the chance to discuss the problem pupil with the parents, it is best to do so. It is not a confession of failure to discuss the pupil in trouble and most parents will be willing to help in dealing with the matter.

Being preoccupied with discipline is not unusual amongst young teachers and the management of a class is not easy or natural for all. Most staff go through a learning phase which is part of the apprenticeship to the profession.

To conclude this section on a more positive note, it may be helpful to derive from the York study those ingredients in the lesson necessary to ultimate control being achieved:

1   Pitching the lesson to enable the pupils to have a high success rate.

2   Involving the whole group in the activities.

3   Using the available equipment skilfully.

4   Providing a variety of activities in the lesson.

5   Being flexible with regard to objectives.

6   Building positively on pupil error.

7   Keeping a sense of proportion and a sense of humour.

Getting the class on your side

Following from the above, it may be concluded that the successful language teacher is the one who persuades the pupils that languages are worth learning and that there is a sense of achievement to be had if the lessons are properly structured. To achieve this, teachers do need to feel that they and the pupils are on the same side and the following may help to bring this about.

1   Learning names quickly.

2   Smiling at pupils whenever possible.

3   Being generous with praise – what may be a simple answer to the teacher may be a *tour de force* for the learner.

Praise may be of the following kinds:

a) verbal (of prime importance)
b) merit cards, merit marks
c) written praise
d) house credit points
e) reports
f) prizes (many firms produce badges, stickers, etc.)

    g) letters to parents
    h) display of work
    i) positive marking
    j) diplomas (e.g. graded tests).

4   Setting attainable standards to guarantee success.

5   Setting standards based on good work. The class should be absolutely clear as to what the teacher thinks is good.

6   Using a low voice when talking to individuals.

7   Taking an interest in pupils and their welfare; asking if they are well again after an illness or accident.

8   Learning to size up a class quickly in order to estimate which pupils enjoy repartee or can have their leg pulled without taking offence.

9   Being firm, fair and friendly.

10   Being consistent in class management.

Above all teachers should avoid:

1   Giving the impression that they do not care.

2   Making threats they may not wish to carry out ('The next person to . . .').

3   Setting work that will bring a lot of errors, a practice which demoralises the class and proves the teacher is ineffective.

4   Attempting to mimic and use sarcasm.

5   Wasting time by having long debates in open class on 'Why did she get 14 and I only got ten?'

6   Telling the pupils that 'I was no good' at this or that (it reduces credibility).

7   Making unprofessional remarks about the school, the timetable or a colleague.

8   Keeping exercise books for a long time, forgetting to mark work.

7   The use of resources

Otto Jesperson, father of modern language teaching as it is known today, showed great foresight when, in 1904, in *How to Teach a Foreign Language* (a book which still repays careful reading), he forecast that the new invention, the gramophone, was in future likely to play an important part in language teaching. Professor Jesperson would certainly have approved of what Eric Hawkins has called 'recent panaceas' and would have no doubt taken the same realistic view of such teaching aids as Professor Hawkins does when he comments, 'By the mid-1970s there were few teachers or administrators who still believed that the language laboratory was the panacea that it had been thought to be in the early 1960s'.[1]

Language teachers of today, nearing the twenty-first century, find themselves in a privileged position in one sense, for they are the inheritors of a vast amount of technical development and pedagogical research which together enable teachers to deploy technical advances in the most effective and the most realistic way. There are no panaceas but there *are* many useful teaching aids on the market that keen language teachers will wish to exploit to the full. But, like most aids, they are only as good as the teacher using them can make them. In other words, the hardware can be bought, but to be effective, the software has to be developed by the teacher, using imagination and a vast amount of time and energy.

The tape recorder

The tape recorder (the reel-to-reel) has been common in the classroom since the early 1960s, but in recent years its more portable descendant, the cassette player, has become very popular in schools. Both types of machine have in-built advantages over the record player which has now become almost extinct for school use.

The main advantage of the tape player is that it brings to the pupils very faithful recordings of authentic speech of all kinds. That is to say that one does not merely have the possibility of hearing model native speakers recorded in studio conditions but that the techniques of recording and playback are now so effective that the voice of the man or woman in the street, and indeed other noises of the street, can be had at a moment's notice. Even the small cassette player is obtainable with so refined a loudspeaker that it is possible to hear it comfortably at the back of the classroom. However, for best results, a modest investment for each classroom for the installation of an external, wall-mounted speaker will repay the outlay with

---

[1] E W Hawkins *Modern Languages in the Curriculum* (revised ed.). Cambridge University Press, 1987

vastly improved listening facilities. The permanent fixing of the speaker on the wall with a lead and jack-plug for connection to the machine is a very simple installation task. The tape recorder should then be at the front of the class (away from chalk boards) and in the control of the teacher.

With all these machines, trial-and-error techniques will show how best to use the volume, tone, treble and bass controls. (A little more treble than bass is usually best.) The wise teacher will experiment by going to the back of the classroom to assess the quality of the sound. It is important to remember that the ear needs a moment or two to adjust and tune in to the loudspeaker and therefore a common remark from classes is that they cannot understand when the tape first begins to play. For this reason, if there is no 'lead-in' it may be necessary to replay the first part a second time. When the classes are sitting public examinations in which a pre-recorded tape is played, it is important to use the kind of machine the pupils are used to and, if possible, to allow pupils to hear some familiar material on the machine before the examination begins.

Group listening facilities with tape recorders

In recent years, a cassette recorder has been developed which allows five or six pupils to listen to the recording via a dedicated headphone system. Some machines also allow recordings to be made. These machines are perfect for facilitating a variety of activities to be carried on in a group work situation. In such a way we can allow a differentiation of activities in the modern classroom. A full discussion of such possibilities is to be found in the section 'Group work' on pp. 34 – 41.

Individualisation of work with tape recorders

As more and more pupils have their own personal stereos and cassette recorders, the possibility of setting new style tasks for homework becomes a reality. Instead of asking the class to write or to read, it should be possible to issue them with cassettes to listen to or even record their homework. This is not as far-fetched as it seems. A lot of schools are doing it already. To cut down the marking burden for staff, it will of course be necessary to have some kind of self-marking scheme for such work – or else the prospect of listening to 30 cassettes would be too daunting.

For the sixth form it becomes a very attractive idea. Instead of sending them to the library to research from books, why not have the library equipped with listening facilities? A tape recording is at least as attractive for some purposes as a book. There is less valuable teacher-pupil contact time taken up, so that more personal, face to face activities can take place during the timetabled lessons. It need not be an expensive investment – the English, music and humanities departments may share the facilities and the cost. Preplanning is needed of course, but done on a departmental team basis it is not a burden.

Notes on pre-recorded material

1 It is important to protect the cassette from accidental erasure by removing the protection device at the back of the cassette.

2 Some recordings are sold to schools on the understanding that a sub-master can be made for classroom use only. The label indicates when this is allowed. If so, make a copy and keep the master in a safe place.

3 All tapes should be catalogued and stored in a central point. A borrower's book is essential and all tapes should be returned to the central store as soon as possible after use.

4 Damaged or twisted (reel-to-reel) tapes should always be repaired before being returned to store. A colour code for side one (green) and side two (red) is a useful reminder. This can be applied by a self-adhesive sticky dot bought in hundreds from stationers.

5 Care must be taken at the end of the lesson to wind the tape back to the beginning.

6 When a reel-to-reel tape is indexed (a very helpful procedure) the box should indicate the machine the tape is indexed for and the size of the take-up spool. On a cassette tape, the order of the items is probably useful and if the recorders have counters the index number as well. (It is useful to choose machines with counters if at all possible.)

7 On a reel-to-reel, a rough and ready way of quickly marking a reference is to insert a slip of paper at that point and to wind back. Next time, wind forward till the paper drops out.

8 Preparation of tapes beforehand is vital. Time-wasting while the teacher fiddles with the tape is frustrating and the class loses confidence. All sorts of tricks can be employed – getting ready at break; getting ready while pupils write or are engaged in some other occupation.

9 It pays to have the printed script to hand if there is one. Any mishap with the tape – a blown fuse or worse – can then be overcome by reference to the script.

10 It is important to grade the use made of the tape recording carefully. Can the class benefit from short extracts or is it ready for longer passages? Has the context been set for the listening? It is rare in real life to listen in a vacuum. There is usually a context giving clues to aid comprehension. Setting the scene is therefore more realistic and more likely to help understanding. '*Maintenant vous allez entendre une conversation entre deux élèves qui parlent de leur*

école. . . Vous allez noter d'abord leurs classes d'aujourd'hui et puis leurs opinions sur la journée scolaire. . .' Such an introduction helps focus on the task and is more likely to lead to success than coming cold to a conversation.

11 Teachers should also keep in mind that listening is a difficult skill. The text is not under the control of the pupil as it is when reading, where one can flick backwards and forwards at will. At least at the beginner's stage the text may need to be replayed to help pupils understand.

Other uses for the tape recorder

1 Recordings made in the school to use for listening material and essay stimulus material. Assistants are invaluable for this kind of work, particularly in areas where they are thinly spread. Schools can usefully pool in-house material via consortia or the LEA advisory services.

2 Recordings made abroad by pupils (street interviews) and by colleagues (interviews with tradesmen, etc.).

3 Recordings made by pupils in exchange schools describing life at home and school.

4 School bulletins contributed to by many pupils. Recordings done in the mother tongue and in the target language are an excellent beginning to pupil-to-pupil exchanges.

5 Recordings made by assistants and staff for home listening (see above). To do this effectively, fast copiers have to be acquired and the services of a technician are invaluable. Ideal for fifth and sixth form work, for essay preparation and listening tasks. Good also for absentees.

6 When the school has no language laboratory, it is useful for the pupils to hear their own voices, e.g. as practice for oral tests.

7 Off-air recording involves copyright problems of all kinds. The BBC allows copying of schools broadcasts (particularly when they are broadcast at unsocial hours). It is usually stressed that recordings should be erased after the end of the school year. Colleagues working in schools abroad, who are often persuaded to record off air material for use in the UK, should be advised to check up on the regulations.

8 Transcription exercises are good in small doses for advanced classes. Whole passages or gap filling can be useful for calling attention to details and particular structures, or to a particular sound and a multiplicity of spellings.

9   A variety of musical activities is possible:

   a) listening to songs in the target language
   b) music to precede or accompany an activity – to give atmosphere
   c) musical accompaniment pre-recorded to allow the class to sing live
   d) home-made recordings of choirs.

10 Remedial exercises with built-in self correction for home use. These are not difficult to devise. Many traditional grammar books will supply the raw material the value of which is increased if the pupil can hear the exercise. The assistant can help with the recordings. A better effect is produced if two voices are used – the assistant gives the stimulus and the teacher supplies the response after the necessary pause. Then there is a further pause for the pupil to repeat (though not record) the correct version. Many language laboratory exercises will go easily on to cassette for home use.

The language laboratory

The rise and fall of the language laboratory is a story yet to be related in detail. Suffice it here to note that the first primitive laboratory was in use in the United States in the late 1940s and, by 1961, 2500 schools had been equipped in the United States, whereas in the same year Ealing Technical College was the first educational establishment in the UK to install and operate a full-scale language laboratory.[1] By 1965 there were almost 250 schools so equipped. The high-water mark was probably about 1970 when the decline then began because of the high cost of maintenance and the doubts raised about efficiency except in the case of highly motivated pupils. The most relevant study of UK schools was the carefully controlled York Study (Green 1975). This showed that exploited in the most typical way, the costly language laboratory did not improve the performance in German of 11+ beginners, when compared over three years with the use of the same materials played on a single tape-recorder in the classroom.[2]

Before dismissing the language laboratory, note the caveats: exploited in the most typical way and 11+ beginners. The York study does not belittle the use of the language laboratory or minilabs for sixth formers or in further and higher education, where greater maturity coupled with high motivation make the laboratory a valuable open access teaching aid.

The move in the past few years away from the Skinnerian behaviourist approach to the cognitive psychology of language learning has meant a new approach to the relationship between teacher, learner and machine. The need to *acquire* language

---

[1] D H Harding *The New Patterns of Language Teaching*. Longmans, 1967, p. 103
[2] E W Hawkins *op cit*, p. 180

rather than *learn* it has led to pupil-centred learning which views the teacher as facilitator. This is the message of many of the chapters of the present book.

It should be noted that if the four-phase drills beloved of the laboratory and the early audio-visual language courses are now frowned upon, there are nevertheless some uses for the lab in schools, for example, in the sixth form:

- listening comprehensions
- transcription exercises
- stimulus material for essays
- dialogues and simulated telephone conversations
- remedial pronunciation
- four-phase drill and testing
- drills for *ab initio* courses
- open access/private listening.

The slide/film-strip projector

A few years ago, every department made extensive use of the slide and film-strip projector. However, today many of the materials which were used then look somewhat dated; but this facility could be used in the department when appropriate materials are to hand. Relatively inexpensive and easy to maintain, there are occasions when slides and publicity material can be of use. Most language teachers are keen travellers and although we do not advocate tedious slide shows of a visit to Torremolinos, there can be value in the well-chosen shot to give background to the language study. Departments should have a collection of appropriate material in their departmental resources bank. Gone are the days, however, when every self-respecting course had a film-strip for each chapter. Children are often so sophisticated and used to the video cassette at home that this apparatus has largely stepped into the privileged place once occupied by the slide and film-strip. This will be dealt with later but, nevertheless, a few fundamental points about using the projector need to be noted.

1   It is important to be a showman and give the slides some impact.

2   A careful choice is necessary in order to illustrate the point in question (background or linguistic).

3   The pace of the lesson should be brisk. Film-strips and slides should be used sparingly. No entire lesson should be devoted to watching or the teacher will lose the two or three pupils on the back row all too quickly. A maximum of ten frames per lesson is really enough.

4   With older pupils, they can be used to spark off discussions/descriptions/debates, etc.

The overhead projector (OHP) _____

For most language teachers these days this is a basic tool. In some schools it has supplanted the blackboard. It can accept writing instantaneously and, in addition, slides can be easily prepared and very easily transported into the lesson. Indeed, much lesson preparation can be done beforehand which in former times could only have been done by taking the blackboard home! A further advantage lies in the colour presentation which can easily be achieved by home-made line drawings. And the most important point is the power of revelation it offers. It is easy to mask the distractions on the slide and hence present work in a logical sequence, sure of the fact that pupils are only looking at the part the teacher wants them to see at that moment. This is what is meant by progressive revelation and is achieved by a simple piece of paper or, for more complicated procedures, by paper cut out into various shapes to hide/reveal a more complicated design.

From the point of view of class control, the OHP is ideal, since the teacher can be facing the class all the time without having to turn round to write on the blackboard.

Again, as with all aids, it should be used properly, not over-used or the effect is diminished. It is always best to *switch off* once the OHP is no longer needed.

Using the OHP

1　Water-based fibre pens should be used if it is intended to erase writing later. Spirit-based fibre-pens are best for permanent slides. (Cellulose thinners can sometimes be used to clear this if needed.) For an even more professional look, the printing can be done on a computer desktop-publishing program and from the paper copy a slide made on special acetate via a photocopier. (NB It must be acetate specially produced for the purpose – ordinary OHP acetate will *not* do and may ruin the photocopier.) It is even possible to reproduce photographs and pictures in this way, so the teaching possibilities are endless.

2　Any picture can be traced on to the normal acetate.

3　Overlaying is a good way of building up the scene or a sequence the teacher wishes to reveal in stages. The layers can be added loosely or stuck on to the base sheet with sellotape rather like the opening doors on an Advent calendar. Different colours can be used on the overlays to represent the point being made. For example, a new colour for a gender, for a tense, for a verb ending, for speech bubbles – the list is endless. Once the idea has been grasped, further possibilities soon become obvious.

4　It is important always to check that the lens is correctly focused. It is best to do this from the back of the room.

5　Cut-out shapes in coloured plastic can be used to build up stories – they give a shadow-play effect.

6　Pupils can be invited to superimpose or remove layers at the teacher's instructions in the language.

7　For sentence patterns, lists of beginnings (subjects) middles (verbs or pronouns) and endings (objects) can be moved up and down to help weaker pupils compose new sentences.

8　Words and/or phrases can be written and cut into individual pieces of acetate to also help pupils compose sentences, by physically moving them over the OHP for projection.

9　The actual process of writing a composition can take place in front of the class. Pupils compose the sentences and the teacher (or pupil) writes them up as the lesson progresses. This can be later extended for use in the next (revision) lesson. The final story is written down, cut up into individual sentences and presented in jumbled order for rewriting.

10　Acetate transparencies which are to be stored need filing and keeping in transparent pockets.

11　Very impressive transparencies can also be obtained by using 'Letraset'.

12　In departments where the OHP is used on a shared basis, it is as well to apply the principle 'use one, make one'. In this way a substantial number of transparencies will be built up.

13　Some good transparencies are produced commercially, but the best ones are those made by teachers.

The spirit duplicator

This is often referred to as the 'Banda', from the well-known make. No teacher needs to be told of the existence of this invaluable tool which accepts handwriting or typing equally well, though bigger type is more successful than small. In addition to producing individual worksheets quickly and cheaply for reading, it is useful for staff notices, agendas and minutes if a computer is not to hand.

Publishers have recognised the appeal of the spirit duplicator and offer sets of masters which the school runs off as they are needed. Users should be aware that the carbon dries off fairly quickly and the number of copies obtainable is then reduced.

It is a noticeable trend, however, for publishers to turn more readily to photo-copiable masters. These produce endless copies for schools, but the photocopy fee is higher than with the spirit duplicator and departmental budgets need to take this into account.

The photocopier

No machine has improved more rapidly and become more widely available than the modern photocopier. The conventional one uses a powder to produce the copies. There is another type on the market which actually cuts a stencil auto-matically and then runs off the copies. (The stencil is like the old 'Roneo' type, but the whole process is automatic and not messy as in the past.) This is excellent if fine line drawings are not needed. It is also cheaper.

The photocopier is so handy that it brings dangers to schools in respect of the copyright laws (see p.9). Cut and paste methods, used attractively, produce high-quality work material. However, in some schools pupils seem to suffer 'death by worksheet', so we suggest that a proper policy is worked out to avoid the worksheet becoming overused (see pp. 74–5).

Blackboard v. whiteboard

The traditional blackboard and chalk are still the standby of most teachers. Dustless chalk has made the task of erasing slightly less hazardous for clothes and lungs, but at the same time the modern language classroom has filled up with the wonders of modern science listed above and chalk dust is ruinous to all of them.

Any teacher able to design a modern language classroom should therefore ban the blackboard and substitute a whiteboard which will do no harm to essential hardware. However, care must be taken to protect the whiteboard. Pupils and staff must be warned against using spirit markers which are difficult to erase. Markers left around for staff quickly disappear and are used for graffiti. Erasers need to be charged with clean water to work. Whose job is this and how does the teacher prevent the water getting into the cassette recorder during horseplay? A policy is needed.

One point against the whiteboard is that the surface offers less resistance than the traditional wooden board and handwriting appears to be more careless. Most whiteboards look messy at the end of the lesson and it cannot be good to set them as an example to pupils whose books have to be neat. Practice is needed with these boards and care at all times. Finally, the chisel-edged type of felt tip gives better handwriting than the pointed variety.

Better in many ways than the blackboard or the whiteboard is the OHP (see pp. 71–2) which, given the choice, is by far the best bet for the language room.

Display boards

All language classrooms should have plenty of display boards. Not only for display of posters, *realia*, etc. and pupils' work (properly mounted and regularly changed), but also as a teaching aid. Most primary schools make good use of display for teaching purposes and secondary schools can do as well. There will be the days of the week, the months, numbers, colour charts, etc. Especially in the early days of language learning, these are useful. Why not have the perpetual calendar? Why not have a German map of the world? Why not get the pupils to do a picture/word alphabet as a wall frieze? A visit to a local primary school will be worthwhile and it is often useful to look through infant/primary catalogues for display ideas.

Flashcards

Sets of flashcards can be devised to introduce, reinforce and revise many different linguistic topics. Concrete vocabulary is an obvious area but there is no need to draw objects. Excellent illustrations can be cut out from magazines, colour supplements and mail-order catalogues. Pictures can even be made by pupils. Collections of cards in series can be used to practise patterns, for example, reflexive verbs, verbs of motion, impersonal weather verbs, etc. A set of cards illustrating a story, later to be written up by the class, is another possibility. Flashcards with numbers can be used for mental arithmetic as well as weights and measures in other situations. Cards should be stored in marked envelopes and catalogued.

It is a mistake to think that flashcards are only for use in the early stages of language learning – quite complex structures can be developed (e.g. for the teaching of comparisons and superlatives) and can be used for role playing. Cards are also useful for group work (see pp. 34–41).

Worksheets

Having touched on the means of reproducing worksheets, it is also appropriate to mention some of the pitfalls in the design of such aids.

1   Worksheets must be clear and serve their purpose.

2   It is important to remember that it may be quicker to allow a pupil to write on the sheet – but then it cannot be reused. Handing out a work sheet and then

making the class copy into an exercise book is time-wasting and also when it comes to revision, answers in an exercise book don't help much without the original.

3   Worksheets can be graded for the mixed-ability class (e.g. an A or B version). This allows for differentiation of task and is essential for good teaching in many classes.

4   Using a mixture of upper- and lower-case writing is often easier to understand for the pupils.

5   Bandas in various colours can help decipher the work to be done.

6   The arrangement of exercises on the paper must be neat and self-explanatory. If the presentation is too cluttered it will risk confusing the pupils – especially the weaker ones.

7   Instructions must be clear at every stage of the sheet. Can pupils see exactly what they have to do? Do pupils know if they should write on the sheet or elsewhere?

8   If the sheet is to be handed in with their efforts, is there a space for pupil name and class?

9   Handwriting. Is it legible? Is it clear on all parts of the sheet? Does it fade at the edges?

10   Illustrations. Are they without ambiguity? On the other hand, teachers should not let themselves be so carried away by their artistic efforts that the time spent producing them outweighs the benefits to the pupils.

11   A useful book to consult is *How to Produce Better Worksheets* by Robin Lloyd-Jones (see Bibliography).

Radio and TV

The following categories are of most interest to teachers:
- schools programmes devised for secondary school pupils
- language programmes for adults
- foreign films broadcast in their entirety
- foreign news broadcasts from British broadcasters
- off-air recordings from foreign stations

- cassettes of foreign programmes sold by foreign stations
- relevant current affairs programmes largely in English
- some local radio station programmes.

These are dealt with below under separate headings.

For schools the advantages of using broadcast material and of recording it on a regular basis are obvious.

1 Cost is negligible apart from the outlay on tapes and cassettes and, initially, a time switch for recordings to be done after school.

2 The most up-to-date material becomes available immediately.

3 A whole new range of voices comes into the classroom.

4 The quality is excellent and in particular the background noises superb.

5 New topics of immediate interest which might well have escaped the teacher's notice are brought into the lesson.

6 For sixth-formers, the more adult approach makes the programmes more appealing.

Schools programmes

These are put out by both the BBC and ITV. Language programmes, from beginners to sixth form, are available in French, German, Spanish, Italian and Russian.

Full details are available as follows:

BBC The Schools Broadcasting Council (Annual Programme),
The Langham, Portland Place, London, W1A 1AA.

ITV The Education Officer,
The IBA, Brompton Road, London, SW3 1EY.

Language programmes for adults

These can provide very useful programme material to listen to and to watch. In addition to the basic programmes themselves, there is now a vast amount of excellent support material in the form of illustrated books with exercises (often self-correcting), notes, and audio/video cassettes of supplementary material not necessarily broadcast, though the texts themselves will be found in the course books devised to accompany the broadcasts.

Such materials are excellent for supplementing classwork and, in addition, can be safely recommended to pupils wanting extra practice. Sixth-formers whose oral work is not good simply because they have not been abroad will benefit from listening even to the more elementary programmes for, without exception, good native speakers are heard, some of them professionals but many of them men and women 'in the street'. When schools do the recording themselves off-air, pupils can be encouraged to borrow tapes on a library system for home use. Most broadcasts are well made in that the language work is broken up into manageable sections. But there is no substitute for the teacher knowing the material thoroughly and deciding exactly how much to play at any one time in order to make it digestible.

A third use for such material is served by the more varied further education language courses. They provide excellent material to recommend to pupils thinking of doing a different language after leaving school. To get an idea of what the language involves, books and tapes might be borrowed from a library. There are such courses as Arabic, Russian, Greek and Japanese.

Exploiting the broadcast materials

Further possibilities include:

1 Proof marking. Pupils underline discrepancies between an amended script and what they hear.

2 True/false questionnaire on material heard or seen.

3 Summaries of material heard or seen.

4 Reconstituting the dialogue of part of the programme.

5 Commentary over pictures with sound muted.

6 Transcriptions of part of programmes.

7 Note-taking for report on broadcast.

8 Comparing news items with printed items in newspaper.

9 Essay writing with broadcasts as stimulus

Foreign films

Happily these are now appearing more frequently on TV and often in subtitled versions that allow the sound to be heard without interruption. They are an excellent source of language and civilisation material. However, there are drawbacks. It is very unwise to push a film as yet unseen by the teacher, not only because it may contain unsuitable material but, quite simply, it may be a bad film and more harm than good is done by suggesting the wrong things. Again, films date and what may be remembered with affection from 25 years ago may be now so dated as to put sixth-formers off watching films.

Foreign news broadcasts from British broadcasters

The overseas service of the BBC can often yield good material, especially for sixth-formers. Such broadcasts cover British as well as foreign news, though reception varies in different areas of the country.

Off-air recordings from foreign stations

These can be obtained by asking friends and colleagues abroad to do recordings in their own homes, using a good VHF set, and to post the cassettes. To be effective, one needs to give them a list of topics since it is difficult to know what is coming up other than news broadcasts. However, these are worth having on any topic.

Alternatively, teachers who are well placed to pick up sound broadcasts direct can do their own recording. France is obviously the country in the best position to do this form. France Inter is on 1829 metres (164kHZ) on long wave and is usually very clear. Close to it on the long wave is Europe 1 (1674 m: 182 kHZ). The signal is not quite as strong but the programmes may appeal to teenagers more than France Inter.

Table 2: Useful radio wavelengths

Radio stations	Long wave	
France Inter	1829 metres	164 kHZ
Europe 1	1647 metres	182 kHZ
Westdeutscher/Norddeutscher Rundfunk	309 metres	971 kHZ
Deutschlandfunk	1986 metres	151 kHZ
Radio Nacional de España	518.2 metres	584 kHZ
	439 metres	683 kHZ
RAI Programma Nazionale	333 metres	899 kHZ
	225 metres	1331 kHZ
RAI Secondo Programma	335 metres	845 kHZ
Radio Moscow	1734 metres	173 kHZ

A useful source of information on French broadcasts is the London office of *Radio France* (France Inter, France Culture, France Musique), 64/6 Great Portland Street, London W1. This office issues a list of French radio stations with brief details of forthcoming broadcasts (see also the publication *Quid* edited by Dominique and Michèle Frémy which is detailed in the bibliography. This well-known French publication contains much information on this topic in its *Informations* section). Sixth-formers can be encouraged to listen in their own homes to such broadcasts though, regrettably, many cheap transistor radios are not equipped to receive programmes on the long wave band. In advising pupils to listen it is important to remind them that they need to develop a listening habit, i.e. it is better to listen for ten minutes every day at the same time rather than for two hours once a fortnight. They need to become familiar with voices and personalities.

A good source of of information for all wavelengths is the publication by George Wilcox *Dial-Search* (see 'Bibliography').

Cassettes of past broadcasts

These are sold by France Inter and a catalogue of some 500 cassettes is available from France Inter, 116 Avenue du President Kennedy, Paris 75786, Cédex 16.

Current affairs broadcasts

These need no explanation. Teachers should always be on the lookout for relevant programmes for their pupils. Having recommended pupils to listen or to watch, it is important to follow up the recommendation by asking for comment and opinion on the programme.

Local radio broadcasts

As far as we know, there is no local radio station putting out a regular series of language programmes. However, a number of BBC radio stations do take a general interest in local schools programmes and may be prepared to help with language programmes if asked to do so. Possibilities include:

- interviews with foreign assistants living locally (these could be in English and the mother tongue)
- broadcasts of lectures recorded at local sixth-form days and put on by the local college, university or language association
- broadcasts with phone-ins covering local exchange schemes, town-twinning events, ideas for entertaining foreign visitors in the area, etc.
- broadcasts of foreign carol concerts
- interviews with foreign speakers who have settled in the area to work or marry (the local chef?).

Teachers interested should contact the local radio station direct to propose programme ideas (and perhaps seek the support of the local authority when the area arranges a European Week or similar event).

One final word on all broadcast material used. All programmes must be previewed by the teacher first. Pupils can then have advanced warning of the language difficulties and sometimes receive background information which clarifies the programme. The teacher's preview also ensures that the programme is broken down into manageable portions for use in the classroom. It is helpful to interrupt the recording for questions and discussion to take place at the end of each topic covered by the broadcast.

Many broadcasts obviously make excellent listening comprehension tests, but for these to work well there has to be time between the broadcast and the lesson to allow the teacher to prepare suitable work covering both the subject matter and the language content.

Details of all broadcasts are also on the NERIS database: telephone 0525-290364.

Satellite TV

Exciting new possibilities are now available to enable the viewer to watch foreign TV satellite broadcasts. A modest dish aerial plus the decoder and electronic connections will enable the school to receive foreign broadcasts. As yet there is no single system and it is difficult to choose one system to capture all the available programmes. No doubt rational decisions will result in the future in some compromise but at the moment it is best to take advice.

Things are changing so fast that it is important to keep an eye on the specialist press to see what is becoming available. Live TV is difficult to handle for obvious reasons. Edited recordings (e.g. Olympus material) are much more effective.

However, what we have said about radio, TV and videos in the classroom applies also to satellite. It is important to be selective and above all be prepared to spend a lot of time editing in order to get a moderate extract of taped programmes for class use. It is certainly best to record and select for most classes. Direct reception, for example, of the news, will be interesting for sixth-formers, but more problematic for younger pupils.

How is it possible to know what is on the air and suitable for schools? There are various magazines and it is a good idea to subscribe to *Satellite TV Europe* which gives all the listings. The main satellites beaming programmes for language use are shown in Table 3.

It will be important to decide on the equipment as there are three systems for broadcasting and they are not mutually receivable. One of the best ways of

Table 3: Satellite stations useful for language work

Satellite	Language	Standard
Eutelsat 1 F4	German French	PAL
Eutelsat 1 F5	Italian Spanish	PAL PAL
Telecom 1C	French	SECAM
Gorizont	Russian	SECAM
Olympus	Variety	D2-MAC
TDF 1	French	D2-MAC
TVSAT	German	D2-MAC

exploiting this new medium would be to form a cooperative users' group so as to prepare work to enhance the programmes.

Video _____

There are many advantages to the video for the language teacher:

1   They bring authentic foreign culture into the classroom.

2   Expense is not great since the machine will belong to the school and can be shared. Tapes are not expensive.

3   Sound quality is usually better on video than it is on film.

4   Video is very convenient to use as there is no need for blackout facilities. It is reasonably portable for use in different rooms. It is flexible, with replay, freeze frame, fast forward, etc.

5   There is no need to disrupt the whole timetable to show a full length film since it can be seen in episodes in successive lessons.

6   Video is a modern medium and as such appeals to teenagers.

7   The addition of the visual element will greatly help understanding of the language element – language is put into a real context.

And there are certain dangers:

1   Watching television is such a ingrained habit that pupils may quickly allow attention to wander.

2   Teachers may be tempted to use the video because it is handy and 'keeps them quiet'. To avoid this trap it is essential to ensure that pupils are watching to a purpose and not just passively viewing.

3   Pupils used to slick professional TV production may be disenchanted with less sophisticated material.

Features to look out for are picture-search facilities for ease of finding the place on the tape, rapid fast-forward and rewind, a clearly displayed tape counter and a remote control to enable the teacher to adjust the volume, colour, and so on at a distance. A freeze-frame option is valuable for teaching, providing an opportunity for questions, such as 'What happens next?'

Software materials are easy to come by and, as well as broadcast materials, many publishers produce video tapes for their courses.

Golden rules for the video

1   A video should always be previewed before showing to a class, if necessary selecting and editing the sections to be shown.

2   It is important to give careful thought to the reasons for watching the video. What language purpose will it serve?

3   Even when using extended viewing, teachers should check from time to time that the class is with them.

4   Teachers should decide in advance on support material: handouts, questionnaires, blackboard support, OHP, etc.

5   The video should never be treated as a soft option; that is the surest way to waste time.

6   The activities should be varied, especially at the comprehension stage.

7   The teacher should exploit the prime quality of videos: moving pictures.

The use of the video in the home and the school has now almost completely taken over from 16 mm film. It is a much more flexible form of viewing and has thus opened up so many new possibilities.

The video camera _____

Most schools now have access to a video camera and the language department can make good use of this versatile piece of equipment. It is a motivator for all sorts of groups and can be used to great effect to record class progress, especially at the end of a topic which may culminate in a role play or more elaborate acted scene. Pupils like to see themselves perform and the result can be used to teach other classes or for parents' evenings. They are easy to operate even in restricted space. The teacher must be familiar with all the operating procedures, but pupils are always eager to help. *Like any other electronic gadget, it is only as good as the use it is put to.* Another idea well worth consideration is to use the results as INSET material for departmental use.

Possible ideas for the video camera:

- filming sixth-form debates for analysis afterwards
- making a news programme
- making a programme such as 'Blind Date' (lots of questions/answers)
- roving reporter' interviews in school
- interviews with visitors to school
- videos to send to twin schools detailing everyday school life.

The library

Some schools have modern language books stocked in the library in the care of a librarian while others maintain a departmental library for both pupils and staff. Yet other schools have a system which keeps a foot in both camps.

In the library, whether departmental or school, the following stock should figure:

1 Main reference books: dictionaries, (bilingual and mother-tongue), grammar books, language textbooks, self-correcting exercises, up-to-date year books (e.g.*Quid*).

2 Languages and careers: details of courses beyond the school.

3 Books on languages in general; examples of languages not taught in school.

4 Literature texts: set books and works by the same author.

5 Critical works.

6 History and geography: in English and in the language.

7 Social sciences.

8 Graded readers. Ideally one or two copies of all books on current catalogues.

9 Foreign language strip cartoons.

10 Pedagogy; books for staff; journals; magazines; newspapers.

11 Cassettes for readers – with listening carousel facilities; video cassettes.

12 Travel brochures.

13 Applied texts in the language: science, business material, etc.

Computers and IT _____

The new technology so often talked about by colleagues in other disciplines has now made considerable inroads into the world of language teaching. One hears of machine translation, automatic dictionaries, word processing, databases, Email, concept keyboards and the like. Many linguists have kept up to date and are now beginning to appreciate what IT can do for them and for the learner in the classroom. What is more, they cannot afford to ignore what is, for most children, a fact of life in almost every other subject in the curriculum. The developments over the past few years in CAL (Computer Assisted Learning) and CALL (Computer Assisted Language Learning) have been vast.

In the early days, there were computer courses in most schools and pupils were given one or two lessons per week as part of their PSD entitlement. As a result, it is now rare indeed for a pupil not to be computer literate. Indeed it is rare for an eleven-year-old to arrive in the secondary school without keyboard experience.

While it is true that in most schools the computer room is the central facility, it is now apparent that the next few years will see a devolution of this centralisation of teaching and learning *about* and *through* Information Technology. It is only when teachers see the computer and IT in general as an integral part of all teaching that they will truly appreciate the power of IT in learning and its true place in the classroom as a tool and aid for pupil development. As has been said about all teaching aids, IT is only as good as the material to be exploited. In this way it is no different from the TV, the cassette recorder or the OHP – it is the teacher who makes use of the new strategies available and who has the vision to exploit technology for what it is – a human invention.

Another factor which is now very present in teachers' thinking is how to motivate those pupils who, up to now, have not had the opportunity to learn a foreign language or who chose to abandon their study at an early stage. In particular, the special needs pupil, who needs motivation and also to some extent new methodology to make possible and enjoyable this new experience. Information technology is certainly one path to explore to help these disadvantaged and possibly disaffected pupils.

And so our vision for the computer in the language classroom is that it will be an integral part of activities available for the pupil and the teacher. Of course on some occasions it would be useful to have access to the computer room for a whole class, but a better way (avoiding also the need to prebook the IT a long time ahead) is to have a keyboard, monitor and printer on a trolley in the language room or at least available in the language suite. *Such decisions will be a matter for a whole school policy.*

Subjects which have brought computers into the centre of their teaching gain popularity with pupils. That is an important consideration; teachers cannot afford to teach in the Dark Ages.

As well as involving the pupil in IT activities with the aim of delivering the Modern Language attainment targets (ATs), language teachers should be aware that they can also make significant and meaningful contributions to the IT National Curriculum requirements where it is clearly stated that students should be able to use IT across the *whole* curriculum. By looking at the IT programme in this way and including it in the traditional subject areas, there can be some lessening of the pressures on the timetable as a whole.

IT is specifically referred to in the National Curriculum programme for Modern Languages. In the final report IT features in:

AT 1 at levels 3, 5 and 7;
AT 3 at levels 1, 2, 3, 5, 6, 7 and 8;
AT 4 at levels 1, 2, 4, 5, 7, 8, 9 and 10;
though it should be noted that other ATs may be enhanced via IT.

It is stressed that IT should be a means to an end and not an end in itself, so that it enriches the experience the pupils have. It will bring problems of management but at the same time it can free the teacher in the classroom to do other things. What we have in mind is a carousel of activities, based on group work (see pp. 34–41). There would be an input by the teacher and then at some point in the lesson or sequence of lessons, pupils would break into groups or pairs with well structured activities in individualised or group form to work in a semi-autonomous manner.

One of the possible reasons for the relatively slow uptake of computers into the language classroom (apart from the paucity of programmes when compared to the other 'obvious' subjects like Maths and Science) was the early output of the programmers. They devised materials rather on the lines of arcade games requiring input and output on predetermined lines and which took little account of the new trends in communicative methodology. What teachers were unable to do on a computer was to allow real communication if they were seeing the micro as a 'drill' machine. True, some of the monotony could be taken out of the learning sequence, if only in that it allowed pupils to work at their own pace as individuals. In short, what teachers had was a reflection of the traditional grammar-based teaching where the emphasis was on mastery of forms rather than on communication.

Over the last few years, with the advent of the communicative methodology and the inevitable shift from teacher-centred learning to pupil-based interaction, there has been a new thinking on the ways of integrating the computer into the 'new' classroom where there is more emphasis on pair work and group work, and more pupil autonomy.

The Education Reform Act and the advent of the National Curriculum have made it clear that the delivery of the IT component is to be done via the 'regular' subject areas and not in special lessons. Hence our claim above that the change from a single IT room to a facility in every subject area has strong official support.

What can be done within the language area, and bearing in mind the National Curriculum advice?

Word processing

- allows the pupil to create and edit texts, redraft material and produce high quality finished products (writing skill area)
- allows tentative experiments to be made without the terror of fixing the printed word too early in the process; takes away some of the trauma of committing words to paper
- correction of error is less threatening; the intimidating red pen is less present
- spell-checks help and support
- some users can concentrate on the message rather than the form – others can concentrate on the form *and* on the message
- children with special needs are less inhibited and intimidated when helped by computers
- a lot of language discussion can go on while using the software, especially if used in pair/group work
- creative linguistic experimentation is encouraged since drafting and redrafting is possible
- a tentative text can be entered by the teacher, for redrafting by pupils, and this can be one of the early stages of writing in the language; this involves the reading skill as well as writing
- software is available which involves on-screen instructions in the target language and the ability to use foreign characters and accents.

Desktop publishing

- allows word processing to be aligned with graphics and the subsequent manipulation of layout leads to the production of high quality finished print-outs for display and teaching
- creative teamwork in producing a class or school foreign language newspaper comes from discussion, reviewing and editing
- cross-curricular development is a real possibility in this area.

Databases

These collect, store, sort and retrieve information which the pupils collect and enter or simply act upon from a previously prepared database. The advantages are:
- a variety of simulations is possible to make real, for example, a visit to a tourist office for information or simulated office work in a foreign country
- a lot of language activity can be generated by the use of a database which is directly relevant to the world beyond the school
- the print-out of the information on such databases may enable the creation of appropriate role-play cards
- there are in existence some 'dedicated' databases (for example 'at the hotel') which can be used in simulations.

Databases can also be used in administration within the department – see the discussions in Part Two.)

On-line databases

These allow access to vast stores of information by means of a modem, telephone line and computer. They offer the following benefits:

- the material is up-to-date and topical
- it allows simulation of real life situations with FAX type material
- it is possible to access, for example, the French Minitel system with its thousands of facts and the German system called Telebox; this can be expensive in telephone time and another possibility is to use the indigenous systems such as Campus 2000 (formerly TTNS) or the Derbyshire database (for details of this, contact East Midlands Development Centre, SEDC, Ilkeston Road, Heanor, Derbyshire.)

Electronic mail

This allows conversations to be carried on electronically with others connected by the Email system. The following should be borne in mind:

- it opens up vast possibilities for communication with schools and other establishments abroad
- it is expensive on-line, but it is real use of real language – not an artificial game in the confines of a classroom
- messages received can be saved to disk and the real material thus obtained is very much up-to-date and brings immediacy to the classroom
- to save money in transmission, rather than type while on-line, the word processing should be done beforehand and the disk content transmitted
- to use the Email system, the school must subscribe to Campus 2000 (formerly TTNS). It will then be provided with the correct software and an individual identification code. As well as contacts within the UK it is possible to contact France, Germany and Quebec. Other countries will soon come into the system.

Drill and language practice

- via the numerous software packages available, the pupils are able to take remedial action with a computer to repair areas of confusion, to reinforce areas of weakness in the language as well as to engage in puzzles and other educational games
- some interactive software is available to guide the pupils in a self-tutor mode through branching activities.

Specialised packages

Special tasks can be set up, especially with more advanced students, using 'authoring packages' based on texts and exercises. For the more independent-minded this can be a useful self-tutorial system. The teacher is able to input a text or series of texts and the computer can then handle a variety of exercises on the text. Most have the possibility of instant feedback after each question and this is a source of motivation for the pupil, especially as the on-screen reply is to the individual and in that sense mistakes are a private affair. Some programs are so sophisticated that they can analyse error, suggest alternatives and even print out an analysis of the pupil scores!

There are packages which combine 'authoring packages' (with preset texts) and word-processing abilities (text manipulation). In these cases, for example, the pupil calls up a series of prewritten sentences which they can then re-form into (say) business letters.

Games and fun

Computers can be fun. And through them language learning also can be fun! Simulation packages such as the famous Granville can be used in very imaginative ways to stimulate interest. (NCET has an interesting video on the use of Granville in the classroom.)

Those teachers who have plunged into the world of IT have always been amazed at the results achieved by pupils which often go beyond what the teachers themselves can do! And there is a hidden bonus too. For by using IT in the language classroom, pupils are also acquiring other marketable skills for the world outside.

Most LEAs have an adviser for IT and very many also support development centres. There will always be advice from such people and, if teachers feel unsure about operating with computers, the advice is take the plunge and learn about them.

The hardware

What does the classroom need? Obviously if starting from scratch, planning in detail is needed. It will be good idea to start from year 7 and build up the facilities over the years so as to allow all rooms to have access. Security will be important and so will the need to have a language suite in order to share expensive equipment.

The ideal would be the following:

- microcomputer – the type will be important; in many schools it will be a BBC or Master, the increasingly popular Archimedes or the RM Nimbus.
- monitor
- dot-matrix and various other printers allow Cyrillic and other scripts to be printed as easily as Roman script
- concept keyboard – this is discussed below and is especially useful for SEN work
- access to modem for Email work.

Software

A variety of software for language use has been developed and the latest information can be had from NCET (see address section). We have not given a list of software as so much depends on the machine in school – your LEA will have an IT adviser who can help.

Suggested lesson sequences using a computer as a teaching aid

1   Finding out information for a holiday.
    (Assuming basic structures are known by pupils.)
    Pupils decide on the area of the country they wish to holiday in. They use a database in an imaginary tourist office to find out the facilities. A telephone conversation to the hotel to book rooms is simulated. A database is used to do this at the 'reception' end of the conversation. Pupils write a letter on the word processor to confirm. This could be done as group assignments.

2   Applying for a part-time job.
    Pupils use a database to find out what part-time jobs young people do in other countries. They then use the word processor to write a letter of application.

3   Setting up a penfriend service (imaginary or real).
    The teacher or the pupil can set up a simple database with various fields (name, age, interests, family, etc.). English applicants are typed in and then matched up with foreign pupils.

4   Producing a class newspaper.
    Pupils use 'French/German/Spanish Folio' software and real 'cut and paste' or a DTP program. News is made up or gathered from Email sources or simulated Minitel from a homemade database.

Special needs and IT

The micro can play a special role in the learning process for pupils with learning difficulties.

1   Word processing can help in writing. The fact that the end product is in an acceptable form helps motivate and the process of redrafting helps build up confidence.

2   Social skills are encouraged as pupils work together to solve problems.

3   Programs can give intermediate rewards for small successes – something which is appreciated by pupils.

4   A machine never tires with repetition!

5   Pupils with physical handicaps can access the curriculum via the computer. For example, the pupil who cannot physically write with a pen can produce written work via word processing.

The concept keyboard

Although this touch sensitive keyboard was developed in the first place for special needs, schools are now finding that it can be of real use in the early stages of language learning for all abilities.

Essentially the concept keyboard is linked to a screen and it can be very easily programmed by the teacher. Several possibilities are available. One square touched by the pupil can bring onto the screen a word, a phrase or even a whole sentence. Thus a pupil can easily compose whole stories on the screen without too much worry. Alternatively, the overlay on the keyboard could feature pictures or symbols in the squares rather than words. Thus, for example, a map on the keyboard overlay will produce the shop names on the screen when you press the correct square.

A more sophisticated program can work at different levels (for example 'Touch Explorer Plus'). The rich variety of language work that can be built around such software is only just being explored.

CD-ROM (Compact disc – Read-only memory)

This development offers a vast store of easily accessible information. It may not yet be possible to envisage them in schools, but the day will come when this will be possible. Examples so far seen are dictionary discs, for example, *Le Robert Electronique* and *Harraps Multilingual Dictionary*. The complexity of tasks available range from spelling checks and word searches to provision of synonyms, antonyms and quotation finding.

Conclusions

1   Each modern language department should have a representative on the school IT committee.

2   A whole school policy is needed.

3   Language teachers should know what skills the pupils bring with them from the primary school so that they do not reinvent the wheel.

4   Cross-curricular working should receive high priority.

5   IT must not be an afterthought; it should be part of the whole department's teaching and learning strategies.

Courses, course books and materials_____

Any work purporting to give an overview of resources for the classroom must refer to the wealth of materials produced regularly for and by teachers to enable them to do the job most effectively, and with the most suitable equipment for the courses as they are perceived at the time. As philosophies of language learning evolve, so the teaching materials must respond to new classroom needs. Anyone looking at a language course book published 25 years ago will immediately see the truth of this. Indeed, even ten years ago many books were in common use which have now almost totally disappeared from classrooms as pupils' needs have changed.

The rate at which new materials are coming out and old favourites are gradually being dropped means in fact that any publication which tries to include everything will be out of date in less than a year. For this reason we have chosen not to attempt to produce complete lists.

There is also a second reason which dissuades us from attempting a huge and fruitless task: namely that much of the work has already been done and is continually being revised and brought up to date by CILT. Consequently any teacher seeking a comprehensive review of teaching materials including recorded and visual courses, supplementary material, textbooks and grammars, general readers, background readers and vocabularies need only turn to the guides issued by CILT for any of the languages in the National Curriculum.

These guides are extremely comprehensive and well annotated, giving, in addition to author, title, publisher and date, a simple classification by levels. For full details contact CILT at the address given in the address section in Part Four.

Finally it should be said that every conscientious teacher must keep up to date with the publishers' catalogues which appear annually. An even more effective way of keeping up to date is to attend the annual conference of the Association for Language Learning (ALL), which usually takes place in March. At this course-conference all the educational publishers put together a most comprehensive exhibition of the latest teaching materials that can be seen anywhere in the country and probably in Europe. Details are sent to ALL members and to all schools.

The foreign language assistant (FLA) _____

Now that teachers operate under the Local Management of Schools (LMS) regulations, it is obvious that there is close scrutiny of all expenditure in schools. All the more reason, therefore, for using the assistant to the best advantage when teachers have one and for agitating for the services of an FLA in the light of the recommendations of the National Curriculum that there should be regular and sustained contact with native speakers for all learners of foreign languages.

The notes which follow are intended to suggest how to derive maximum benefit from an extremely valuable resource. Details of how to prepare for the assistant's arrival and settling in school are given in Chapter 15. In this part we are concerned with the work in the classroom.

Preparation   The assistant must understand from the start the need to prepare beforehand and keep records of what has been done. All staff should be involved in helping in this respect.

Levels   Initially the main difficulty for the assistant is to get a clear idea of what level of French, German, Spanish or Italian they can expect from pupils. Observation will guide them, but teachers should also ensure that the assistant has the chance to listen to recordings of oral examinations if possible.

Progress   The assistant should be warned that pupils learning English as a foreign language make much more rapid progress in the early days, because of the analytical nature of English and because of the relatively simple basic English grammar – no genders and little agreement.

Wide ability variations   This needs to be talked about as do personality differences. Is the reticent speaker to be left alone to listen? Should he or she be pushed or ignored? Home difficulties need to be pointed out occasionally.

Correction of error   The assistant should be warned against overcorrection, which tends to inhibit contributions. On the other hand, ignoring basic errors does no good whatsoever. The departmental policy on this matter should be shared with the assistant.

Speed of delivery   It is wise to warn the assistant not to speak at the speed he or she would use with a similar group of native speakers. This certainly applies down the school and even in the sixth form for many pupils. The assistant should understand that speed is not the most essential acquisition. All foreign speakers have at some time to ask a native speaker to slow down until they reach near-native speed themselves. Much more important than speed is the acquisition of a range of expression – vocabulary, idiom and established forms of speech (e.g. '*Ils sont sages comme des images*') which one only learns from the native speaker.

Problems to be encountered

It is a great help to assistants if the language teacher goes over the problems they are likely to encounter in the classroom. The following points may be a helpful guide to staffroom chat:

1   Behaviour – the departmental and school policy should be explained. In particular how to get help quickly as well as some elementary guidelines on avoiding trouble. A period of pre-teaching observation is useful here to help establish confidence.

2   Lateness to classes and/or failure to attend – the assistant should keep a register and report back to the class teacher.

3   Learning difficulties – each assistant should understand that his or her language presents particular problems to an English speaker:

   a) *Pronunciation*   The 'u' in French and the 'ü' in German, for example. Each language has its own pitfalls and these may never have occurred to the native speaker. The assistant should be encouraged to give a few minutes' practice at the start of the lesson to a particular pronunciation problem, e.g. the nasals in French, the Spanish 'b', 'd', and 'v'.

   b) *Gender*   Practice will help. So will the giving of rules: e.g. 'All words in *"ment"* are masculine except for *"la jument"*.' But warn against too much practice as it will inhibit fluency.

   c) *Numerals*   These are a real problem for foreign speakers, especially when written in 'number' form. Teachers should encourage regular doses of arithmetic, multiplication, addition, telephone number games, dates, etc.

   d) *Questions*   The assistant needs to be reminded that the foreigner abroad needs to *ask* questions more often than to answer them. The assistant therefore should ensure that every lesson affords the opportunity for pupils to put questions either to the assistant or to fellow pupils. It is helpful for the assistant to do exercises in putting questions, particularly colloquial forms which are widely used orally but not so common in the written form.

   e) *Tenses*   Practice with tenses is essential and fortunately such practice can take the form of games. For example, the assistant says what he or she is doing. Pupil A has to say what they did yesterday, and pupil B what they will do tomorrow.

Authentic materials

Reference will have been made to the need to ask assistants to bring authentic materials with them, but guidance will be needed on what to do with such materials. The following may be helpful:

Postcards   The assistant should show the postcard to the class, explain what it is, but always insist on a reply from the pupils in return, i.e. saying what the picture represents then questioning the group: 'Where do you think it is?', 'How far is it from Vienna?' The assistant should then hand the card to a pupil to do a present-ation to the class. Any type of picture can serve for this.

Mail-order catalogues   These are not just to look at. They can be used for imaginary shopping expeditions, for example, involving comparisons: 'This is bigger than . . . more expensive than. . . .' It can involve number work. All pupils have 100 Deutschmarks to spend and they choose and justify their choices.

Telephone directories   Pupils look up telephone numbers and say them to each other. They can also read and explain the introductory pages on emergency calls.

The Highway Code Pupils look at the details and say what they would do (conditional) at the various signs. The subject can lead to driving, passing the test, accidents, road safety, making posters for safety, being witnesses and answering questions etc.

Newspapers, journals, comics All to be looked at, but more importantly to be talked about. For example, pupils could interview the main character in a story. In the sixth form comparison of several versions of the same story would be useful.

Official forms If the assistant will plunder the local post office, etc., a large number of useful forms will provide excellent role play material.

Maps Town plans from the local tourist offices provide extensive work for pupils at all stages – direction finding is just one way of exploiting the material. The use of geographical maps of the country is important, firstly because pupils need to be familiar with the location of the main towns and regions and secondly because practice with the names of places can be important to the traveller.

Some general ideas for the classroom

Pass the parcel (Using an old telephone instead of the parcel.) The telephone is passed round. When the assistant makes the 'ringing sound' that pupil has to hold a short conversation with the assistant on the topic appropriate to the class work at the time. This can be competitive, with 'dropping out' if needed.

Bingo Instead of numbers, words or even pictures are used which the caller describes simply for the pupils to cross out on their cards. Topics for words or pictures vary according to the current work/topic of the class.

Balloon game Pupils decide who should be dropped overboard and why!

Desert island game Pupils have to decide (in teams) what they will need to survive on the desert island and justify their choice. They should use everyday items from vocabulary areas of present subject/topic.

20 questions The person who has chosen the hidden object can only answer with 'yes' and 'no'. This is good for eliciting questions from pupils.

Blockbusters As in the TV game.

Wanted posters Pupils draw wanted 'mug shots' after a verbal description.

Spot the difference The assistant gives out two almost identical pictures and asks for the differences. If they find it difficult to obtain these, they should photocopy a picture, using correction fluid and pens to make slight differences.

Interviews These can be at any level – from simple conversations with pop personalities to real-life scenarios such as job interviews.

Songs

It is important that the assistant is warned against becoming known as the one who does nothing but play records. Songs are learnt in schools for sound pedagogical reasons as well as for pleasure. But the song must be chosen carefully for its language content, the clarity of the singer's voice and the subject matter. The assistant should play the song, then ask simple questions about it. Then the work begins. The assistant does a vocabulary/grammar study of the song, commenting on detail and whenever possible asking for synonyms for the actual words used. To round off this section the pupils receive a copy of the words (NB: not first). The assistant then reads the words and the class follows. The record/tape can then be heard again and the pupils may join in. Finally, the pupils learn a verse or two and exercises may be brought in ('fill the gap', etc). This sort of activity may well be tried in the school language club.

Help with compositions/essay work

The assistant may often be asked to help with essay planning in the sixth form. To do this most effectively, he or she must encourage the group to talk around the subject, to pass ideas from one person to another, possibly based on a stimulus text, picture or even recording. Equally important is his or her role as provider of appropriate language. In any discussion on *Atomwaffen*, the sixth-former is not short of ideas and opinions to express, but *is* short of the language which will permit him or her to express the ideas. Here the assistant is very useful.

Very important is the structure of an essay and most assistants are well versed in this. They bring the ideal antidote to the 'splurge-type' approach which so many sixth-formers mistake for essay writing.

Finally it should be remembered that the assistant will have a better idea of the standard to be expected and the problems encountered by the pupils if they are involved in some way in the marking (see p. 97).

Spelling and the alphabet

This is often neglected. The assistant can help in various ways.

1   The assistant should be asked to make sure that every pupil knows the alphabet in the target language.

2   Spelling bees can be used as five-minute fillers.

3   All pupils should be able to spell their name, the name of their street and country in the French way (a useful telephone skill).

4   Making up words from a long one such as *anticonstitutionnellement*, *prestidigitateur*, *Kraftfahrzeugmechaniker*, or *Lungenentzündung* involves calling out letters.

5   Crosswords are good group activities. Plenty of collections are available or can be made up and put onto OHP or worksheets.

Sixth-form literature

The assistant may help with this in several ways, but the wise teacher will ensure that there is a willingness to assist in this area. A negative approach from a less than enthusiastic exponent is likely to counteract the teacher's approach. If the assistant is agreeable, give him or her time to read the book carefully and, if possible, discuss it with the teacher. The main thing is to avoid duplication of the literature class. Examples of activities are:

1   Class readings of scenes from the play, with some basic analysis.

2   Class discussion on certain roles – the parts are taken by pupils and each character defends his/her action in the first person.

3   Class reads and discusses other works by the same author.

4   Discussion of topics from past papers.

5   Quiz of 'Who said what . . .?', 'Who did what to . . .?' or, after reading part of text, 'What happens next . . .?'

6   Narration. After reading a scene, pupils retell the events in the first person.

7   The class listens to an extract on tape and discusses the interpretation by the actors.

Having said this, we recognise that many teachers have perfectly valid reasons for not involving the assistant in this sort of work.

Civilisation topics

As the A-level syllabuses change and as other examination courses are introduced, there is a greater emphasis on *civilisation*. The assistant can play an important role in this area, especially for updating information. The following suggestions are not just meant for the sixth form, though they are all possible there. It is hoped, however, that skilful treatment of these and similar topics will provide a stimulus which may encourage some pupils who want to continue their language(s) in the sixth form.

Assistant's home and home town as a microcosm of the nation The assistant talks and presents illustrations of all kinds and insists that the class gives back all they learn. Some individuals write to the tourist bureau of the town being studied. Other places to write to include the local newspaper (following up promising adverts), the town hall, *mairie, Rathaus,* Chamber of Commerce, town-twinning bureau.

Schools Not a talk on 'Education in Germany' or 'Educational Policy in Barcelona' but 'What I did when I was at school.' Assistant shows books, primary readers, marked exercises, etc. Class asks questions as well as replying.

Major industries Cars, *haute couture,* wine, electronics, etc. The assistant collects examples of publicity, etc. Some class members could write for further information.

The capital city History, geography and growth. Involves slide show with commentary.

Youth activities, colonies de vacances, classes de neige etc. Scouting, religious and political movements.

The role of women in . . . Some talk from the assistant but this should stimulate discussion.

Language varieties within the country

Food Regional specialities. Pictures and recipes. Some class members may be asked to bring recipes (e.g. for Yorkshire pudding). At the end of term the assistant could cook a simple dish.

Involving the assistant in the school

As stated earlier, teachers should do their best to make the assistant feel he or she is fully a part of the school community. The following suggestions will help in this direction:

Marking Here we distinguish between marking and assessing. All parties benefit if the assistant and the teacher read the pupils' work together – especially sixth-form work. The teacher up-dates his knowledge, the pupils gain from the authentic suggestions made by the assistant and, finally, the assistant gains himself by acquiring a first-hand knowledge of what the pupils are capable of. The *evaluation* of the work is, however, entirely the teacher's responsibility.

Preparations for visits abroad Exchange visits should be a high priority on the department's list of activities. Preparation is vital and the help of the assistant should be sought.

Preparation of teaching material All good teachers prepare new materials for teaching or testing and the assistant will be an ideal consultant.

Modern Language days Assistants can make a valuable contribution.

Language evenings for parents/open days   If the assistant is invited, real authenticity is guaranteed. Such meetings can lead to invitations for assistants to visit homes.

The choir   The carol service puts the language department in a good light if there are one or two carols or even Bible readings in the foreign language. The assistant can help train performers.

Displays   The assistant can help produce lively classroom display material.

Authentic written material   The production of authentic written material such as penfriend letters is a useful activity and handwriting styles are genuine!

Recording   Recorded material can be produced which is appropriate to the age and experience of the pupils.

Interviews   Assistants can be interviewed by pupils on sound or video cassette.

Helping staff   Teachers' linguistic skills can be updated.

Information technology   The assistant could prepare texts for use on the computer or material for a database.

Withdrawal groups or working with the teacher in the classroom?

As part of the departmental strategies for its teaching and learning styles, the role and the deployment of the assistant must be taken into account. As teachers evolve a methodology involving more and more group/pair work, the assistant becomes even more valuable. In the section on group work (pp. 34–41) we have discussed this scenario. The assistant becomes an extra expert in the normal classroom and if involved in the planning stage for such activities a whole range of possibilities becomes available. It is one way of reducing the pupil/teacher ratio.

Don'ts for the assistant

If may be helpful to the assistant if the regular class teacher says at the beginning of the year what he or she should *not* do if the class is to have good, effective and worthwhile lessons:

- don't lecture on the subject – ensure the class contributes
- don't give the impression that you don't care if pupils attend or not
- don't allow pupils to cause major distractions which demand lengthy use of English
- don't allow time-wasting
- don't ask pupils to do things that are way beyond them
- don't ask pupils to speak at length on subjects without preparation
- don't mimic a pupil's attempts
- don't overcorrect as this may inhibit

- don't play records/tapes every lesson
- don't expect pupils to be knowledgeable about institutions in your country
- don't be disappointed if pupils are not very interested in politics or film as an art form.

Dos

While the class teacher lists the above points, it is essential to be positive as well. It is well worth stressing the following:

- cultivate a good attitude – pleasant with a serious attitude to work itself and language in particular
- develop a good voice manner for public speaking – one which expresses confidence and which is not monotonous. If the class seems lost, *slow down*
- prepare material carefully
- present material effectively. Don't use all the best material in the first few minutes
- learn names quickly. Use name cards or labels
- conclude the lesson by telling the class what will happen next time. If a topic is to be prepared, give some guidance and help.

Outside the language class

Finally, it will be worthwhile underlining the fact that many assistants may be able to make valuable contributions to the classes of colleagues outside languages. This is especially true as nowadays many assistants do not intend to become teachers and may be following courses in disciplines outside the traditional teaching subjects. The best way is to ask colleagues to invite the assistant into their lessons, in the first instance mainly to improve their English. From this, spontaneous offers can arise from the assistants and this helps cultivate the European Dimension within the National Curriculum.

Miscellaneous resources (things to make, do and collect)

1 Visual aids can be made which illustrate those things and actions not demonstrable in the classroom. It is a waste of time and resources to draw hands, faces, figures walking, etc.

2 When abroad make an effort to collect: old telephone books; post office forms; car-showroom literature; tourist leaflets; food packets; posters from cinemas and supermarkets; timetables from the railway and bus stations; shop-window dressing – pictures of food, plastic fruit, pictures from photographic shops, etc.

3   Calendars and diaries are useful for many purposes. Out-of-date ones can be bought very cheaply after March. The language room must have an up-to-date calendar. Old calendars from friends often contain illustrations of an area.

4   Catalogues of all kinds are worth hoarding. Mail-order catalogues are good for number work and role play, as well as for arousing general interest about things from abroad.

5   Old magazines, preferably well illustrated ones, are good value. They provide cut-out material for flashcards and games. Magazines specialising in radio and TV programmes are useful.

6   Children's indoor games no longer wanted by the French, German or Spanish family who bought them can have an extended life in the classroom.

7   School stationery purchased abroad is always attractive. If all language notices are put up on French squared paper they will always be distinctive. Some pupils like to use it too. It is worth encouraging them to do so and makes a cheap and different present brought back by those able to go abroad.

8   Maps, town plans and out-of-date red Michelin guides are all ideal material for group work and role play.

9   Stamps do not seem to have the appeal they once did but a subscription to the Philatelic Bureau of the country whose language is taught will provide advance information on new issues which makes excellent display material.

10 Food is of primary interest and a wonderful collection of pictures of food, menus from restaurants, recipes, etc. can quickly be assembled.

11 Pupils' hobbies can be reflected in collections made. Interest in computers, fashion, sports, etc. can be stimulated. A group of pupils might maintain an up-to-date chart of the French/German football leagues.

The aims of building up such collections is pedagogic in that useful teaching material is virtually free of cost. At the same time the interest value is high when the material is put on display and the psychological impact should not be overlooked. Pupils should be invited to help with displays and it is a fact that if they help to produce wall material themselves, there is less likelihood of destruction by vandalism.

For a development of the theme of using *realia*, it is worth consulting *Using Authentic Resources* by Barry Jones (see 'Bibliography').

8 The sixth form

It is in the sixth form that so many of the problems concerned with modern language teaching come together and in this chapter we shall consider the most important of these and note the solutions already available or those proposed for the future.

The students

It has been the fashion for a number of years to speak of the 'new sixth', meaning by this the much broader intellectual range the sixth-form teacher is required to provide for as post-16 education becomes increasingly necessary.

As a result there are sixth-formers who fall into the following categories:

1   The traditional sixth-former doing two, three or more A levels, having come into the sixth with a number of high grade GCSEs.

2   Students doing a mixture of GCSEs plus A levels.

3   Students intending to leave at the end of the L6 year.

4   Students starting a language *ab initio*.

5   Students preparing for examinations other than those set by the traditional GCSE/A level boards and at different levels and for different reasons.

6   Adult students 'dropping in' to do, say, one A level.

Organisation

Not only has the number and type of sixth-formers increased over the years, but also the type of establishment in which they are taught may have changed. This will largely depend on the pattern for sixth-form work chosen by the LEA:

1   A conventional sixth form in the same building as lower forms;

2   A conventional sixth form serving a consortium for a group of local schools;

3   A sixth form or tertiary college;

4   An FE college.

We are not embarking here on a discussion of the merits or the problems of each system, for it is obvious that from the students' point of view the work will be the same in any kind of establishment. The social ambience may be different, but to a large extent that is not our concern here, except to note that the student-teacher relationship will be important in all cases.

The induction course

Whatever the students' background, the language teacher has to beware of thinking of them as sixth-formers from the word go. Usually they are fifth-formers of two months ago and some, if not all, will not be too sure of themselves. They will need an induction course to initiate them into the mysteries of the sixth form. This aspect of sixth-form life may be particularly demanding in languages, but not a unique phenomenon, and as such will require sympathetic handling from teachers.

Before looking at some of the problems particular to the post-GCSE students and the need to address some linguistic challenges, it is important to face up to some more fundamental skills: study skills, study habits and attitudes.

Methods may vary according to the kind of establishment in which the teacher works but nevertheless the wise sixth-form teacher will ensure that whatever the background and past experience of the students it will be very helpful to initiate them into study methods appropriate to the sixth.

Study skills

The ultimate goal is to produce students who are capable of working by themselves effectively so that they are ready for the next stage, whether it is in higher education or the world of work. For the language student we suggest the following study skills need to be fostered.

1   Reading to some purpose: for this a programme of guided reading needs to be evolved which will require the student to discover information and evaluate it.

2   To achieve success in 1, the student has to acquire the skills of questioning what they read and reaching their own conclusions. This will come about only if teachers avoid 'feeding answers' such as were often provided by the old literary histories. In a few cases uncritical reading habits have also been a direct result of poor tenth and eleventh year teaching methods.

3   Dictionary use is a vital skill for sixth-form studies, and useful exercises can be set which will require the student to read carefully before selecting a word, e.g. looking for synonyms and antonyms, taking an English word such as *what* to

find how many different translations are possible. Work with bilingual dictionaries and foreign language dictionaries with definitions is essential.

4 Specialist dictionaries and reference grammars should also be properly introduced, e.g. dictionaries of proverbs, dictionaries of difficulties. With tasks assigned, students should become familiar with these works. Other reference works such as Roget's *Thesaurus*, Brewer's *Dictionary of Phrase and Fable*, the *Statesman's Yearbook* should also be introduced.

5 Reference books such as *Quid* and *Duden* should quickly become friends and this is also best done by setting assignments such as comparing basic details about towns and countries, or by requiring the student to find out the meaning of acronyms well established in the foreign language.

6 The ability to use recorded material correctly is a positive skill. Students should be given the chance to explore the use of recorded cassettes, etc. as an aid to learning. The same applies to video recordings which are now part of all well equipped resource centres. Computer software has now become an information source and students need to be trained to use databases and the like (see Chapter 7).

Study habits

In addition to the process of familiarisation with the tools of the trade, there are habits of work which the students should be encouraged to develop.

Listening habits Students should be encouraged to listen regularly to foreign radio. If this is too remote or if the material is unsuitable for any reason, the provision of cassettes for home listening is equally effective and probably easier to control (for a list of the major foreign stations which can be heard in the UK see p. 78).

Reading habits Unless teachers take newspapers and magazines into the classroom and show students what is in these publications, they are unlikely to be read. It is worthwhile spending 15 minutes per week going through the papers and handing out papers with requests for brief summaries to be presented orally in class. If this is done on a regular basis with the teacher and/or the assistant, it will serve not only linguistic ends but also a more general educational aim of widening horizons and combatting chauvinism.

School library Students will not be confident in the library unless they are shown what is available. Half an hour in the library at the start of the course is time well spent.

Local resources A visit to the public library will pay off later. If there is a good working relationship with a local college or university it may be possible for sixth-formers to visit the library even if they cannot borrow books.

Habits of study should already be well fixed but they may not be. It is therefore the teacher's duty to foster habits of regular study by setting and marking work on a regular basis.

Coupled with this is the need to teach students how to take *criticism* positively. To do this there does have to be a regular discussion with individuals about standards of work.

Revision skills should not be neglected. In the present A level where separate texts are taught it is wise to require students to return to work already covered to revise on a regular basis.

General attitude

All the above might well be labelled the bread and butter of all sixth-form instruction, but without it the average student will not get far and this is why we advocate some kind of induction course at the start of the sixth form. Perhaps more difficult to inculcate are the right attitudes to language study. Here it is not so much a matter of *precept* as of *manner*. Right attitudes are contagious and the keen sixth-form language teacher can pass on almost imperceptibly his or her enthusiasm for the subject by:

1   Creating an opportunity to hear and better still speak the foreign language – teaching in the target language should be the norm.

2   Setting oneself translation problems when one suddenly hears an English phrase; it may be silly ('his candyfloss is next to the fire hydrant!') or it may be a grammatical teaser – teachers should want their students to be curious.

3   Taking a general interest in the happenings abroad – political, social and cultural.

Appropriate language activities _____

The induction course outlined above might well take up the first half term in the sixth. Side by side with these general study methods the sixth-form teacher is introducing a whole range of language activities; this process will go on throughout the lower sixth year.

Below we set out a range of activities we would hope to see sixth formers involved in.

Although the following are listed under separate skills, it should be noted that mixed-skill activities will often be possible. It is to be seen also that the activities may lend themselves to other skill areas.

Listening skills

- transcription
- dictation
- comparing spoken text with written text on the same topic
- taking notes in the target language
- summarising
- listening to a recorded version and filling in gaps in the written version
- listening to material and using a true/false exercise
- listening to a passage and finding equivalents to phrases from a list (jumbled?) supplied in English or the target language
- listening to a conversation and filling in a form (eavesdropping), e.g. at a hotel
- listening to text and noting down points for and against in an argument
- listening to text and marking in a pre-prepared grid, items such as 'when', 'where', 'who', 'how', etc.
- listening to text and having to put jumbled sentences in correct order
- playing 'Chinese whispers'
- listening to answers and then supplying questions
- listening to text and then supplying all words/phrases expressing (say) disgust, etc.
- listening to text and then with the help of key phrases having to reconstruct the argument.

Reading skills

- answering questions in English or the target language
- finding definitions from the text
- finding opposites from the text
- finding synonyms from the text to suit a given list in the target language
- true/false exercise
- transposing from one tense to another or from one person to another
- finding words/phrases from the text to match equivalents in English
- finding all ways in the text to express (say) anger
- reading two different accounts of an incident, then trying to find the truth or differences
- making a *résumé* of the text
- translating
- mixing up pictures and captions then unravelling them
- filling in a form (e.g. a police report form) after reading an account
- reading a tourist brochure. Writing an equivalent in English (could be the other way round)
- reading text and presenting a for-and-against summary.

Oral work

Some of the ideas above can be done orally. Other ideas include:

- verbalising visual material – cartoons, maps, pictures, photographs, etc.
- reporting
- interpreting some material to a native speaker (e.g. a newspaper article)
- role play
- debates
- interviewing – this can be a mixed-skill activity involving writing a job advert (or using real ones from the paper), writing a job description, writing a CV and applications, telephoning for an appointment, interviewing candidates and appointing a new employee
- carrying out an opinion poll/survey.

Written skills

Many of the above ideas plus:

- translation
- essays
- summary
- newspaper reports
- letters of all kinds
- guided writing
- interpreting statistics, etc.
- CALL exercises
- Grammar exercises.

No doubt the teacher will be able to devise other ideas in the light of the demands of the particular syllabuses being used.

Examination syllabuses _____

To cater for the much wider range of needs of sixth-formers, a varied range of courses can now be offered which are summarised here to remind teachers of the possibilities open to them. The important thing of course is that not only should the language teachers be aware of the existence of such a variety but also pupils and parents need to be well informed long before the pupils enter the sixth form. This is why a departmental book listing courses available is essential. Good advertising lower down the school will help produce viable groups.

Advanced level

There are a number of innovative syllabuses now available from the various boards and certainly things are changing. Perhaps there will still exist for a long time to come 'traditional' A levels with proses and unseens – but the newer syllabuses emphasising other skills, based on authentic materials in a wide range of registers, seem more appropriate to candidates whose basis is GCSE. New syllabuses are appearing and while literary studies will probably not disappear totally, the type of exercise which requires long discussion in English almost certainly will. New content areas from spheres other than literary ones will provide the substance of much discussion and enquiry. To operate such schemes with a substantial course work element will involve a rescheduling of teaching and some greater emphasis on autonomous learning. Certainly teachers must take these developments seriously since their students now arrive with skills markedly different from their predecessors. If teachers do not take such considerations into account, they will end up with disgruntled students before the end of term one in the lower sixth. One major problem to be addressed is that of materials. It seems unlikely that at the moment there will be one single suitable textbook available for all the options available for study and so a departmental bank of materials will be needed.

AS level

Again there is a variety of syllabuses on offer. The most important thing to remember is that the AS is designed for A level students, as a complement to other A levels. It is not meant to be the course for those new, non-A-level students now in our sixth forms. If this is borne in mind it may be possible to timetable A and AS together for part of the week. Careful scrutiny of the syllabus details is needed. The original intention was for the time allocation to be about 50 per cent of that for A level.

The Institute of Linguists

Grade II is often said to be roughly the same standard as A level and a number of colleges will accept a grade II pass as equivalent to an A level for entry on a language course. For some, the attraction has been that there is little or no literature but there are other subjects for which a considerable depth of knowledge is required to pass. Until recently the exam has been a bigger favourite with the FE colleges than it has with schools. Syllabuses are available direct from the Institute of Linguists (for address see 'Organisations useful to the language teacher').

The Royal Society of Arts

The RSA organises vocational and nonvocational language examinations. There is a series of examinations designed to reflect the recent emphasis on communicative language learning and testing. Stage II is rather above GCSE and stage III is defined as rather above A level. There are also examinations in languages for business – French, German, Italian and Spanish.

City and Guilds

Examinations are arranged in English, French, German, Spanish and Italian at two levels. They are designed for a variety of candidates:
- those leaving school at 16
- those following a programme of further education and training
- mature candidates
- those in employment seeking work in the foreign country
- those who need to work with foreign nationals.

The syllabuses are vocational in orientation.

The Business and Technical Education Council (BTEC)

BTEC validates language courses proposed by centres. As the name clearly indicates, courses will be of a vocational nature. The emphasis is on the realistic use of authentic material through assignments and tasks for communicative purposes, rather than on conventional language exercises, e.g. 'Making a telephone call for a third party', 'Greeting a visiting sales team', etc.

Foreign Languages at Work (FLAW)

The London Chamber of Commerce and Industry runs FLIC (Foreign Languages for Industry and Commerce) and from this grew the FLAW scheme. Here again, teachers propose the syllabuses for their centres and the aims are defined as skills to be acquired. The most exciting part of this scheme is that it is specifically aimed at pupils in the sixth form who would otherwise have dropped all connections with languages. Full details from LCCI (for address see 'Organisations Useful to the Language Teacher' in Part Four).

General studies

Some general studies syllabuses require work in foreign languages. Though limited in scope, it is better than nothing, though some of the requirements are not very imaginative.

Technical and Vocational Education Initative (TVEI)

TVEI projects offer exciting possibilities in the sixth form. Courses are centre-based and are typically very much integrated with other areas of learning. Such courses have to be practical, involve interpersonal skills, have outcomes useful beyond the classroom, foster student independence and involve a variety of modern communications such as IT. Most LEAs have a TVEI coordinator who will be happy to discuss developments.

Links with other subjects _____

An important attitude to foster is one which ceases to see modern languages as a subject apart from other school activities. Instead we would hope that more and more of our pupils and our colleagues would come to see languages as a skill which can enhance other subjects. To this end we consider it important to seek to involve other colleagues in sixth-form classes which have direct links with other areas of the curriculum – history and geography are obvious links and so too are the various literary movements that are reflected in the different languages.

The use of IT _____

As in lower down the school. the computer can be used to enhance the language lesson. In the sixth form, it may very well be possible that the students could present their written work directly from a word processor – IT put to a very real practical use. In other ways, a database can be use to enhance the language programme. Furthermore, one of the most innovative and exciting ways is to use a desktop publishing system to produce a foreign language newspaper. Ideally this will be a team affair. News items are received in the 'news office'. Items can be taken from written sources, from interviews by sixth formers, etc. and even downloaded from Minitel or other on-line data services. The stories are word-processed in the target language and then the editorial team gets together to design the pages and make up the copy via the DTP system. The final version is then photocopied for sale in school (or to parents and beyond), hopefully beating the deadline! It can be in several languages and can involve a variety of skills – linguistic and others – all to a very real purpose. The idea of producing a news-paper in a day has been one of the most exciting events imaginable in a number of schools.

Preparing for beyond the sixth form _____

All sixth-form teachers should have in mind what the aims and ambitions of their students are. For those who have none, teachers should try to provide some! The following are some ways of arousing interest beyond the sixth:

- talks on languages other than those taught in school
- careers talks by modern language staff and others
- visiting speakers (former pupils, college lecturers, industrialists, etc.)
- organised visits to universities, polytechnics, colleges and industry to hear about languages
- careers days.

Visits abroad

The sixth-former has almost certainly outgrown the traditional trip abroad, unless one or two go as escorts for exchange visits or schemes. Generally it is far better to get them abroad with another aim in mind – school visits, work placements, etc. The following ways are all possible:

- exchanges
- au pair posts
- visits to reside and work in school for a period
- working holidays or placements.

The Central Bureau for Educational Visits and Exchanges (CBEVE) publishes a useful book *Volunteer Work Abroad.* (This is an occasional publication available from the Central Bureau whose address is to be found in Part Four.) With careful planning and good contacts, it may be possible to organise overseas work placements in banks, restaurants, industry and offices. If it can be done on a reciprocal basis, accommodation problems are less pressing. The benefits can be enormous, but one must not underestimate the amount of planning needed. The CBEVE may be able to help.

Social contacts

The assistant can become a real friend of the more mature sixth-form pupils. It is well worth encouraging as both parties can benefit from the formal and informal contacts.

Students should be encouraged to seek out every opportunity to attend conferences, study days, sixth-form days, plays and films run by ALL branches, the local colleges and universities.

Some sixth formers benefit enormously from being asked to help lower down the school. They effectively consolidate their own sometimes shaky grammar and benefit from additional self-confidence acquired from teaching someone else how to do something. In some schools, this practice has been developed as a major teaching technique and is capable of extensive application.

9 Five-minute fillers and end-of-term treats

Every lesson probably has a five-minute corner into which the imaginative teacher can tuck a language activity which will:

- provide the bridge between one main activity and another (variety will be more important in the increasing tendency to teach in double lessons)
- provide a well-needed change of activity
- relax a class or permit more noise when noisy activities are going on in adjoining rooms
- get over a difficult patch (e.g. after a ticking off)
- provide a very necessary extra practice in an area which needs constant revision (e.g. numbers, counting)
- introduce pupils to an activity well worth doing in itself but unrelated to a tightly constructed course in use.

In addition such activities can be very welcome when, for unseen reasons, the planned lesson has to be changed or abandoned for reasons such as a room change, timetable change, tape recorder or projector breaking down. Or again substitutions for an absent colleague are a daily problem; here is something that does not interfere with the normal course of the lessons planned by the absent colleague. Finally teachers have all occasionally got through their material more quickly than they thought possible and switched on this kind of activity at a moment's notice. It will be very well worthwhile for the department to have a bank of such ideas at the disposal of colleagues and supply staff.

This is the point of the five-minute filler. It can be turned to quickly and little or no material is required to make the thing go.

Games

General games

Jacques a dit . . . (using imperatives but only to be obeyed when preceded by the phrase '*Jacques a dit. . .*')

I Spy . . .

I am thinking of . . .

Where is the . . . (a hunt-the-thimble game).

Spelling games

Spelling Bee   (easy word but spelling in the foreign alphabet to be used).

Word Chain   Choosing a letter, going round the class with pupils giving other words beginning with the same letter.

Anagrams   Teacher puts anagrams on the OHP or pupils each have to make an anagram.

Word formation   How many words can be formed from one long word?

Hangman   Teacher should not allow letters to be called out at random – pupils do it in turn.

Counting games

Bingo   Does need equipment.

Counting   Round the class backwards and forwards.

Cocorico   Every three or multiple of three is dropped and *cocorico* is substituted. Wrong number and the pupil is out: this can be used as an elimination game for staggered departures at the close of the lesson.

Arithmetic   Little sums to do mentally, answering in the language. Also reading telephone numbers and car registration plates in the target language and in their style.

Number recognition   Filling the board with random numbers; pupil has to point to correct number called out by teacher. Or vice versa: calling out number pointed to.

Memory games

Grandma went to market and there she bought . . . Good for vocabulary revision.

What do you see in the picture . . . or on the tray? Two minutes to look and then the objects are hidden. Pupils have to recall what they saw (in the target language), rather like the rules of 'Kim's game'.

Question games

20 questions

What's my line?

Yes, no   (The two words must never be used.) Pupils question one individual about anything. Must survive one minute.

Whispers   Passing a sentence down the line. Sentence becomes distorted. 'What we want is efficient ships' becomes 'What we want is fish and chips'.

Matchsticks (for groups)   Pupils arrange matchsticks in a pattern then stand up book to conceal it. Pupils who cannot see have to make the same pattern based on information found by questioning. With *Cuisenaire* rods, colours can be involved too.

Picture completion   Similar technique to above. One pupil has to complete his/her incomplete picture or map by questioning other pupils who have a more complete version.

Talking games

Tongue twisters

Counting-out rhymes

Opposites   Teacher says a word – pupil says the opposite.

Animal noises   Hearing the noise – saying the animal.

Riddles

A quiz

Drawing games

What is it?/Qu'est-ce que c'est?/Was ist das?   Pupil thinks of an object and gives one fact about it (e.g. '*C'est un animal*'/'*Das ist ein Tier*'). They then draw one line to begin the picture of it and ask 'What is it?' Any pupil who can tell or guesses scores ten points for the team. If no one guesses, pupils add another detail and say 'I add . . .' and again ask 'What is it?' Correct guess scores nine points. Game continues down to one point.

What's the difference?/Was ist der Unterschied zwischen . . .?   Banda'd pictures that are almost the same.

Commercial games

Monopoly   This is available in all main languages. Good for a long session at the end of term.

Cluedo   As Monopoly. Certainly not a five-minute game.

Départements jigsaw   Learning where every *département* in France is (up to four pupils).

Card games   Happy Families, etc.

Writing games

Cartoons   Providing cartoon story in wrong order – pupils reorder. Or providing cartoon story with speech bubble blanked out – pupils fill in speech.

Adverts Providing products – pupils provide captions.

Wordsearches

Dictation competition Words from the day's lesson.

See W R Lee *Language Teaching Games and Contests* and A Wright *et al. Games for Language Learning* (Bibliography).

Class discussions

For the odd five minutes every now and again, teachers will find it very useful to invite a general discussion in English on topics to do with languages and language learning. The following are simply suggestions and teachers will easily think of many others.

1 Why do you think we learn languages? (Suggested answers to this question are given in Chapter 11.)

2 What can you do with languages? – Careers.

3 How can we make language classes interesting?

4 What have we learnt from this week's (today's) lesson?

5 How can the teacher best help you to improve?

6 What do you like least/most about Spanish?

7 Who has been to France/Germany? Tell us about it.

8 Why do we have different attitudes towards nations? The traditional views of Germans/French. Are they fair descriptions?

9 How do other nations see the British?

10 Books to look for in the library.

11 What is a foreign accent. Does it matter?

12 What are the qualities of a good linguist?

Discussions like this reward both teacher and pupil.

Eric Hawkins' book *Awareness of Language* makes many more similar suggestions.

Songs

It may be that songs mainly appeal to the younger pupils though if a good tradition of singing can be built up in the lower school it is possible to continue, possibly with a choir or a music colleague. If teachers fail to provide their children with this rich tradition of culture then, to that extent, they are selling them short.

Songs should be taught properly. They are not just a means of passing away a pleasant twenty minutes. They must justify their place in the school day and this they can do on clear pedagogic grounds:

- pupils are helped to improve accent and intonation
- some new vocabulary is acquired painlessly
- pupils have an insight into tradition and/or popular culture
- those not particularly gifted linguistically may have the opportunity to shine because of musical talents.

A serious attempt to teach a song does not admit the mere playing of pop music records. This is probably almost always fatal anyway, for the sophisticated pop experts of today will have nothing but scorn for what they may think is just the teacher's taste in French, German or Spanish music.

For this reason it is better to choose a traditional song with an 'everlasting' tune, with words that are not too complicated nor too contaminated with Anglo-American. Such traditional songs have often lasted for centuries and this must say something for them.

There are many collections of traditional songs which the teacher may get hold of in the UK and an even richer choice is to be found abroad. In addition, the school may exchange tapes and cassettes with a twin school abroad. At Christmas, carols can be taught which often have English versions and tunes anyway.

Rounds, drinking songs and traditional nursery songs can be taught; these often sound attractive on record with modern orchestration.

10   Emergency lessons

Emergency lessons fall into three categories:

1   Cover for a language teacher's absence for illness or INSET reasons.

2   Cover for another colleague.

3   Cover to deal with the unexpected.

1   When a teacher knows he or she is going to be absent for any reason, it is normal to leave appropriate work for a class to do. This is not strictly speaking an emergency lesson. Nevertheless some of the suggestions below may be of use at such times.

The first advice we would give is that it is always possible to be prepared for an emergency by holding a stock of material which can be brought out at short notice which will prevent pupils wasting their time:[1]

a) sets of readers stored according to year: magazines are also possible
b) sets of worksheets on specific topics for revision and also for new work, especially if there is some self-correcting element or autonomous learning
c) sets of comprehension passages with questions for reading comprehension
d) sets of past examination papers stored according to year
e) tapes and cassettes for the substitute teacher to use
f) recordings for sixth formers to listen to themselves; in addition to exercise-type tapes, pre-recorded material of interesting areas of literature and civilisation, such as lectures and talks produced by Exeter Tapes, are useful.

Any of the above can take place *in the absence* of a language teacher.

2   If a language teacher is able to cover for a fellow linguist, all of the above are possible and, in addition, the following apply:

a) all the five-minute fillers referred to in Chapter 9 are capable of being extended if necessary
b) a set of colour slides on the towns of a country make an excellent talk
c) a set of OHP slides for essay work for those pupils who do this sort of task
d) a talk on language – how languages change and other linguistic topics, such as why words change their meaning and form
e) producing worksheets/posters, etc. for use in other classes.

---

[1] This should be part of the departmental planning and so agreed by colleagues. The production of a good scheme of work and cooperation between colleagues is dealt with in Chapter 18 and will prove helpful.

3 The unexpected is usually due to mechanical failure or sudden changes in the timetable when the usual facilities are out of action.

a) if the OHP breaks down, the teacher should go back to chalk and talk
b) if the tape recorder breaks down, the teacher should read from the script
c) if a change of timetable means that pupils have no books, the teacher should use OHP/tapes and issue scrap paper to write on
d) if vital notes are left at home, the teacher should set a quick test of yesterday's work with assurances afterwards that marks will not be 'taken in', finishing the lesson with five-minute fillers. And don't do it again!

11 Answering difficult questions

Every teacher has to face questions from time to time about the subject, its rationale, aims and objectives, methods and results. Such questions may come formally from the governing body and in the post-Educational Reform Act (ERA) scenario, as governors become more influential, this will grow. On other occasions, parents will quite rightly ask the same sort of questions, perhaps at a parents' evening. Finally, and not infrequently, pupils will themselves question the teacher on why they have to learn languages at all, why this particular one and what will they get out of it.

Wise teachers will have answers ready when this sort of questioning occurs, not only because they will have conscientiously thought deeply about such issues, but also because they know that part of their professional duty is to be able to speak up for their subject and defend their actions. The following ideas should be seen as suggestions which may very well come in useful when the teacher is already under heavy pressure and needs to draw up quickly a response to a request from on high, or else faces a class which suddenly feels they have to challenge the assumption that French is good for everybody.

Formal requests for statements _____

These will usually come to a head of department from the head teacher or from a governing body via the head. Questions may cover any of the following topics.

'Why is French the first foreign language?'

Tradition and teacher supply are the two strongest reasons. 'A routine of French teaching has been set up.' Proximity to France and close cultural ties together with the origin of much English vocabulary are further strong reasons.

'Could a good case be made for making another language first language?'

Yes! Especially in view of the DES policy on diversification of first foreign language and the new position generated by the 1992 regulations in the EC. Spanish is a strong contender. The proximity argument applies almost as well as it does to France. Spanish is generally regarded as an easier language for English beginners because of its pronunciation and phonetic spelling. The same arguments apply to Italian. German, with admittedly more complex grammar, gets beginners off to a good start.

'Could the school staff offer another first language?'

Many teachers of French have a second language they could turn to. Even more important, those with first languages other than French have to teach French to get a job. To ensure fair coverage the best plan is to devise a pattern of diversification. Practicalities such as resources (staff and materials) will have to be considered. For a full discussion on diversification see pp. 214–19.

'Should slow learners do a language?'

With the advent of the National Curriculum, the entitlement of all pupils to full access to all parts of the curriculum is a right. While we admit that they will be unlikely to use the language at work, there is a good chance of deriving personal satisfaction from what they do achieve. They will become aware of the nature of language and, at the same time, be learning how to learn a language which may serve them well later. Ability to take part in a bilingual dialogue is a realistic possibility. A language has a positive effect on other subjects. Slow learners need to do a language to ensure they are of equal status within their year group. For fuller discussion on this topic see Chapter 21.

'Who should do a second foreign language?'

More pupils than at present. The ability band is too narrow and produces a particular kind of teaching. With a broader band, teaching methods would be adapted and a greater proportion would succeed. If the group the teacher starts with is small, it will never provide a viable sixth-form group.

'Why do girls do better than boys in languages?'

The question is not so simple. True, more girls get higher grades at GCSE and at A level but this is in part due to the option arrangements in many schools. Schools are now enjoined to offer a balanced curriculum for all and to ensure that sex bias is not in operation. For a well developed study of this problem see Bob Powell *Boys, Girls and Languages in School.*

Parents' evenings _____

Some parents may come with the intention of seeking advice and guidance. Others may casually put a question in the course of a discussion about Tracey's chance of a good grade at GCSE.

'Were your examination results as good as St Thomas' School's?'
Comparison with one school is meaningless and a comparison over one year even more meaningless. The important statistics are the city/national ones. All schools are now obliged to publish their results and some comparisons are possible. The average pass at A, B, C, D grades, etc., taken from the national statistics and the examination boards, is x per cent and this school had y per cent last year.

'My neighbour's daughter does three languages. Why can't Karen?'
In this school we try to ensure that all pupils have a balanced curriculum which suits each child's ability. The language policy in another school is not one we can discuss here.

'If she does French and German in the sixth form, what job can she do?'
The careers teacher is well briefed with all the possibilities open to linguists and there is a display in the careers room listing these. (This list can be based on the advice in Chapter 26.)

'What sort of books should I buy to help with languages?'
Not necessarily books in the language. They may be far too hard and very expensive. Many are really published for adult learners. A dictionary of reasonable size is helpful as we teach the correct use of dictionaries in our course. Buying tapes that advertise mastery of a language in a few weeks is a waste of money.

'Three years Spanish and last year in Malaga he wouldn't say a dickybird. Why?'
Lots of children don't like performing in front of parents. Did all the hotel staff speak good English? Were they nearly all English at the hotel? Any of these reasons will put a shy person off. If he had had to sort himself out he would have done.

'Two years in the sixth form and she still can't translate the letter I've received from France about the spare parts I've ordered. Why?'
Up to now we have not been able to offer business French and it's a specialist field. The A-level syllabus is so full that it would be wrong to take up time doing things that are untested in the exam. Things are changing.

'We have two children doing the same language and yet they never speak it. Why?'
It is slightly unnatural for two people who know each other well in one language to use another. Language is a very basic reflection of personality.

'In my day we learnt our verbs well – and knew them! Now they don't.'
Verbs are learnt nowadays as well but they are learnt by using them in real

conversation. When you recited *Je suis . . . Tu es . . .* could you say anything worth saying?

'She hates French. What can we do? Can she drop it?'

Mary has shown she has the ability to succeed. It would be wrong to drop it and we need to find out why French is so unpopular with her. Is there an activity she is frightened of? A test she hates doing? This needs investigating further.

'My son is getting bored with French. What can you do to arouse his interest?'

Will he come to our language club? We are having a day trip to Boulogne in November. Could he come with us? We take magazines from various sources. Can he subscribe? We have an exchange scheme with France. Could he take part?

'Why can't George do Latin? He might need it later.'

A lot of teachers regret that Latin has had to disappear from the curriculum but we have had to change to make way for new areas of knowledge such as computer studies. It is not likely that it will be a compulsory subject when he wants to go into higher education. We do try and teach them all about language in our 'language awareness' course.

'Fiona has always wanted to do Russian at university, but how will she get along when you don't offer it at school?'

There is a whole range of languages which can be started *ab initio* in universities and polytechnics, these days. They are normally four-year courses and this is made clear in the prospectuses. (See 'Bibliography' *A Guide to Courses with Languages*, published by SCHML.)

Pupils' questions

Teachers are frequently asked to justify to their pupils why so much time is spent learning a modern language, and it is right that they should ask and vital that teachers should be able to give answers which satisfy.

Nonetheless, the question is not always put because of a burning desire to argue the philosophy of education. The time chosen to put the question and the manner in which it is asked indicate clearly enough whether the question is seriously intended. If the teacher suspects it is a 'try-on' he should offer to deal with the question after school.

The question 'Do we have to do French?' is a fair one. Equally fair when applied to other languages, or indeed to any school subject, and it is one that teachers have to be prepared for and anticipate. In other words the teacher should remind the class periodically why they do this. When introducing something new, the class can be told why they need to know it. Revising number, the teacher can remind the class how important number is. 'You might need a telephone number in an emergency.

You want to know what things cost'. 'Verbs of motion? You are always wanting to say where you have been or where you are going'. Before a repetition session it pays to remind pupils how much repetition practice a baby puts in learning its mother tongue. Think of small children's stories in which the same phrases are repeated again and again; children love to join in.

Anticipating the question 'Do we have to, Miss?' is a sensible way of preventing the question arising as a distractor. Children soon spot the airy-fairy answer and have respect for the concrete and practical. Consequently in some areas it may be wrong to overplay the line 'You'll need it when you go to X on holiday' – although it is fair enough to recall how easily people do move around Europe these days on package tours.

To start the ball rolling, we give below a selection of possible reasons which might be put in class to the question 'Do we have to, Sir?' Some will suit certain situations and certain types of class: others may be regarded as totally inappropriate. Any experienced teacher will have his or her own stock of answers to add to these. If so, all the better.

1 When you leave school you will often find that a qualification in a foreign language is regarded by an employer as a good sign that the applicant is an intelligent and hard-working person – even if the job itself does not require a language.

2 Later on in life you may need to learn another language quickly for your job or perhaps just for a holiday. When you've learnt one language you take to another one more easily.

3 Think of the wide range of jobs for which a knowledge of a language is very helpful if not essential – the hotel trade and tourism, long-distance lorry driving, coach driving, and journalism where an ability to skim through the foreign press easily may lead the journalist to pick up a good story for his paper.

4 Foreign travel gets easier and relatively cheaper every year. You will almost certainly go abroad for a holiday and perhaps even to work within the next few years.

5 You never know when you may meet a French, German or Italian person in your own town and not *all* of them speak English.

6 We are Europeans now. Other Common Market countries teach English in their schools but not every pupil is good at English. It is only fair that we in Great Britain should make every effort.

7 Everybody should be given the chance to find out whether they are good

121

linguists just as everybody should have a try at tennis or football. We aren't all star footballers but many people get satisfaction from it. In the same way we don't expect every language learner to become a fluent linguist.

8   Even if you feel unable to express yourself fluently in the foreign language you will often find that you can *understand* what people say to you. You can, in addition, *read* and understand many notices and signs in the street.

9   Using a foreign language is fun and you feel a real sense of achievement when you come out of a shop with exactly what you went in for.

10 You will make many new friends that you would never have got to know if you had been unable to communicate in a foreign language. There is no knowing what such friendships can lead to.

11 The coming of many more TV channels and satellite TV gives us greater opportunity to see foreign plays and films and news programmes.

12 Learning a foreign language certainly helps you understand and use English more effectively. (Here, the teacher should explain by referring to words directly derived from French and German cognates.)

13 It's interesting to look through foreign magazines and even mail-order catalogues. (It is useful to build up a collection of foreign comics, women's magazines, car and sports mags and catalogues for use as five-minute fillers.)

14 Many pop records are made in Europe. Is it not better to be able to understand some of them? It is possible now to listen to European pop music programmes on long and medium wave.

12 How to avoid fatigue

All jobs conscientiously carried out make heavy demands on the worker. This we recognise, of course, but the burden placed on the teacher is a particularly heavy one as a result of the constant need to provide for 30 or so individuals. Within the teaching profession it is often said by language teachers that the constant demand to provide material for oral work makes the linguists the most hard pressed of all.

True or false, such a statement requires us to pause and think for a moment about ways and means of easing the burden, even for a short time, to allow the teacher to gather strength for the next major contribution.

The following suggestions are to be taken in the spirit they are intended and are in no way dodges to avoid work. They are included here to make more efficient, and hence more effective teachers.

Voice

1 No one will deny that a modern linguist has to talk! A lot! But need they shout? To emphasise a point, it is important to slow down and even *reduce* volume slightly. Less strain, more effect.

2 The teacher should make plenty use of others' voices: using tape recordings instead of always reading aloud (getting a variety of input as well); using teacher substitutes for questions – an essential part of pupil practice. In group work some of the talking will be done by group leaders and members. With shadow reading it is not worth trying to be heard over the top of 30 pupils all the time.

3 There is a legitimate place in language lessons for silent activities; a 15-minute reading session once a week can, if properly planned, make an excellent contribution to the week's overall programme. At such times, the teacher moves silently from pupil to pupil having a word or two about the reading and the pupil's understanding.

Marking

A very heavy burden since detailed checks must be made.

1 Keep up to date with marking.

2 If pupils write in class, the teacher can mark in class by going round from desk to desk.

3 To avoid major misunderstandings about homework, the teacher should let pupils begin the homework task in class and check the well-known muddlers – and a few others.

4 Class tests (but not homework) can be marked by changing papers but the teacher needs to take in a sample to check that they have been marked correctly.

5   Good presentation eases the strain of marking. It is important to insist on this at all times. Pupils can only benefit from high standards set by the teacher.

Preparation

Fatigue often stems from strain and strain is caused by anxiety. Anxiety comes from a lack of preparation. The teacher should be prepared as follows:

1   An academic year diary/planner is essential. It is important to ensure all dates and deadlines are put in immediately – exam dates, dates for exam paper completion, parents' evenings, reports to be completed by . . ., number of weeks in the term gone out of the total so that the teachers know exactly where they are. Important dates should be marked in red – including holidays. If the head of department is so minded there will be all this information in the departmental handbook (see Chapter 18).

2   Good preparation is also based on good record keeping. Twice a day it is worthwhile jotting down exactly what was done in each class.

3   Teachers should have handouts ready to distribute as they need them.

4   Preparing OHP transparencies before the lesson is far better and less wearing than scribbling on the blackboard.

Discipline

Fatigue is often caused by wear and tear on the nerves caused by poor discipline (see Chapter 6, 'Discipline in the classroom'). Very often discipline problems can be seen in embryo by the experienced teacher. Two pupils starting to talk, perhaps even argue, can be distracted and even brought back into the lesson by asking one of them a question or by requesting one to give a hand with a piece of apparatus: result – the problem goes away. It is always vital to step in right away, before there is a real problem. Finally, it is unwise to allow known disturbers to sit together.

Some discipline problems stem from the fact that the class does not know where they are or what they are supposed to be doing. See the next point.

Routine _____

Everyone is more relaxed when they are following a regular routine. It is important to get classes used to particular ways of doing things and used to certain standards. Teachers should:

1   Have a reputation for always starting promptly.

2   Always take in and mark written homework.

3   Return marked work promptly.

4   Insist on quiet before the lesson starts but avoid, at all costs, making tempting offers such as 'I won't start until you are all quiet.'

5   Be consistent from day to day – if there is a seating plan, it should be kept to, except in flu epidemics!

6   Do as much administration in the language as possible.

7   Not raise their voice until *really* necessary – calm is infectious.

8   Plan well ahead, and not be caught out.

All the above will help ensure smooth running of classes and a feeling of control, with a consequent reduction in fatigue.

PART TWO

Running a modern language department

13 Managing the department

The quality of leadership _____

While we may reasonably start with the proposition that members of the department ought to work together as a *team*, sharing a common interest in a particular part of the school's curriculum, we must also acknowledge that it is the quality of leadership shown by the head of department which is a prime factor in creating a happy and above all an efficient team of teachers.

The HMIs have recognised this:

> The vital importance of the role of the Head of Department is that it lies at the very heart of the educational process: it is directly related to teaching and learning; whether a pupil achieves or underachieves is largely dependent on the quality of planning, execution and evaluation that takes place within individual departments.
>
> HMI *Departmental Organisation in Secondary Schools*. 1984

All schools are different: structures and management styles vary, but it is increasingly obvious that with the advent of LMS and other reforms consequent upon the implementation of the Education Reform Act, a high degree of professionalism is required from all staff and in particular from the head of department. Some departments *appear* to run themselves, other seem to need cajoling and pushing. Whatever the case, those responsible for reporting on teaching in schools and colleges in this country are quite clear on the need for firm but enlightened leadership:

> HM Inspectors are more than ever convinced that the Head of Department is a key figure, the most important single factor governing the quality of language work in the school. His effectiveness is seen above all in the help and guidance he gives to colleagues.
>
> HMI *Modern Languages in Comprehensive Schools*. 1977

There would appear to be two extremes of style in running a department. The first is authoritarian and dictatorial: schemes of work and suchlike are handed down from on high and all other teachers are expected to follow a pattern of teaching which they have had little part in devising. The other extreme is simply a collection of individuals who are left to go off in various directions to meet occasionally at the end of the term. Both extremes will leave a message of incoherence and unease with the pupils. Both extremes are less than satisfactory from the point of view of the pupil, and the frustrations caused by having to work according to someone else's ideas, or cut off from any real help, thrown back entirely on one's own resources, are not good for staff morale.

Furthermore, the advent of the National Curriculum has made forward planning and the efficient and responsible use of available resources a prime need in schools. Teachers are now all to be monitored in various ways, by staff appraisal schemes, by results and by the mere fact of competition in the market-orientated scenario of the late twentieth century.

We are sure that the department will be most efficient, coherent and happy when decisions are taken by the group as a whole after careful debate and research, with help from associations, advisers and other agencies. The head of department should be seen as a first among equals, an organiser and leader, and certainly not the only source of wisdom and ideas.

> **The two principal aspects of the head of department**
>
> He or she will be a first-class practitioner in the classroom.
> He or she will be a manager of resources, human and material.

Our concern in this part of the book is therefore with management and the strategies to be employed. It is not to be an exploration of the *theory* of management, but rather a guide through the complexities of the job. It will be descriptive rather than prescriptive, seeking to lead rather than direct.

What will leading mean?

Sharing by example

There can be no effective management or leadership at departmental level if the head of department does not take a full share in all aspects of the departmental work, including the teaching of all types of classes in the school. The situation in which the head of department has contact with the sixth form and the top-band classes only, to the exclusion of all else, is not the ideal to be encouraged. Such an attitude will almost always lead to jealousy, tensions and accusations of wanting an easy life.

Delegation

Leading does *not* mean doing everything oneself. There are only 24 hours in the day and shouldering all the burdens of the department is the surest way to a breakdown and the quickest way to lose colleagues.

Being responsible and responsive

Being responsible means listening to the wishes, ideas and aspirations of others. Being responsive means being able to weigh up these considerations with the needs of the pupils and coming to a reasoned decision that all can accept. It means being constantly available to colleagues and pupils (and parents as well); it means having foresight to smooth away potential troubles before they overwhelm. It does *not* mean trying to be superhuman.

Efficiency

Good leadership means being efficient. It means having the information and systems ready and working to enable all members of the department to function to their highest standards. It does *not* mean making efficiency the aim of the department – it is a means to an end, a way of making life as pleasant as possible in an increasingly complex profession.

Broad view

Leadership means being outward looking, to other parts of the school and to the world outside. This aspect of the job has become increasingly important of late. Working in cooperation with other departments and colleagues to provide a coherent programme for pupils, with an eye on cross-curricular themes, for example, is vital. In the post-1992 world, working with outside agencies to provide the appropriate modern language curriculum will be essential.

Concern

This will mean being aware of colleagues' career aspirations by providing appropriate INSET and guidance.

Perhaps the best image is that of the conductor of an orchestra, but in this case with no stick!

14 The image of the department

Relationship with the head and governors

The school will not flourish effectively unless there is cooperation between all members of the teaching staff and others. Under the new arrangements for governing and managing schools, where the leading role is played by the governing body and the head is seen as a managing director, then the active participation of the head of department with management responsibilities will be crucial. For the benefit of all members of the school community, the relationships between the head and the heads of department must be based on trust and confidence on both sides. It is to be hoped that in appointing the head of department, the head will have laid out a statement of the duties and responsibilities of the post in order to provide an agreed framework of operation. Such a job description is vital if the advantages and the responsibilities of this level of management are to be taken seriously. The agreeing of targets and the definition of the means to reach those targets will help to provide a guideline for assessment of success. In return, heads of department must agree to carry out conscientiously those tasks *delegated* to them. At the same time there should be some freedom within which to operate, with room for initiative in a climate of open discussion.

A wise head will see to it that the head of department is a member of the school management team. At this level the HoD must:

1   Represent the subject area within the context of the whole curriculum.

2   Be clear as to the contribution modern languages can make to the education of *all* pupils in the school.

3   Be able to take a broad look at the whole perspective of the school and to take part in a whole school debate on curriculum and other important issues.

How can these ideas be put into action?

First of all, heads of department will see themselves as specialists advisers to the head on a whole variety of matters. These will arise from the particular subject area and will demand a broad knowledge and appreciation of the aims of the school and the special needs and contribution of the subject in question. The head of department must be a specialist on the latest methodology and developments in the subject's technology. He or she should ideally also have an open mind on new developments and be able to see and evaluate new ideas as are appropriate to the subject. The HoD should also be up to date on syllabus and curriculum developments and this will involve reading reports and publications, being a member of the subject association (ALL) as well as attending courses and other INSET meetings designed to help and improve teaching. A keen eye should also be kept on examination syllabuses and on the demands of the world beyond school. In interpreting such issues to the head (who will see the head of department as a special adviser in this field), the departmental leader must be able to translate all such ideas and theory into action, being conscious not only of the department but also the more general needs and constraints of the school situation.

In keeping the head briefed, the head of department must be able to discuss openly the ideals and aims of the department and the constraints of the available resources.

Relationship with the school governors

As a result of the 1988 Education Reform Act (ERA), governors have much extended powers and responsibilities in schools. Heads of department have to make sure, via the head, that they are informed and able to act positively for the school. One of the obvious ways is to ensure that they have copies of the departmental syllabus and handbook (see Chapter 18). Another way is to respond positively to any invitation from the governors to 'present' the department. A short talk, display and even a walk around the departmental area will be welcomed. It will also be useful to prepare a printout of the departmental external examination results (with comments). Indeed this will probably be a normal routine in September for the first governors' committee. If there are reasons for concern, there may be an enquiry and the head of department may be asked to outline an action plan. It is to be hoped that this is approached in a professional manner and not in a threatening way, but it is as well to be aware that the governors have the powers to act in a much more pro-active way in respect of their schools. Keeping the governors well briefed is a positive move.

Tools for the job

Time

Discussion and negotiations will centre on the allocation of teaching time for the subject at various levels in the school: the balance with other departments, the balance across the age and ability range and the need to carry out the programmes of study of the National Curriculum.

Money

Discussion of 'capitation' allowances and 'capital' money to service the department in the framework of the provision for the school as a whole will be necessary. An understanding will be required of the arrangements in place within the school and the LEA for allocating funds for the running of the school (LMS).

Staff

Negotiation with the head and maybe with the LEA to allocate sufficient staff with the appropriate specialisations and allowances to carry out the departmental programme.

Space

Planning sufficient specialist classroom space and a departmental base for efficient operation.

The head of department will also be seen as a link between the head and the departmental team. He must keep them fully informed on school policy, and also, just as importantly, keep the head informed on ideas and perspectives from the department. In these days when the head has many more managerial functions to carry out, it will be increasingly the case that the deputy and middle management layers of the school will provide specialist advice to the head. This role as 'link' will involve putting a positive case for the subject and defence of its position in the school, but also demands tact and diplomacy.

Perhaps the best way to review the crucial importance of the job and the position of the head of department is in the 'job description' itemising the various areas of responsibility devolved by the head.

The role of the head of department _____

The staff

- seeing that staff work effectively
- advising the head on the level of staffing required
- assisting in the appointment of new staff
- devising appropriate help and support for new staff as well as continuing to care for all the team
- ensuring that all staff are informed as to school policy and are able to carry it out in so far as it affects their area of responsibility
- allocating responsibilities within the department according to needs and also with an eye on the professional development of colleagues – ensuring that such duties are carried out
- organising effective departmental meetings
- ensuring that school and LEA administrative procedures which affect the department are carried out
- overseeing staff development and assisting in the writing of references
- overseeing the work and contribution of language assistants.

The subject

- devising, in conjunction with colleagues, and keeping under review, an agreed scheme of work and departmental handbook
- being informed and informing on all aspects of curriculum development.

The pupils

- overseeing the work, development and behaviour of pupils within the department
- arranging appropriate teaching groups
- maintaining adequate pupil records
- advising in matters of option choices and careers, including opportunities for further and higher education.

The timetable

- liaising with the school timetabler to ensure the correct allocation of timetable space – both in terms of total time and also of lesson spacing in the school week.

Parents

- informing parents of departmental aims and objectives
- overseeing the writing of reports and other communications with parents.

Resources

- ensuring that equipment of all kinds is provided, maintained and kept secure
- determining, in conjunction with colleagues, the priorities for allocating the departmental capitation monies
- liaising with the school librarian and resources officer
- advising the head on the need for equipment
- ensuring that the staff are informed about and can use the equipment to the best effect.

Students and teachers in training

- planning students' timetables and programmes of work
- liaising with training establishments and providing supervision
- preparing reports and references.

Examinations

- ensuring that all internal examinations are set, marked and evaluated
- ensuring that for all external examinations the correct syllabus is studied and that pupils are entered appropriately
- seeing that all information from the examination boards is distributed to all who need to know and in particular that examiners' reports are noted.

Records

- keeping appropriate records of all pupils (information from previous schools, internal assessments and external examination results as well as such other information for the records of achievement as is decided by school policy)
- keeping staff records to assist in writing references, etc.
- minuting staff meetings and circulating as agreed.

Extra-curricular activities

- overseeing activities such as visits, exchanges, penfriend schemes, etc.
- maintaining links with other bodies such as LEA advisers, HMIs, FE and HE establishments, subject teaching associations, etc.

As head of department, it is well worthwhile joining the language teaching association ALL (The Association for Language Learning – see 'Organisations useful to the language teacher'). The local branches provide a forum for ideas, meetings and INSET. Nationally there are conferences, courses, exhibitions as well as a range of professional journals and other books designed for the language teacher.

Relationships with other departments ____

It is extremely important for both pupil and teacher to feel that the work carried on within the language department is not isolated from the work in other areas of the school, remote in aim and character from the activities which engage the attention of the pupil groups during the kaleidoscope of the rest of the school day. Of course there are differences because of the very nature of the subject being taught, but there are many areas where there can be fruitful cooperation. This has become more important in the last few years since the introduction of the National Curriculum with the crowded timetable and the concept of cross-curricular themes. There has also been a growing recognition that the aims of language teaching have changed somewhat in the emphasis teachers now place on communication. It is now being slowly realised that if teachers are to communicate, they need something other than the trite transactional messages of the early GCSE days. A link with the other subjects of the curriculum as well as an acceptance of the body of knowledge and interests that the pupils bring into the classroom will help provide such material. As well as this admission that teachers can benefit from sharing ideas, subject matter and even techniques with others, there is the important need even in the post-1992 world to convince colleagues of the importance of language teaching, of its challenges and especially of the important educational benefits which come from exposure to a foreign tongue. It follows that the head of department and all colleagues must be willing to establish points of contact with other subject areas and the benefits will be mutual. Other colleagues will have a better understanding of the aims and objectives of the language staff and, more importantly, they will come to appreciate the challenges and difficulties of teaching a modern language in today's schools. The language staff should also be able to see how their work fits into and complements the work in other areas, particularly in respect of the language policy of the school. This latter consideration is of prime importance. It must be a priority for the staff teaching language – English, foreign and 'community' languages – to come to a consensus on aims, methods and approaches.

The head of department is a key figure in this respect, initiating and maintaining contacts with other sections of the school, both as a matter of routine and on 'special occasions'.

Ideally, the language department, in common with other groups in the school, will

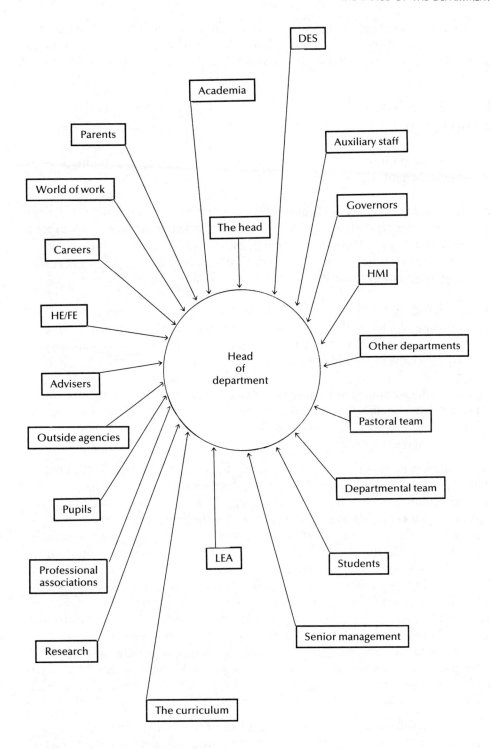

Figure 4: The head of department as manager

feel part of the total team of the school and, in offering its specialisation, it can also contribute to a whole-school approach on matters of policy, ideals and thinking about the education on offer to the community.

First steps towards informing and cooperating with colleagues

1   The HoD should circulate departmental syllabuses – or at least summaries – to other colleagues.

2   At the heads of department committee it is worthwhile arranging a special time (it can be incorporated into several meetings) when departments talk in turn about their aims, objectives, new developments and ideas. The HoD should be ready at such times to answer questions and debate their point of view. It is surprising how informative and well received such sessions are.

3   It is important to arrange for departmental 'at-homes'. When possible, the HoD should allow colleagues to see and examine rooms, equipment, texts and other aids *in situ*. When teachers are all teaching a full timetable it is not always easy to see the latest additions to the computer workshop or the CDT area.

Equally, colleagues may not know how teachers use the foreign language in the classroom as a medium of teaching, or how they use that scarce resource the assistant. Such 'at-homes' could very well be in the lunch hour when pupils may be on hand to make the visit more 'real'.

As linguists, special attention must be paid to the work of colleagues in the English department and any policy they (and others) develop in respect of 'language across the curriculum'. Such topics can very properly lead to discussion about real classroom issues, rather than filling the staff meeting with administration. Such matters, once thought the private concern of the English staff, must be actively taken on board in the language department. Incidentally, but very importantly, teachers of foreign languages can also learn a great deal from EFL (English as a Foreign Language) colleagues and from teachers of mother tongue languages. In many schools, especially in inner-city areas with a multicultural intake, there may very well be an EFL specialist and such a teacher can most positively contribute ideas and methodology to many departments. Active, communicative lessons are often the hallmark of such teachers who do not have the heritage of traditional grammar methods behind them. If there is not such a teacher in your school, there will possibly be a centre in the LEA for advice or it may be possible to join in INSET for such staff.

In their search for communicative competence in the foreign language, teachers must look to more flexible methods and shift the focus away from teacher-centred lessons to the classroom with multi-centred activities, where the pupils interact among themselves and not merely with the teacher. A fuller discussion of this approach is given in Chapter 2.

In this respect, it will pay to investigate how the English department organises small-group talk, encourages independent reading, involves personal experience in pupil work, and encourages creative personal contributions from pupils.

It may also be possible to cooperate with other departments as well – geography, history, music and art come to mind as well as areas such as maths and science. Cooperation can be simply a matter of timing. For example, if dealing with the 'Dreyfus Affair' in the sixth-form literature course, mention of it may coincide with it in the study of this period in the history course. The textbook chapter set in the Basque region or in Berlin, can coincide with some project work in geography. In dealing with the Channel Tunnel the possibilities of cooperation with several other subject areas are enormous. The introduction of cross-curricular themes in the National Curriculum also requires planning and cooperation if teachers are to avoid topics such as the environment occurring five or six times in a short period of time for the same pupils. They will pall at a repetition of the same topic area and show their disapproval. There will be room for some imaginative cooperation in this area if a whole school approach is adopted.

On the other hand, cooperation should be at a deeper level, with all departments adopting a flexible teaching strategy, child-centred rather than teacher-centred, as a result of discussion amongst staff. An interesting discussion on such an approach can be found in Douglas Barnes' book *From Communication to Curriculum*, and on his distinction between 'transmission' and 'interpretation' styles of teaching and learning. This is also echoed in many parts of the National Curriculum document for modern languages.

Cooperation will also be called for in other areas of the school, for example, in timetable planning and in the sharing out of the timetable space within the school week. This will be looked at in the section on timetabling (Chapter 17). However it can be mentioned here as one aspect of cooperation – that of seeking a correct balance of subject choices for various age groups, ability groups and between the sexes. To some extent, the choices are more limited now than a few years ago, with the prescriptions of the National Curriculum. All pupils will have to follow a language course up to the age of 16, but the way the timetable is constructed is still a matter for the judgement of the individual school. The construction of groups and sets can still be a matter which affects positively or not the success of the groups. Teachers will still need to avoid single sex groups and come to a decision on the way they deal with special needs. The language department will need to discuss and present its case to the senior staff in the school, so that the best of what will inevitably be a compromise can be reached. Tact and diplomacy are called for, especially when lesson allocation is at a premium and rivalries tend to come to the surface. This may be particularly so when trying to fit in a second foreign language, where it is highly desirable to begin such study at the latest in year 9.

Putting the department on show _____

Putting the department on show in the broadest sense of the term is an important part of the work of the departmental team. It will always be vital to bring languages out of the classroom routine and to seize every opportunity to bring languages to life throughout the school. The public in general is slowly beginning to appreciate the need for language competence in a wide variety of situations and so in schools, the language department must try to create the feeling that languages are to be used in 'real' situations, that they are not just a funny game to be played in the classroom, with no relevance to the world outside. It is therefore important to exploit every opportunity to show off the department to the school and the world outside – parents and the community at large. Contacts with parents vary from school to school, but a readiness to meet parents will always be much appreciated and a good, encouraging image can do much to foster a positive atmosphere in the classroom.

Possible activities – ideas to exploit

Use the foreign language

The HoD should encourage all staff to *use* the foreign language as much as possible and in the most natural way. If visitors arrive in the middle of the lesson, the teacher should talk to them in the foreign language. It does work even when the head comes in! It will soon get about that it is totally natural to use French, German, etc. without embarrassment and such a reputation will rub off on pupils. When meeting pupils in the corridor or dining room it is worthwhile greeting them with a cheery '*Bonjour, Marie*' or '*Guten Tag, John*' and so on. With a little practice it will seem the most natural thing in the world and not at all eccentric. Being a showman can bring satisfaction and can be contagious.

Helping others with language problems

It is important to be willing to help staff with their language queries, for example, by translating letters or writing for the holiday *gîte* in Normandy. Helping people in this way to go to the continent can be rewarded in surprising ways – by the bottle of brandy from the cross-channel boat or the unexpected poster for display in the classroom. The same applies if requested by pupils or parents. Any such help may very well spark off a lasting interest.

A news blackboard

The HoD should arrange to have a departmental blackboard in a permanent prominent position in a school corridor or lobby. It can easily be constructed out of plywood and painted with special matt blackboard paint available from DIY shops or educational suppliers. It should be put on the wall, headed in white paint as shown in Figure 5. Daily news items can be chalked up by staff or pupils for all to see. It creates a lot of interest and can be done in a variety of languages. A good source of information is the foreign newspaper or the daily radio/television

140

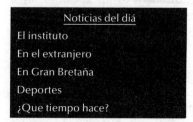

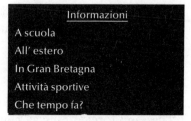

Figure 5: Foreign language news blackboards

broadcast. French and German radio can be received quite easily in the UK and with the advent of satellites TV programmes are now within reach.

A foreign dining corner

It is often easy to create a French, German or Spanish corner in the dining room. Tables are designated where only the target language is spoken – it can bring to life the role plays acted out in the classroom.

A foreign tuck shop

Why not have a special day in the school tuck shop? In the local area there may well be a baker who sells *croissants* or other continental delicacies. A stall can be set up at break time to sell them to pupils and staff using the foreign language as the medium of communication. A variation is the French breakfast which can also be for fund raising.

Languages at the school concert

On the occasion of the annual school concert or carol evening, an item in the foreign language can be offered. It could take the form of a reading, sketch, carol or song, etc. and is invariably well received. Some schools even run to a French, German or Spanish choir. This will depend on the staff, but is a useful avenue of cooperation.

Helping other departments

The HoD should always be ready to meet the requests of other departments. For example, a collection of slides from travels abroad may be of use to the history or geography departments or simply help a pupil engaged in a project. The PE department may also ask for help. They may have an interest in dance, for example, and the 'Breton' evening after your school trip to Britanny may be livened up with a local folklore dance contribution.

141

Cross-curricular events

It is increasingly common for schools to hold special days or even weeks based on a cross-curricular theme. For example, the environment, European awareness, the Channel Tunnel, etc. The language department can play a full part in such activities and indeed initiate them.

A language club

Many activities can be tried out, especially with the help of an assistant, and depending on the age of the pupils. The main aims of the club will be enjoyment and to do those things that might get squeezed out of the normal classroom because of pressure of time.

Suggestions for 'club' activities:

Showing films   Many can be hired free from commercial bodies such as tourist offices and foreign railway companies. Commercial distributors should not be forgotten; if the fee they charge is high, it may be possible to join up with other schools to share the cost. The local ALL branches often show films and may help put schools in touch with those who can help (see Chapter 27).

Showing slides   These can come from pupils, teachers, local teachers' centres, etc.

Making cassette recordings   These can be sent to your 'twin' schools as a sort of *correspondance sonore.*

Food   By 'borrowing' the housecraft room, it is possible to prepare simple dishes for the pupils. It is a good idea to print out the recipe in advance in the target language and hand them out to the pupils at the beginning. Making a *salade* or even snail butter can be great fun and something which the pupils remember! 'Bought-in' food can also be used if there is a good delicatessen or baker in the area.

Playing games   Depending on the ages of the pupils, it is possible to play games, do foreign crosswords, use foreign versions of 'Monopoly'. On trips abroad it is often possible to pick up children's games cheaply at the supermarket or beg them from friends whose children have outgrown them.

Looking at satellite TV   It may not be possible in the normal lesson, but this activity can be interesting. It may be that you could swap videos with the twin school. A word of warning – videos recorded from French TV come out as black and white in the UK unless you have an expensive converter or a dual system – PAL/SECAM. However, French language broadcasts from Belgium are usable.

Producing foreign language newspapers   With the use of word processing software – or even better with a desktop publishing system, it is a wonderful experience to put together a foreign newspaper. It can be done in a simple way by using for example *European Folio* – software designed for the BBC computer and with the added advantages that the on screen instructions are in the target language. Desktop publishing software can be used with, for example the Archimedes or AppleMac computers which are now in many schools. Detailed discussion of this activity will be found in Chapter 8.

Open days

These events can be very time-consuming, but if properly planned and thought-out they can play a very useful part in promoting the cause of the language department. It doesn't always seem easy to compete with the spectacular displays that attract spectators to the science or computer departments. But here is an opportunity to show to visitors, parents and prospective pupils (very important in the days of LMS) that language learning can be *fun*. Some ideas for open days are given below.

French/German/Spanish café

Croissants, cakes, etc. and coffee are bought in for sale in the café. This can be arranged around a *terrasse* created from garden parasols, tables and chairs. In the background a cassette of local pop music will be playing to create the atmosphere. In the course of the language lessons the pupils can be trained as waiters and waitresses and the 'script' for the customers to act out as they order in the other half of the role play can be written on the back of the menu cards/price lists. It will soon be evident how much the customer/visitors will enjoy playing the game for the benefit of the pupils. With careful budgeting it is possible to make a profit for the departmental fund to help towards the extra cassette recorder badly needed and at the same time provide real motivation for the pupils.

Slide show

It is a good idea to have a slide or video show on open day of the latest school visit to the continent. This is not only good for those who participated but is also a recruiting ploy for the next planned excursion. It is important to make sure, however, that there is a substantial contribution from the pupils themselves – such as their diaries, etc. – as this attracts parents.

The twin school

If the school is fortunate enough to have a twin school in Europe (via the LEA twinning committee, the Central Bureau for Educational Visits and Exchanges[1], or even by your own contacts), then it is a first-class idea to arrange a display of material which may include timetables, slides, posters, letters and projects. This can be part of an ongoing project with the other school.

Demonstration lessons

Depending on the aims of the open day, much can be gained from putting on demonstration lessons. If the aim is to reveal what the pupils can do, then the opportunity for the visitor to see what a 'real' lesson is like can be invaluable. It may be possible, for instance, to arrange for the afternoon sequence of lessons to

---

[1] For address of CBEVE see 'Organisations Useful to the Language Teacher' in Part Four.

take place in the evening and so allow parents and others to witness classes in action. On the other hand, the aim of the demonstrations may be to allow the parents to have a 'taster' lesson of a language that they know little about, in order to better appreciate what it is like to be a learner, as their children are in their everyday experience.

Displays

It is useful if the displays are normal – that is of the work that arises from everyday school activities.

The HoD shouldn't forget the hardware available in the department. Visitors can usefully be shown how it contributes to the work of the pupils.

Open days are usually (thank goodness) single events in the year. However, there is much to be said for keeping parents and other interested people very much in the picture throughout the school year. Many researchers have found that one of the most important factors in helping pupils towards successful language learning is a positive attitude held by parents and a supportive family. Therefore always be ready to answer questions about methods, aims and objectives, both verbally and in writing, for example in the school prospectus or any other communications sent out. Many schools, in order to compete and attract pupils, publish a newspaper for distribution to the neighbourhood. Some are professionally produced and are most convincing. Is there a contribution in every issue from the language teachers? When sending out lists of results is the language department prominent? Is the local paper informed of visiting groups from Europe with a photograph?

In some schools, the writing of reports on individual pupils may be the only form of communication to parents; these should be well written in a positive way.

Parents do have the legal right to be well informed about the school and the progress of their children (or lack of it, before it is too late!). It is not always appreciated by staff how reluctant some parents are to ask questions and find out about school matters, and so anything teachers can do will be beneficial.

The school information booklets _____

A large number of schools produce, in addition to the statutory prospectus for intending pupils and their parents, a series of other publications, booklets and handouts at certain critical times in the life of the pupil – at option time and before entry into the sixth form, for example. The recent changes in the Education Reform Act make it obligatory for the school to provide all relevant information for parents who may have legitimate cause to use such information. These are very important documents and the modern language department must be properly represented. The head of department should consult with colleagues to determine the kind of image it is desirable to present. It is advisable to write the contribution in language which is non-technical and easy to understand, avoiding the jargon which the expert may understand but which can so often confuse others.

A suggested format for a chapter in the new pupil booklet might be as follows:

Midshire Education Committee
Midtown High School
Midtown

The Modern Language Department

Introduction

The modern language department in this school, teaches French, German and Spanish. We have six full-time staff, together with the help of the deputy head and two foreign language assistants.

The staff are:

Mr B Jones, *Head of Dept*	French and German
Mrs S Brown, *Second in Dept*	French and Spanish
Mrs G Smith	French
Mrs R Lewis	French and Spanish
Miss V Ormerod	French
Mr D Wheeldon	French and German
Mr R Wood, *Deputy Head*	French

Our assistants this year will be Mademoiselle Bernadette Denoyelle from France and Herr Joseph Lehman from Germany. They will work in close cooperation with the staff.

Over the past few years, we have enjoyed good success. We have steadily built up the Department so that now all our pupils follow modern language courses from ages 11 to 16. Many of our pupils go on to study languages in some form or other at university or polytechnic. However, we also aim to give a good grounding and lasting interest to all our pupils who will work in the new situation of the open market in Europe.

General aims

We try to develop the various language skills with all our pupils. For all, the skills of listening, reading and speaking are important, and for many we would also add the skill of writing. As a nation, it is vital that we increase our knowledge of languages, especially with the changes in 1992, and because of the needs of work and leisure beyond school. We believe that the apprenticeship of language learning at school will lay good foundations for

---

the future, so that our pupils will be adaptable in their future lives and careers.

We do not forget that learning and using a language can be fun and can also help you enjoy your foreign holiday even more.

Examination aims

We encourage as many pupils as possible to enter for public examinations at the age of 16 (end of Key Stage 4). The exact combination of skills at a particular level is decided at a later date.

In the sixth form, the aim is A level, or for nonspecialists, the AS level. The latter qualification is particularly important for those students who do not wish to specialise in languages, but who wish to keep their language alive as an extra skill which will add a further dimension to their chosen course of study. For the non-A level student we run a 'Foreign Languages at Work' course especially suitable for those following a more general course in the sixth form. There is also the possibility of continuing language study in our CPEVE scheme and with NVQ in mind.

All our pupils are encouraged to enter as appropriate for the various levels of the Graded Examination Scheme run by the LEA (a series of stepped examinations rather like the various grades of music examinations).

Classes

As with all other subjects in the school, in the first year (YR 7) the foreign language is taught in mixed-ability groupings, and in the second year (YR 8) in broad bands. Pupils study either French or German and you will be asked if you have a strong preference (otherwise the choice will be made by the staff). In YR 9 the groupings are by ability sets. All pupils are offered the chance to study an additional language (French, German or Spanish) if they so wish. Please note that this option is *not* restricted to more able pupils. Sixth form students may also begin a new language from scratch.

Since naturally we adhere to the National Curriculum all pupils must continue with at least one foreign language until 16.

Methods

We try to develop skills that will be of real use in the foreign country and so we put a lot of emphasis on speaking, listening and reading of real language. Writing is not neglected, nor is the teaching of grammar and language structures.

Resources

Each language room has a cassette recorder and group listening facilities. We have the use of projectors, and a library of tapes as well as a computer for pupils to integrate their language with information technology skills.

Visits and exchanges

Each year we arrange trips and exchanges to various countries, usually for a week to ten days. A one-day 'taster' visit on a 'Boulogne flyer' is a regular feature for all YR 7 pupils. We have a system of exchanges with twin schools in France and Germany and are in the process of setting up such a system with Barcelona. Other forms of regular contact are the exchange of penfriend letters, tapes and videos, and soon we will have contact via electronic mail.

At our school open day in November, why not pay us a visit and see us at work? Come to our continental café and attend our demonstration lessons. You will be very welcome.

15 Making the most of staff

It is a basic assumption in this section that the modern language department will function most effectively when the members of the department are cooperating as a team. This is more and more true as teachers take on board the implications of the National Curriculum. Positive planning of the curriculum, the programmes of study and a consensus on techniques and methodology are vital if teachers are to give a positive message to their pupils that language learning is worthwhile. However, it would be naïve to assume that in the hurried life found in schools, such a spirit is everywhere. But such cooperation is more likely to bring personal and professional satisfaction and thus the head of department will be wise to do everything possible to foster this cooperative spirit. Nothing is worse than major decisions being taken in isolation, without debate, amongst the colleagues who will have to work with such policies.

The bringing together of a team like this is partly in the hands of the head of department and begins with the process of appointing staff.

Making appointments _____

Appointing a new colleague to the departmental team is not a task to be taken lightly. On the contrary, it is a process that demands great thought and tact in order to foster the well-being of the department as a whole. Very careful consideration must be given to all stages of the process. It goes without saying that heads of department should not be excluded from any part of the procedure. They should make every effort to act on behalf of the whole department throughout, and their opinions should weigh heavily with the team making the final decision.

Ideally the head of department should be involved in all the stages outlined below:
- deciding on the needs of the department – an 'audit'
- drawing up the advertisement
- shortlisting
- meeting the candidates
- interviewing.

Each of these stages will now be dealt with in detail.

Deciding on the needs of the department

As part of the continuing consultative process, the head of department will have informed the head in good time of the need to make a new appointment. This may be because of expansion or resignation. In a well-regulated team, the unexpected resignation should not really happen, because the head of department would have kept his ear close enough to the ground to know the intentions of the staff well in advance. The continuous review of the school and departmental needs, and a clear idea of collective policy, taking into consideration also any future changes brought about by legislation such as the Education Reform Act, will make an audit of needs a reasonably easy task. The head of department should take careful stock of the staff resources required to carry out the policy of the school and, in so doing, should try to maintain a balance between experience and inexperience, full- and part-time commitments, language balance where more than one language is taught and, if possible, a balance between the sex of the staff; the image so often given is that language learning is a female business (though this latter consideration may be a matter of supply). As well as the present situation, they must look to the future, where flexiblity will be vital, especially in those schools where a policy of diversification is to be introduced. Staff with a two-language capability are valuable.

All this preliminary planning must be done, if possible, in good time, in order to avoid last minute panics which often lead to hasty appointments from a reduced field.

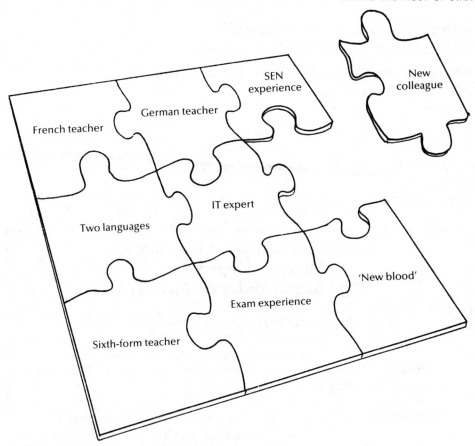

Figure 6: Deciding on the needs of the department

Drawing up the advertisement

It is unlikely that the head of department will draw up the final version of the press notice giving details of the vacancy, but nevertheless, they should have a clear idea of the image they seek to project. This is the first contact the school has with potential candidates and as such it is worthwhile giving some thought to the wording. The advertisement should be precise in the description of the post so as not to waste time and attract unsuitable candidates who cannot possibly fulfil the requirements. When enquiries are received, it is a good idea to send with the application forms a short job description, well written and honest, in order to tempt as wide a range of candidates as possible.

The head of department should certainly be closely involved in drawing up this document, which should be of maximum A4 size. Information will vary from school to school, but the first part should contain factual information as follows:

- school name, address (including post code) and telephone number
- geographical/social location
- number on roll, age range, single-sex/mixed

149

- language(s) and qualifications required
- level of teaching required: GCSE/A level, etc.

Information about the department will contain such details as:

- external examination aims
- composition of classes
- resources available
- special projects, etc.

It will include the date by which applications should be received.

Here is an example of such an information leaflet.

Midshire Education Committee
Midtown High School
High Street, Midtown, MD1 1DD
Telephone 0123-123456

(An 11–18, mixed comprehensive school. 1,400 on roll.)

Headteacher: M Pearce BA MEd

Modern Language Department – MPG teacher

Required for September 199–, an enthusiastic teacher of *French* and *German* up to A level

Midtown High School is situated on the northern edge of the market town, with a socially mixed intake. The campus is self-contained with its own playing fields and purpose-built accommodation. Because of expansion six temporary classrooms are also in use.

Two languages (French and German) are taught in half-year groups as first foreign language to the complete ability range (including pupils with special needs). The first year (YR 7) is taught in mixed ability groups, with broad banding in YR 8. Pupils are offered the chance to study a second foreign language in YR 9 (French, German or Spanish) and this is not confined to high ability pupils. In line with the National Curriculum, all pupils must study at least one foreign language until they are 16. All the department's syllabuses are based on communicative lines and we enter pupils for the Midtown Graded Tests Scheme and in YR 11 for the GCSE run by the — Board.

In the sixth form there are courses in A and AS levels and FLAW courses in French, German and Spanish.

The modern language department operates in a well-equipped suite of rooms, each with audio-visual aids and ready access to computer facilities. There is usually a French and German Assistant and the shared use of a technician.

We have a thriving link with the Lycée Courvoisier in Cognac and the Mozart Gymnasium in Trier. We are looking to establish a new link with a school in Barcelona. Pupil exchanges and contacts with Europe are seen as a vital part of our work and help in this area would be appreciated.

Candidates should state what extra-curricular help they would like to offer, both in the language area and outside.

The successful candidate would be expected to teach the full ability range and to contribute positively to the life of this busy community.

Application should be made by letter to the headmaster, enclosing a full curriculum vitae and the names and addresses of two referees. We welcome applications from qualifying students as well as experienced staff. Applications should be received by April 30th 199–. Please enclose a stamped, addressed envelope for acknowledgement.

Shortlisting

The sifting of the applications is often a tedious and frequently unscientific job. It is best done by two or three people who have clearly in mind the job description for the post in question. Each application form deserves careful consideration from several points of view:

- the needs of the school and departmental timetable
- the present composition and strength of the departmental team
- the future needs of the school and department
- the expertise the new teacher can offer
- possible contribution to the general life of the school.

When reading the applications and the references, note should be taken of what is said as well as what is left out. However, it is advisable to avoid being too cunning a reader and imputing qualities or failings which are not really there. It is important to try to consider positive questions about the applicant as well as looking for such things as gaps in the sequence of experience and career. The choice and the reasons for deciding on a short list should be discussed with the head or the deputy concerned with staffing. It is only professional to put on the short list the candidates who at least have a chance of being appointed. It is unfair and expensive to waste the time of those who do not really fit the vacancy.

When concerned with appointments to modern language teams, as well as these general considerations, there are particular items to look for:

- qualifications and fluency in the language in question
- residence and experience in the country of the target language
- continued contact with the target country.

An investigation of these matters should form a major part of the total interviewing process described below.

Meeting the candidates

Before the formal interview, there is an equally important stage in the selection process which should not be ignored or treated lightly. It is essential to invite candidates on the shortlist to visit the school before the formal interview, so that this relaxed more informal session will allow the head of department (and colleagues) to assess the potential strengths of the candidates *and* equally important allow the candidates to make *their* assessment of the school and the department, prior to entering into any sort of commitment.

The 'informal' visit

As the candidates arrive, the HoD should introduce them to the other staff in the department and show them around the whole school as well as the departmental area. If possible this is best done on a 'normal' working day, when it is possible to glean some idea of the atmosphere of the school.

It is worth trying to arrange visits to one or two lessons (or at least a look into a working classroom) with the consent of willing colleagues. It is also important to allow the opportunity to look at the departmental resources, to get at least a glimpse of the pupils and to see something of the departmental style. In order to get a balanced view of the work of the department, the HoD should make a point of letting other colleagues have a chance to talk to the candidates – after all the candidate will be working with other staff and not just the head of department.

It is important to talk with the visitors over a cup of coffee and give them a chance to ask questions and air their views. Throughout this 'informal' half-day or so it will be possible to judge the reactions of the potential colleagues in a way which should complement the impression gained in the formal interview. Such insights will also enable the HoD to put more probing and pertinent questions at the formal interview.

Interviewing

It may be the policy of the school and the governors *not* to invite the head of department to participate in the formal interview. We take the view that this is to be regretted and the increasing managerial responsibility of the head of department is a sign of the maturity of the school management structure. If nonparticipation is the rule, it is essential that heads of department make known their point of view on the candidates and ensure that the interests of the department are represented. It can be argued that the work of sifting the potential candidates during the earlier stages outlined above is the proper concern of heads of department, and their views, carefully considered, should in the final stage be but one aspect of choosing a new colleague. However, we consider that the special expertise of the linguist head of department at the interview is most valuable in offering a particular point of view in the proceedings.

If HoDs *are* included in the interviewing panel, they are just one of a team and *not* the star in the limelight. The aim of the panel is to allow each candidate to be seen at his or her best and to allow a proper judgement to take place in the interests of all concerned. Since one does not sit on interviewing panels every week, it is essential to think out the strategy very carefully beforehand if the opportunities in the brief 15–20 minutes are not to be wasted.

Interviewing techniques

1   It is essential to have a clear idea of the person needed in the departmental team. Only those who have the essential requirements should be invited for interview.

2   When the shortlist has been drawn up, all members of the interview panel should study the documentation very carefully, noting the strengths of the candidates in the light of the job specification.

3   Interviews should be carefully planned, both individually and collectively. This will mean that the areas of questioning for each member of the panel should be decided beforehand and the individual member will then be able to plan the contribution to the whole interview.

4   All candidates must be given a chance to settle down in what is often a stressful situation. A comfortable waiting area should be provided and the procedure explained to everybody before the first candidate is called in. The candidate order should also be indicated.

5   The interview room needs to be arranged so as not to intimidate the candidate. Sitting behind a formidable desk puts up a physical as well as psychological barrier and is not advised.

6   The chairman should welcome each candidate in a friendly manner, making sure that all the members of the panel are introduced in turn. Some basic questions should be asked of *all* candidates to enable comparisons to be made, followed by other questions to individuals to suit the circumstances. Questions should be prepared beforehand on the substance of the *curriculum vitae* in order to pose follow-up questions in the light of the candidate's answers.

7   All questions should be clear, precise and positive. Trick questions and those designed to convey the questioner's own point of view are best put aside. Leading questions such as 'Wouldn't you agree that . . .?' should be avoided.

8   All interviewees should be given time to answer.

9   All candidates should be given the chance to ask their own questions.

10 The HoD should not dominate the questioning, but should allow all the panel to take part in the interview as will have been agreed.

11 When interviewing modern linguists, opinions are divided on whether part of the interview should be in the foreign language. Should it be in the informal or the formal part of the interview? Whatever view is taken, it is essential that at some time during the whole selection process, the candidate is heard speaking in the foreign language. Given the inevitable stress of the day, it is probably better on balance to use some factual topic such as 'Tell us about your time abroad as an assistant or in a placement . . .'

12 At the end of the interview, the candidate must feel that he or she has been able to perform at optimum level and that the interview was fair.

13 Finally, as a matter of courtesy, the unsuccessful candidates should be given a few words of counselling and advice – the debriefing – so that they too have some positive feedback. In these days of image building, such courtesies count for a lot.

Samples of questions that can be used at interviews

- Why did you choose to teach?
- Have you any experience in other jobs?
- What attracted you to this post?
- Where else have you taught *or* where did you do your teaching practice?
- How do you keep up to date with your language?
- How often do you go to (France)?
- What are the aims of teaching a modern language?
- What views do you have on a languages for all policy?
- How do you motivate the reluctant learner in the classroom?
- What in your opinion makes a good teacher?
- What in your opinion makes a good lesson?
- What does a modern language contribute to the education of children?
- Do you see any problems in a large school?
- How do you foster a good atmosphere in the classroom?
- How do you cope with the high flier in the class *or* the weaker pupil?
- Should you teach *in* the target language?
- What importance do you attach to a departmental scheme of work?
- What are your views on group work – its organisation, aims and techniques?
- What is the most important innovation you would like to see in the language classroom?
- What else can you offer the school in general?
- What is the role of the form tutor and the pastoral staff in general?
- Where do you see yourself in the profession in five years' time?

And finally:

- Have you any questions *you* would like to ask?

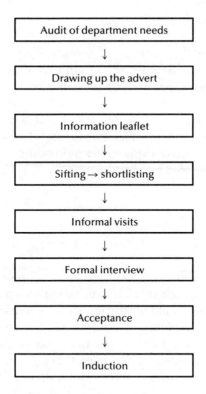

Figure 7: Appointing staff

The new colleague _____

The process begun at the interview is but the beginning. The important work of integration starts as the selection process ends. It is all too easy to forget what it is like to be a new teacher, especially if it is a first appointment. Once teachers are established in a school, all the familiar routines are taken for granted, simply because experienced teachers have trodden the path many times over. However, the wise head of department will take every care to ensure that the integration is as smooth as possible.

Ideally there will be a coordinated policy in the school and indeed across the LEA, and if this is the case, then the head of languages should be a part of this policy. If the school does not have such a positive attitude, it could be suggested to the head. What is totally unacceptable is that a new member of staff (and especially a probationer) should arrive on the first day of the term without the benefit of both formal and informal contact with colleagues beforehand.

A welcoming letter

As soon as the new appointment is confirmed, the head of department should write an informal letter of congratulation and also confirm the dates of visits to the school before the beginning of the new term.

Arranging visits

The informal visit should be arranged in term time, if at all possible, when the school is in action and colleagues are around to allow for full consultation, including, if appropriate, a chat with the outgoing teacher whose classes are to be taken over. Much valuable information about individuals, methods and the class atmosphere, can be passed on at this time. It may also be appropriate to hand over class lists and records if that is possible. It is also useful for some classroom visits to be made and also a selection of the main textbooks and such-like to be given out. Much anxiety can be avoided by considerations such as these.

The staff file

In order to help the new colleague, it is a good idea to present a staff file containing the whole range of information that has to be assimilated before the rush of the first few days in school. This should ideally involve a whole school policy and many good schools already have a file (loose-leaf) that is given to every member of staff. This may not happen, and if that is the case, then an approach to the senior management team is a good idea. However, there *is* a firm responsibility on the head of department to produce a departmental staff file or at least a supplement to the general school information documents. The file should contain information on departmental routine and room numbers, including a school plan, times of lesson change-overs, etc. All this can boost self-confidence in the presence of pupils and help towards efficiency.

The departmental staff file should be in a loose-leaf folder that can be added to (or taken from) as circumstances change. It should contain at least the following information:

- A copy of the departmental policy file and syllabuses
- A detailed scheme of work for each year group
- A plan of the school
- A full staff list and the codes used to designate them on the timetable
- The teacher's personal timetable, annotated so as to make sense!
- A copy of the school rules and other papers affecting the daily routine – fire orders, duty rota, etc.
- A copy of all relevant set/class lists
- A calendar of major events in the school year – parents' evenings, holidays, etc.

In addition, if the colleague is new to the district, possible contacts in the area for flats and accommodation may be useful. The LEA often has this sort of information available via the 'weekly bulletin'. If the language adviser does not provide information on the services of teachers' centres and the like, this too should be provided.

The probationary teacher _____

Some authorities and schools have special policies for the induction of new teachers. As the professional life of staff becomes more and more complex with the introduction of increased legislation, it is very important that a real policy is elaborated. A variety of strategies can be called on – lighter timetables, day or half-day release, proper supervision, etc. It is very difficult for the individual head of department to go it alone when such a policy is lacking, but it is precisely in such a situation, when there is no LEA or school-wide policy, that the head of department should take some initiative – and not just at the start of the year. It is just as vital that there is continuing support, for although very few probationers fail their probationary year, it is surprising how quickly the initial stock of good ideas, enthusiasm and inventiveness can be used up in the rush of the term.

How can one arrange for continuing care over the year? Several strategies are possible:

1   Arranging to be 'free' at the same time as the probationary colleague and thus arrange a regular meeting.

2   If the probationer is not given a form to register in the first term or year, using the registration time once a week.

3   If the school is allocated a student for practice, it may be possible to arrange tutorial help in conjunction with the probationer.

4   Pairing off with another colleague (it needn't be a senior teacher) who is sympathetic and who can help the newcomer overcome the inevitable early problems.

5   Above all, being available.

The timetable

Perhaps the single most important factor in the life of the new teacher is the kind of timetable he or she is faced with in the first year. It is clearly unacceptable to give out a succession of 'bottom' classes. It is the surest way of bringing on a breakdown, or at least total demoralisation. The probationer should be offered an appropriate balance of classes, bearing in mind the sometimes conflicting demands of pupils and the question of continuity. If the school has a policy of a lightened timetable load for the beginner, that is excellent. If not, then it is a good idea to discuss it with the head or the deputy in charge of staff affairs.

157

Observation – a two-way process

As students, there are ample opportunities to observe teachers in action in the classroom. But the need to see good practice in action does not stop when teachers take up their first appointment. On the contrary, it is when they have taught for some time, that they can arguably benefit most from seeing others in action, for they are then more able to observe to good effect – they are more likely to know what to look for. There is a clear need for teachers to see each other in action with a variety of classes in terms of age and ability. Equally important is the need for the head of department to see the probationer in action and this must be done in a climate of mutual confidence and not with the atmosphere of student and inspector, with all the stress that such a situation will entail. Without doubt the head of department will be called upon to contribute to the report on the probationary year – how can this be done without proper observation? If the newcomer is to get the most benefit from such visits, it will be important to discuss openly the classes seen and such discussion must be enlightened with proper analysis and follow-up advice. To this end it will be useful to keep proper notes – preferably that the teacher may have access to. This may be achieved by use of double copies made by carbon interleaved notebooks so that instant discussion may take place about the factual contents of the lesson. As with student observation, the written notes are best if they are factual, with a time scale in the margin; subjective appraisal and comments should be added after discussion and agreement.

The problem of discipline

This can be an area of worry for the new teacher. The problem of discipline in general in the language classroom is discussed in Chapter 6 but the head of department will have a very supportive role to play in the life of the new teacher. The discipline problem can be eased if it is discussed openly and with the realisation that even teachers of long experience still have difficulties and cannot solve all problems. HoDs will have to be seen taking the lead in such matters, for example, by receiving the awkward pupil into their class to take the immediate pressure from a colleague. If there is proper support from the school system, it is important that the new colleague is aware of the system. Above all, it is essential not to pretend that behaviour problems are a disease, not to be brought out into the open – for in so doing the HoD will isolate the probationer who is still trying to find out the tricks of the trade, the personal wizardry and the dashes of good humour that can often extricate the teacher from the difficult situation. A departmental policy on discipline that fits into the school policy is important. Time-wasting gimmicks such as writing out verbs are most unlikely to succeed in reforming the ill-mannered pupil and indeed may reinforce a dislike of the subject. A base-line for behaviour, understood by the pupils and collectively agreed by staff – who try to understand what is the cause of any problems and who present a common front – is a more positive response.

Anticipating the problems and deadlines

Real help can be given by the experienced teacher in other ways: by having a sympathetic ear at all times, in the staffroom and the corridor, and in particular by being one step ahead of deadlines and important dates, such as report writing, assessment dates, etc. This will in some way avoid the inevitable rush of the school year and can go some way towards alleviating the general rush of the school term. For example, teachers should look ahead to report time, give advice on such administrative matters as obtaining report blanks and completing them in the school style. When the first parents' evening comes round, teachers should anticipate the understandable nervousness of the new colleague who is facing parents for the first time. They should give advice on the school's system and the individual's approach – for example, how to win the confidence of the parents by knowing all the pupils as individuals. Teachers have probably all made errors in talking about the wrong pupil and it can be embarrassing.

The departmental induction programme __

Patterns vary from school to school and any attempt to prescribe a programme of induction in exact detail would be out of place. However, the 'in at the deep end' approach should have no place in a well-run department. What we suggest below is a list of topics which should be covered by the head of department or a designated colleague at some time during the year. If an organised training session – say one lesson per week – is envisaged, then the order of the various topics will to some extent be dictated by the progress of the school calendar.

Topics in a school- or department-based induction programme

The school day   Lesson change times, assemblies, etc.

Audio-visual aids   Their use in the educational process: tapes, slides, films, cassettes, records, OHP, videos, computers, etc. Duplication and reprographic facilities: when, where and how. TV and radio facilities, copyright laws, etc.

Departmental stock   Whereabouts, age-range, suitability, availability.

Departmental systems   For record keeping, pupil assessment, issuing and collecting of textbooks, recording damage and loss, etc.

School policy   As it effects the department: e.g. how pupils are selected for options, sets, form, groups, etc., school policy on uniform, detentions, homework, etc.

Examinations and assessment   Where are past papers stored? Where is the set-book list? Who sets internal examinations? Who decides on external examination entries? How are SATs administered? How are pupil records saved?, etc.

Homework and marking policy   How many homeworks per group per week. What is the departmental/school policy on marking – is it positive rather than negative?

Overseas links   School, class and individual links; policy on visits and exchanges.

Sanctions   School policy; help available for troublesome pupils.

Parents   Policy for contacting and informing.

Library   Facilities for staff and pupils.

The form tutor   How to carry out administrative duties.

Other staff   Information relating to other staff, caretakers, secretaries, etc.

Outside agencies   Role, functions and use of LEA advisers, teachers' centres, etc.

Cross-curricular themes   The coordination beyond the department.

Educational awareness   Themes such as equal opportunities, etc.

In good schools, there will be a staff tutor whose role is to engage new staff and others on a programme of personal development. It is imperative that the head of department sees his or her role as part of this function.

Other forms of initial training

In recent years, there have been attempts to reform the basis for initial teacher training by the introduction of schemes such as licensed teachers, articled teachers and internships. All have in common a closer cooperation between schools and the training establishments. In working with teacher trainers there is a two-way benefit both for the school and for the trainer. Many of the ideas discussed in the sections on staff training, probationers and students can be usefully focused here if you are in one of the new schemes. However, it is important here as in so many other initiatives to have the cooperation of the whole department and indeed the whole staff. If the newly fashioned induction schemes are to be positively beneficial, then properly thought out cooperation will mean time, resources and commitment from a number of people working together.

Working with the assistant

In latter years, the presence of the foreign assistant has become something of a luxury in many areas. However, the recommendations of the National Curriculum working party place great stress on regular contact with the native speaker. The problem is that in the days of LMS, the assistant could become an easy target for cutting expenditure when savings are to be made. If teachers are to benefit from the presence of an assistant, then they must be seen to be making the best possible use of this valuable resource. It is essential that the normal school staff receive training on making the best use of the assistant and that the head, senior management team and governors are positive in their views on the employment of such a person.

In order to maximise the contribution of the assistant, it is wise to bear in mind the following points, especially at the beginning of the school year:

1 The assistant is *not* a trained teacher (and may not intend to teach at the end of a university course). As an unqualified teacher, with probably only the briefest introduction to the classroom skills that are necessary, he or she will certainly need very detailed advice and guidance, especially in the first few weeks. Simply sending out a group of pupils to 'do conversation' is unrealistic and will certainly be counter-productive for both assistant and pupils.

2 It may very well be the first lengthy visit of the assistant to this country, and he or she will need help, patience and sympathy to settle in.

What to do *before* the arrival of the assistant

Together with the 'official' letter sent by the head and the forms required by the Central Bureau in London, it is helpful to send an informal letter, setting out the following details:

1 Name, full address and telephone number of the school (typed or printed so as to avoid confusion, as handwriting styles can lead to error). It is important to remember that the STD code for the town, if used from overseas, is used without the '0', so Leeds is 532 not 0532.

2 Type of school – comprehensive, mixed, junior high, etc. – with explanation.

3 Numbers and age range of pupils.

4 Dates of beginnings and ends of terms. It should be remembered that the assistant year runs from October 1st to June 30th.

5 Possibilities and/or offers of accommodation with cost.

6 Address of the previous assistant who will be able to pass on advice.

7 HoD's name and address for contact before the start of term.

8 Requests for material.

9 Precise intentions for arrival in order to arrange reception.

10 The school prospectus.

11 The timetable (if known).

12 A request that the assistant bring written proof that he/she is a bona fide student intending to return to full-time study at the end of the year. This will considerably simplify requests for student concessionary rates in many areas.

During the first few weeks of the term, schools are always busy and the assistant may be forgotten. If there is such a risk, it is best to delegate a member of staff to look after the new arrival. A younger member would be best since such a teacher will quite possibly be nearer the age of the assistant and may have recently worked as an assistant in France, Germany, Italy or Spain.

Things to do as the assistant arrives or in the first few days

In order to help the assistant to settle in quickly, there is much to be done both inside and outside the school. It is to be hoped, however, that if the groundwork has been covered before the start of term, and if sufficient information has been forwarded, then the assistant will already know quite a lot about the framework in which he or she will be working. The HoD should:

1 Arrange for someone to meet the assistant at the station or airport.

2 If at all possible, introduce the assistant to the host family. If a flat has been arranged, what about a 'starter kit' – a supply of bread and milk and some other essentials for the first few days? Or better still, even if a flat has been rented, the HoD could arrange for the first few days to be spent as a guest in a family. These days are often awkward and strange and the sympathetic helping hand may be a reciprocal gesture for all the help teachers have had in France or Germany themselves.

3 Introduce the assistant personally to the head, the deputies, etc. This should be done slowly so as not to confuse the assistant with a host of new names and acronyms. Included in the list of 'important people' will be the office staff as well as anyone else who has shown a welcoming hand to previous assistants. It is to be hoped that all the language staff will make a special point of welcoming the assistant. At the first full staff meeting, it is important to make sure that all staff know who the assistant is – staff of all subjects will probably take an interest.

4 Arrange for the assistant to open a bank account at a nearby branch so that documentation may be ready to receive the salary payment. Explain and demonstrate how to write a cheque (continental practice is not the same as British).

5 Pass on full details to the office so that the salaries section of the LEA is informed in good time for paying salaries into bank accounts.

6 Explain about tax liability and National Insurance rules. Tax is normally waived for assistants under a reciprocal agreement ('The Double Taxation Agreement' – the CBEVE has latest details). Assistants must keep an eye on this, because tax is often deducted at emergency code level and later refunded. The local tax office can supply the two forms necessary to complete all formalities quickly.

7 Give the address of a doctor and explain how to register. Sick leave notification should be explained together with the necessity to inform the school of anything untoward.

8 Provide the local A–Z street map and a bus timetable, if possible arranging for a short tour of the area pointing out items of interest, where to catch the bus, etc.

9 Explain the facilities that are available for study and recreation, and those which are provided, for example, by the local university, polytechnic, night schools, assistants' committees, Association for Language Learning, sports centres, etc.

10 Make a special point of introducing the assistant to the sixth form. These students will often invite the assistant to the tennis club, parties, the pub, the local disco, etc.

11 Unravel the mysteries of initials such as HoD, LEA, DES, GCSE, NC, SATs, L6, U6, etc.

12 Ensure that there is proper liaison, if the assistant has to be shared with another school.

13 Make sure the assistant is aware that if they have to be away to sit examinations, for example, they know of the necessity to inform the school well in advance.

Finally, it must not be assumed that if the HoD has done all this at the start of the contract, then all will be well. A year can pass quickly, but it can also drag on despairingly if the assistant is put aside and ignored during a busy term.

The timetable

In making the timetable work there are several points to bear in mind. The maximum weekly contact time is twelve hours. It should be possible to use the assistant in a variety of situations with the various age groups. The sixth form is the obvious starter and groups should be small. Weekly contact for all sixth formers should be the aim. With year 11 classes, again weekly contact should be the ideal but may not be possible. Sometimes small groups can be sent out with the assistant BUT it must be remembered that a great deal of preparation is needed here to ensure that the work is integrated into the normal classroom sequence. Simply sending out a group is not the best solution. It is therefore important to consider alternatives since the small group in a little room – or at worst the 'back of a cloakroom' syndrome – can lead to behaviour problems and less than motivated classes and assistants. Integrated work within the normal classroom is often to be preferred – especially as group work is encouraged. The advantage is that there are two 'native' speakers in the classroom, the teacher and the assistant. This leads to easier dialogues, flexible groups and often a more positive attitude. Above all the HoD should be flexible and try to encourage the assistant to plan with them the sequence of pupil activities.

It is sometimes the case that the assistants can attend classes for English at the local university – this should be checked so as to enable release. Sometimes the year in school reveals periods that are less busy. For example when the trial examinations take place there will be no fifth and upper sixth classes. Then is the time to let other classes, who do not feature on the timetable at other times of the year, enjoy the advantages of the assistant.

In addition it may be advantageous to let the assistant attend English lessons, for example, in the sixth form (with permission of course).

Using the assistant in the classroom

In the first few weeks the HoD should insist that the assistant begins classroom observation, in order to ascertain the school's methods of teaching languages and see the standards that are expected of the pupils. It should be remembered that it will be rare to have an assistant who is a trained teacher and perhaps rare also in the 1990s to receive an assistant who even intends to become a teacher. A year abroad is now part of the scheme of study of a wide range of courses at colleges and universities here and abroad and thus the backgrounds of the assistants will be much more varied than in the past.

Alongside the period of observation, the assistant should study the main textbooks used as well as looking at the external examination requirements and the procedures for oral examinations. A familiarity with the key elements of the National Curriculum programmes of study, the attainment targets and areas of experience will also be useful. Colleagues should also be involved and it is a good idea to discuss, before and after, the contents of the lessons observed. Particular attention should be paid to question and answer techniques and to ways of *actively involving* pupils. Help on the appropriate correction of faults and the use of audio-visual aids will also be useful.

It is a mistake however, to restrict the period of observation to the first week or so – it is in everyone's interest to continue observation throughout the year.

Detailed discussion on the use of the assistant in the classroom is given in Chapter 7.

Preliminary tactics

The HoD must ensure that:

1   The timetable is understood.

2   The assistant has a base in the staffroom and good classroom accommodation. It is not good enough to relegate the groups to the hall, cloakroom or the back of the stage. The assistant deserves a room just as any other member of staff.

3   All teaching group lists are distributed.

4   Assistant groups are kept to a reasonable size – 10 or 12 at the most.

Furthermore, the HoD should:

1   Show the assistant how to use the basic audio-visual aids and give access to the materials used to make flashcards, etc.

2   Give clear and precise instructions as to what to do if discipline problems arise. Pupils must also be told what is expected of them.

3   Vary the lesson format. The assistant should sometimes work with a group in another room for the lesson, sometimes work with a group in the same room, and sometimes work *with* the teacher in some form of double act.

4   Encourage *enjoyment* of the lesson. It is a wonderful opportunity to inject a lively approach (it is to be hoped that it is always present, but the native speaker affords a unique extra dimension). Pupils are much more likely to want to go to the assistant's lessons if they are enjoyable.

It would be foolish to confine the assistant's work to the regularly timetabled classes. With only 12 hours per week allowed, priority will probably be given to the older pupils facing external examinations. However, the motivating factors with the keener younger pupils must not be forgotten. During the year, classes of lower ability pupils can benefit from 'guest appearances'. It may be that such lessons will involve some talk in English by the assistant – but this can be useful as an awareness raising exercise.

Nonspecialists

It is often the case that schools have to employ nonspecialists to teach a particular subject for a shorter or longer period of time. Various pressures force this: falling rolls, redefined catchment areas, changing status of schools, LMS and other financial pressures. Such a nonspecialist may be a part-timer, working for several half-days scattered throughout the week. In this case the problem is often how to provide a coherent timetable for the part-timer and for the pupils. On the other hand the part-time linguist may be a full-time member of staff with commitments to other departments or to the senior management team of the school.

Being drafted into a department or a second department may be a cause of resentment or difficulty from several points of view. For example, the colleague may have developed a style of teaching which is not in keeping with the general ethos of the department or the language classroom of the 1990s. Many non-specialists may be hesitant over new developments and their views may be coloured by their own experience of language learning in pre-GCSE days. If they are members of the senior management team they may be called out of the classroom on frequent occasions to attend to urgent administration.

What can and should the head of department do in such cases? In the first instance the head of department should have a say as to who teaches in the team in a part-time capacity in the same way as being part of the selection process for full-time appointments. What help can be reasonably given to the part-timer?

It would be reasonable to expect the part-timer to do some reading and preliminary research into the state of modern language teaching. To this end, a selection of materials in the staff library would be appropriate.

The nonspecialist should be encouraged to attend the departmental meetings and to contribute beyond the classroom. Involvement in a particular area of responsibility is a good way of increasing expertise.

It is very important that the nonspecialist be made aware of the books, materials and audio-visual aids that are in use in the school. A simple catalogue is of limited use; an effort should be made to put on show and demonstrate new ideas and materials.

The nonspecialist has the same right to expect support as does the new entrant to the profession. It is a mistake to expect that just because the new colleague has 20 years' experience, he or she will automatically be at home in the new teaching situation.

Ideas worth exploring to help build up confidence include:
- invitations to observe experienced colleagues in the classroom
- pairing the new colleague with a full-time specialist as a 'shadow'
- attendance at in-service courses (contact the LEA adviser)

166

- including the nonspecialist in any training arranged for students in the school (tricky to arrange, but it can be done).

Lastly, the newcomer should be encouraged to feel that he or she *is* an expert in some field and has a positive role to play.

Support staff

With the extension of modern language teaching to pupils of all abilities and the move in recent years to shift the focus in schools from a separate remedial department to a more integrated scheme to deal with special needs (SEN) it has become obvious that all teachers need to consider the use of support teachers. The question of differentiation has been dealt with in Chapter 7 but here we need to discuss briefly the use and deployment of support teachers in the department.

Discussion on the benefits of using specialist (i.e. modern language) staff as opposed to remedial staff will continue for a long time. 'For' a language specialist are such arguments as linguistic competence, familiarity with methodology and sympathy for the aims of the learning and teaching situation; for the nonlinguist are such qualities as special attention to pupils with learning difficulties and an expertise in certain teaching techniques. Whatever the strategy, real help will be positively used only if there is a sharing of ideas. In the first instance, all support staff should have at least an acquaintance with the teaching ideas and philosophy of the department. This is easier when it is a linguist involved, but more important for an outsider.

Steps to be taken

The HoD should:

1 Identify the problem in the classroom and the needs of the pupils – are they arising because of behaviour, the social atmosphere, the intellectual capacities of the students or physical handicaps?

2 Discuss with specialists the various strategies which may be employed – limited withdrawal, extra help for a group or an individual, the use of an amanuensis or the employment of hearing aids, a signer or other help.

3 Try whenever humanly possible to have at least some discussion beforehand about the aims of the lesson or sequence of lessons and be positive in the use of supplementary help, targeting such help carefully so as to utilise the resource fully.

4 Review carefully the deployment of the extra help – long or short term – for particular skills (e.g. listening) and review also the effectiveness of the help.

167

Extra help need not always be in the classroom. One of the findings of recent research is that children with learning difficulties often have problems with, for example, worksheets. Special advice on the layout of worksheets, the language used in such materials can be a great help. Advice on the use of English can also be given outside the classroom. Using the active rather than the passive, using verbs rather than nouns, etc. can help enormously in transforming understanding. This topic could well be a subject for staff, school-based INSET.

Helping students

The possibility of working closely with the local teacher-training institution should be warmly welcomed, not only to enable staff to take part in the vital work of training the next generation of teachers, but also because of the undoubted spin-off effect of having contact with new, and one hopes, inventive minds, when the students and tutors are present. As the proposals for the restructuring of teacher-training take shape, and with the emergence of new schemes such as the licensed teacher scheme, the articled teacher scheme and even a new grade of mentors, it is clear that schools will have a bigger role to play. At first sight this might appear to increase the workload of staff. If handled with sensitivity and imagination this need not be too great a burden. Properly structured, the mutual contact and interaction between school and training department can be a positive relationship. It is clearly part of the job of the head of department to so arrange matters that the pupils will benefit from the experience.

There will be conflicting pressures – chief of which will be to marry the demands and needs of the pupils in the school and their welfare to the needs of the visiting students allocated to the school for a shorter or longer time in the academic year.

At best, the practice period can be refreshing and stimulating; at worst an excuse for the regular teacher to gain a few extra 'free periods'. The head of department needs to plan well ahead for the opportunities and challenges; early contact should be established with the training institution and certain information gathered.

1   What is the overall shape of the training year(s)?

2   What are the main components of the student year?

3   What level of subject expertise and methodological competency can be expected from the student?

4   What is the shape of the school-based practice? If there are several sessions of school placements, clearly there are different expectations of students at different stages.

5   What will be the pattern of supervision? What is the balance between teachers and tutors for supervision?

6   What role does the school have in assessment? What weight does the school report carry?

7   When is the assessment wanted?

The student in training should be seen as a junior partner in the school, enjoying the rights and *some* of the responsibilities of the regular staff. Ideally, as soon as the student has been allocated, the HoD should make contact in the same way as when a full-time appointment is made.

If possible it should be arranged for the student to come in beforehand to meet the staff whose classes will be shared for the duration of the practice. It may even be possible for the student to sit in with some of the classes at this first visit to gain some idea of the atmosphere of the working environment.

What sort of timetable should be arranged? It will of course vary with the type and duration of the practice, but it is very important to liaise with the training institution, and in particular to seek out the curriculum vitae of the student. What combination of subjects is on offer? Will it mean cooperation with another department? The HoD should try to give as balanced an experience as possible over the age-range and ability-range of the school. It is best to avoid 'notorious' classes, yet it would be wrong to shelter the student from the realities of life by going to the other extreme.

Where possible, the student should be allocated the full subject time of the class or group. This does not imply that the student will always take every lesson alone. On the contrary, the inventive teacher will be able to fit a variety of activities into such an arrangement: observation, small-group teaching, team-teaching and whole class presentations over a period of time. Pupils will welcome a carefully planned change in routine and it allows student participation and teacher control as well. Within the classroom, there are diverging views about induction. Some teachers favour the 'in-at-the-deep-end' approach, others the 'toe-in-first-to-test-the-temperature' idea. Experience would suggest the latter strategy, but it should be flexible. After an initial, but not too long, period of observation, the student must be allowed to establish his or her own working relationships with the pupils. This does *not* mean that there is no more observation. It will be important throughout the practice, because it is only as experience increases that the real job of observation begins – as the student learns what to look for in the performance of the experienced teacher.

Careful planning of lessons is important. At first this must be done under the direct supervision of the regular teacher. It is invaluable if members of staff discuss the student's lessons *before* and *after* the event, but gradually the independence must be increased.

Appropriate evaluation is needed of course. A file of notes is useful and it is ideal to use a carbon interleaved note book so as to give a copy to the student as one discusses the lesson. NEVER offer criticism of any sort in front of a class – save all comments for the relative privacy of the staffroom. Encourage self-criticism and self-appraisal, asking the student for their comments on the lessons.

Finally, it is essential that all students get a broad view of the totality of the teacher's work. If at all possible they should be attached to a form tutor, and allowed to see the work of other areas of the school. A session with the staff tutor and glimpses into the role of the year tutor will be invaluable.

Supervision must be positive and discreet – and it should not be forgotten that it can be shared by all members of the team. Many departments allocate on a rotation a teacher to look after students. This is a good idea – it is part of general staff development and can be a good experience.

Appraisal and staff development

The head of department will have an important role to play in the career development of many staff. If the department is to be healthy and forward looking in its approach, it is vital that innovations be considered and that staff horizons are widened.

Inevitably, monitoring the work of colleagues will be important, and at the same time it is that part of the professional duty which arguably calls for the most tact and care. Assessing the work of teachers must not be approached with the attitude of an inquisitor, in an overtly inspectoral role, but rather with the aim of fostering good practice and individual and corporate development. Within the next few years, it is likely that teacher appraisal will be part of the role of the head of department who in turn will be appraised by senior colleagues. It is axiomatic that any such scheme should be within broad outlines agreed by appraised and appraisee, with clear targets for personal developments so that the measuring instruments are open and understood. It is also important that any appraisal should form the basis for future positive development in the career of the teacher as part of the school team.

It will mean treading carefully through a minefield of personal relationships, but having such skills is one of the reasons for being appointed to run a department.

Why assess departmental staff?

1   To allocate staff resources to bring the most beneficial outcome to pupils.

2   To decide if new teaching strategies are possible (e.g. Is there the appropriate expertise to set up an AS course?).

3   To assist in reference writing.

4   To recommend to the head those colleagues who may aspire to scale posts.

5   To assess the need for and best way of delivering in-service training.

Checklist

What should be assessed?

- □   *Administration*   Are mark-lists, minutes, etc. appropriately completed according to previously agreed and circulated criteria?
- □   *Lesson planning and review*   Is the teacher's record book up to date, realistic and meaningful?
- □   *Homework*   Is it set, marked and commented on in an appropriate manner?
- □   *Examination results*   Are they reasonable, given the level of the class, the school expectations and the level of experience?
- □   *General contribution*   Is there an extra dimension to the teacher's work beyond the classroom?
- □   *The work in the classroom*   This is the most important aspect of the review and is dealt with more comprehensively below.

Review and appraisal can be two-edged swords. In any professional relationship, the very existence of appraisal routines must presuppose the existence of machinery to update and retrain the appraisee in the light of agreed targets. Provision of a professional level of INSET is the duty of schools, LEAs and other agencies concerned with assessment and appraisal. It is only when the two processes go together that there will be trust from both partners. This trust is most difficult and delicate to establish and the way it is carried out will depend to a large extent on the maturity of relationships within the department. It cannot and must not be done in an underhand way, such as dropping in on the excuse of looking in a cupboard (though such interruptions can reveal a lot). Ideally the criteria should be discussed openly with the colleague both before and after the event.

Appraisal in a professional partnership is a three-phase business:

1   Establishing trust and the criteria/measuring instrument.

2   The observation/recording process.

3   The follow-up interview and development/action programme.

171

Table 4 is a starting point for devising a classroom observation chart. It is an aid to assessment and must not replace professional judgement. It is based on a five-point scale from positive to negative from observations made in the classroom.

			Negative ⟷ Positive				
			1	2	3	4	5
Relationship with pupils	1	Cooperation with pupils					
	2	Pupil cooperation with teacher					
	3	Reactions to pupils as individuals and their problems					
	4	Class control: a) ability to anticipate problems					
		b) ability to create learning environment					
		c) ability to be consistent and fair					
Organisation	5	Suitability of material used					
	6	Arrangements of materials					
	7	Appropriate use of aids					
	8	Knowledge of subject material					
Communication	9	Clarity of voice					
	10	Ability to receive pupil contribution and to react					
	11	Ability to arouse and keep interest					
	12	Progress during the lesson					
	13	Initiative					

Table 4: Classroom observation chart

Appraisal should be seen as a continuous and systematic process intended to help individual teachers with their professional development and career planning.

What are the benefits of appraisal?

1   Recognition of effective practice.

2   Greater confidence and morale.

3   Increased job satisfaction.

4   Support for systematic development.

5   Better professional relations and communications.

Knowing the qualities of the departmental staff is one step in producing a departmental scheme for in-service training. This must obviously fit into the whole school policy, but it is the duty of the head of department to contribute to such a policy. Teachers are individuals and to some extent they must take the responsibility for their own development. Nevertheless the head of department must also initiate and be in a position to help staff to seize opportunities

Another aspect of the appraisal schemes in schools will be that the head of department will also be appraised. Not only will the qualities of his or her teaching be assessed, but also the quality of leadership provided in the departmental context. It is obvious that the role of 'policing' the National Curriculum has changed the nature of the relationship between head of department and senior management, between school and local/national inspectors. There may very well be a distinction between the role of the inspector and that of the adviser. Whatever the outcome of the negotiations in progress at the start of the 1990s, it would be wise for the head of department to bear in mind the sort of quality control questions that may be asked of him. Below is a list of the sort of questions that may be asked when the head of department is the appraisee and it is offered as a starting point for discussion with the appraiser when the criteria are being laid out.

Leadership   Is the department well led? Is there a good team spirit, high morale, effective planning and efficient organisation?

Scheme of work   Does it offer detailed guidance, especially on a coherent teaching method?

Staff and resources   Are staff and resources adequately deployed to maximum effect? Are the rooms appropriate, well decorated, revealing pupil work and a positive attitude to the subject?

Attitudes, expectations and skills   Is there a positive approach? Is there a good level of teaching skills? Are expectations high but realistic? Is there good use of encouragement and discriminating praise for effort and good work?

Use of the target language   Are the staff willing and able to use the target language in lessons?

Assessment   Is there a good system for recording achievement and profiling? Do the pupils have a coherent experience?

Identifying needs

As a regular item on the departmental agenda, identifying needs is a preliminary step to initiating a programme of self-help and in-service work.

Questions to be asked include:
- Where is the department heading?
- What expertise does it need to implement its policy and the school's policy?
- What is the department's view of the latest developments in the subject area?

Where can one enlist help?

It is important to realise that there is help both within and beyond the school:

- staff within the school and the department may have an expertise they can share
- the LEA adviser, advisory teacher, local college and university in the area may help
- subject teaching associations such as ALL and the local branch may be a valuable source of information and shared experience.

It is a good idea to use part of the departmental meeting for in-service work. After routine matters such as who is setting the year 9 examination papers, why not discuss new ideas?

As a starting point on every agenda should be an item called '*Bright Ideas*' when each colleague is asked to share in one minute an idea that has worked with his or her class since the last meeting. This brief brain-storming session can bring in a rich harvest. More substantially, the head of department (or someone else) could be asked to prepare and introduce a topic for discussion. Very often the invitation to an outside speaker (outside the school or outside the department) will act as a good focus. It will need advanced planning, for it will be of little benefit to invite a contribution on a topic as wide as 'oral work' – that is far too vague. On the contrary, only with careful planning around a specific brief will the venture be worthwhile.

A much more positive approach would be to narrow down the topic area to 'encouraging an oral approach in the lower half of year 10'. Even that may be too wide and a better focus may be, for example, 'effective worksheets in year 7'. If at all possible, staff should be briefed beforehand so that they may be able to offer a positive contribution to the discussion.

The LEA adviser or advisory teacher should be invited to the departmental meeting. The discussion may lead to fruitful cooperation. Many agencies may put on courses and meetings at local, regional and national level. Colleagues have a right to be informed. It is an ineffective (and sometimes threatened) head of department who hides away the circulars!

LEA courses

HoDs should make sure that all information about LEA courses is circulated to colleagues. If kept centrally in the school, they should read it and make sure all are informed. It is often a good idea to delegate a particular teacher to a course if there is seen to be real benefit to the individual and the department. After any participation in a course, there is the important question of follow-up. Ideas that are not disseminated are not beneficial. In these cost-conscious days it is vital that a report is made after participation and an action plan prepared if necessary. This form of self help is often overlooked.

DES courses

Two publications should be seen regularly by staff – *Long Courses* and *Short*

Courses. These annual booklets are sent to all schools and give details well in advance of HMI run courses.

Visits abroad

Staff should be encouraged to maintain and improve the quality of their knowledge of the target country. Several agencies run courses, visits and exchanges or can facilitate such contacts. The local town may be 'twinned' and such arrangements can be of immense help. Finance can be a problem, but it is sometimes possible to tap into various sources; it is worth investigating the different schemes promoted by the Central Bureau for Educational Visits and Exchanges who have a number of possible systems ranging from three week exchanges to visits of up to a year. The European Community has the 'Lingua' scheme for promoting exchanges involving INSET and if you apply for a DES course abroad there are limited government grants. The CBEVE or the local adviser can help. It is to be noted that post-to-post exchanges are not now confined to language teachers and that such contacts can enhance other areas of the school.

Professional reading and the staff library

Members of staff should be encouraged to keep up to date in their reading. In the busy term at school, it is not surprising how much this is neglected. If at all possible, the school librarian and the various departments should cooperate to provide a range of books on curriculum development, methodology, the latest research, etc. An ideal way would be to have a subscription to CILT publications and also copies of the various journals and publications of the Association for Language Learning. A good start is the Bibliography of this publication.

Reporting back

This is essential. In order that the widest possible audience may share experiences, it is vital that anyone who has been on a course or any form of in-service training (especially if it is provided at public expense) should report back to colleagues. This form of self-generated in-service training is often neglected.

Training days

It is often possible to use such days for departmental training as opposed to whole-school initiatives. Such training may be conducted on or off the premises. It is possible to invite in the expert to lead work on a specific topic or to go as a whole team to the computer centre run by the LEA, or the teachers' centre. The value of being away from the school can be very positive, and such initiatives rewarding. For example, it will be possible to have a whole day devoted to awareness raising about the world of computers and IT in language teaching. Such an approach may then lead to individual teachers subsequently developing a specialism of great value to the team.

Career development

The head of department is one of the members of staff responsible for helping teachers to think about their career development. This is not always easy at a time of falling rolls, LMS and financial accountability, but it is important to urge teachers to think ahead and to try and avoid professional staleness. As part of the strategy for sharing out jobs and responsibilities within the department, career development is of prime importance. Wise heads of department do not keep for themselves all the best classes and certainly do not try to keep all the best jobs. HoDs should ensure that each job allocated to other colleagues must be a real job and not just a chore. Senior staff should be kept aware of the work of other staff – especially the good work. It is not always easy for the head of a large staff to know everything that is going on. Keeping an ear to the ground is a sound policy.

INSET

Suggestions for topics for in-service work within the department

The following, not exhaustive, list of ideas could well form the basis for short and long term developmental discussions:

- setting examination questions and other assessment techniques
- testing the various skills
- assessing positively
- continuous assessment
- making worksheets and other aids
- using the hardware available
- introducing Information Technology
- using the assistant
- writing reports and records of achievement
- using the library
- using and developing authentic materials
- cross-curricular themes
- working with other departments, e.g. developing a language policy for the school
- using support staff and cooperating with SEN teachers.

Checklist for INSET development

- □ INSET will be most valuable if it has a clearly defined target group.
- □ A needs analysis will help establish priorities (e.g. the prospect of languages for all, the introduction of diversification programmes, a new push on IT, etc.).
- □ Good materials will help bring about a positive attitude.
- □ Leadership is important as is organisation.
- □ The pedagogy of INSET must mirror good practice, despite possible demands for overly-didactic sessions.
- □ There must be clear links to classroom practice.
- □ INSET is seen as a learning *process* rather than an event.
- □ Follow-up will enhance the quality of the INSET package.

16 The organisation of resources

Whatever grand ideas teachers may have, whatever master plan they elaborate to transform language teaching in the school, sooner or later any such plan has to be worked out within the framework of available resources, the timetable space, the staff expertise, the accommodation and the capitation allowance.

The drawing up of the timetable, agreed by colleagues and acceptable to the timetabler, the head and other departments, is discussed fully in Chapter 17. Likewise the appointment of departmental staff, their induction, further training and deployment have been discussed in detail. This section is concerned with the narrower (but equally important) idea of resources – the rooms, equipment and books.

Teachers are now in an era of greater financial accountability. Waste of resources will certainly not be looked on with favour by those responsible for the provision of materials. LMS has brought to the forefront this question of the correct use of funding. Each school will have its own arrangements for allocating funds down through the institution and each head of department has a responsibility to understand the mechanics of such processes. If the school has a computerised management system, then it is important to get to grips with the system and become familiar with the appropriate software and its applications. Senior management has the job of ensuring the accessibility of the system to those who need to know. As LEA involvement is lessened, it is obvious that management is being devolved and this will mean that middle management, such as heads of department, will be required to assume certain managerial tasks. A whole school policy needs to be evolved.

Rooms

Ideally every teacher in the department will have his or her own teaching room, for in such circumstances they are more easily maintained. Such a regime also allows the development of good teaching styles when the different needs of other occupants do not have to be accommodated. Alas, this ideal is not always possible, so that the minimum to be asked for is a suite of rooms for the exclusive use of the department. The physical conditions in which teachers and their pupils work have a great effect on morale. If the department can create a tradition of tidy, well cared for rooms, so much the better. Such an arrangement will also result in the economical use of expensive equipment which can be shared in the department and will probably be better maintained with the 'ownership' feeling thereby engendered.

The minimum to be asked for is:

1   Exclusive (or major) use of a number of classrooms, depending on the size of the staff. These should be equipped to allow teaching and learning to take place in the departmental style, with the absolute minimum of carrying and transferring equipment.

2   Appropriate storerooms and cupboards, conveniently sited so as to encourage maximum use of resources.

3   Limited rights over other rooms of various sizes to allow assistants and other groups to function effectively.

The advantages of this fixed accommodation are enormous and will enrich the possibilities of teaching and cooperation in many ways.

1   Heavy, delicate or expensive equipment will not have to be moved long distances and up and down stairs – and this will save wear and tear on both machinery and teachers. It will also reduce the temptation for staff to reject the use of equipment because it is not at hand.

2   Staff cooperation will be greater and teaching styles more varied if they are grouped in a language suite.

3   Support for new staff, probationers and students will be facilitated in a compact area.

4   Displays are easier to manage.

5   Borrowing and control of stock is easier to manage.

6   A corporate image can be developed.

There *are* disadvantages in the suite arrangement – the main one being that pupils will be obliged to move for each lesson to different parts of the building. With careful timetabling and the now almost universal double-period system, these disadvantages can be minimised, even in a busy school, and should not be allowed to tip the balance against such cooperative arrangements.

Equipment for the modern language department _____

Basic requirements

- ☐ Carpeted floor and a minimum of soundproofing
- ☐ Tape/cassette recorder
- ☐ External, wall-mounted loudspeakers to enhance quality reproduction
- ☐ OHP and fixed screen
- ☐ Blackout/dimout system
- ☐ Use (shared?) of TV and VCR
- ☐ Electric sockets in strategic positions (shoulder high) and sufficient numbers around the room
- ☐ Cupboards and storage areas
- ☐ Display/pinboard
- ☐ Use of departmental computer including keyboard, screen and printer
- ☐ Listening posts for group listening work
- ☐ Tape/cassette bulk eraser
- ☐ Possible access to fast copier
- ☐ Computer facilities.

This may appear to be an extravagant shopping list, but it is not when teachers look at the requirements of the National Curriculum and also compare it to the funding attracted by science and technology teaching. Of course the case for spending money on capital equipment will be greatly enhanced if the equipment is regularly used and seen to be so.

Further equipment will include such items as satellite TV, modems for linking into databases, etc., and shared reprographic machinery.

Figure 8 shows how a fully equipped modern language classroom might be organised. However, it is not our intention to discuss detailed plans for room layout – that will vary from school to school. Nevertheless, staff must be aware that the way the room is laid out – desks in rows or other flexible groupings – will affect the style of teaching that will take place. Desks in rows may very well favour teacher-orientated styles, whereas group work and other forms of flexible learning may be better in a room with more informal arrangements of furniture. Whatever plans are made it is important that rearrangements can take place with the minimum of fuss and that there is room for the teacher to circulate while allowing all pupils to see the teacher or other lesson focuses. It is best to discuss it with colleagues and work out what suits staff the best. For a fuller consideration of classroom arrangements for group work see Chapter 2, pp. 34–41.

'Gold rush' – or how not to use resources

It is bad planning to use this method, whereby the departmental stock cupboard is

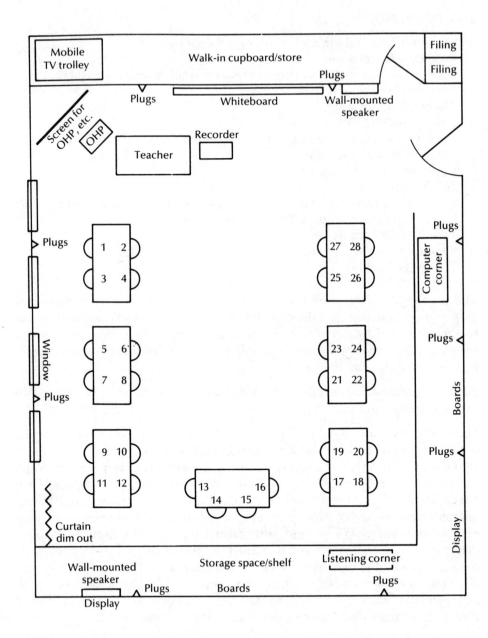

Figure 8: A model classroom for modern languages

180

opened at the start of term and the various members of staff (or at least those in the know!) take away all that they need, (or might need) for their personal use. This is the surest way of building up the staff room 'window-sill' method of storing equipment and files and not using all the valuable material efficiently. It will encourage an individual and not a collective approach to planning. Once this initial rush is over, there is the strong possibility that the HoD will not be able to do anything about it until the end of the summer term when the material is stored.

Furthermore, proper preplanning before the beginning of the school year, and preferably at the same time as decisions are being made about the programmes of study, will go a long way towards easing the frustrations about stock and equipment.

The departmental handbook (see Chapter 18) should contain a list of what is in stock, its location and suggestions for suitable use.

Maintaining the hardware

Equipment will be of no use unless it works efficiently and is available. Whatever method is used for storing, retrieving, returning and monitoring the equipment, *the system must be understandable and easy to use* or it will be abused.

It is essential to have a regular (weekly or even daily) check on valuable equipment together with an efficient system for reporting and correcting faults. Unless malfunctions are reported *and* acted upon quickly, they tend to be forgotten. It will almost certainly be the case that the tape recorder will fail to work at the most crucial time in the school year – just as it is required to record the external oral tests! Maintenance will be easier if there is a faults book in an accessible place. Each page should be ruled out and space left to record the action taken as in Figure 9.

Modern Language Department Equipment Faults Book School Year 19 ___ –19___.						
Date	Machine	No.	Location	Fault	Staff	Action
19/10	Cassette recorder	2	Room 6	No fast-forward	DM	To Teachers' Centre 20/10

Figure 9: The equipment faults book

It is usually possible via the LEA to negotiate a regular maintenance schedule – it is well worthwhile and probably cheaper in the long term. Minor matters can be speedily dealt with in the department. The changing of projector bulbs, cleaning of tape heads, etc. should be part of the training programme for departmental colleagues.

The departmental tool kit

It is a good idea to have a collection of odds and ends in the departmental area in order to effect minor repairs, etc. as quickly as possible. Such a tool kit should contain the following items:

Checklist

- ☐ Spare bulbs of the right sizes
- ☐ Spare plugs and fuses of the correct type – it is important to read the instructions on the equipment most carefully
- ☐ Spare leads, jack plugs, audio and video connectors, etc. all correctly labelled (e.g. with tie on luggage label to indicate that it connects two cassette recorders)
- ☐ A tape editor if reel-to-reel is used
- ☐ Screwdrivers, insulating tape, etc.
- ☐ The manuals of the various items of equipment.

What each teacher should know about the departmental resources

Each colleague should have an up to date list of available equipment and it should include the following:

Checklist

- ☐ Available hardware – recorders, OHPs, projectors, computers, etc.
- ☐ Available software – tapes, slides, cassettes, videos, computer software, etc.
- ☐ Worksheets
- ☐ Flashcards
- ☐ Books and other printed material beyond the basic texts
- ☐ Past examination papers
- ☐ Duplicating and other reprographic facilities in the school
- ☐ Loan facilities from the advisory services and other agencies
- ☐ School library facilities.

Such a list may very well be annotated in order to give an idea of the age/ability range of the materials.

Ordering books and equipment

Much will depend on the policy of the school, but it is usual to allow the head of department discretion in using the funds allocated to the department. It is important to ascertain at the outset what is covered by the departmental capitation allowance. Does it include exercise books and audio-visual aids, etc. or are these the responsibility of some other central funding? It is vital to know in advance what are the needs of the department, as planning is of the utmost importance. One must view the process of the 'requisition' as a long term process and not a matter to be dealt with hastily at the start of the financial year. LMS in schools means accountability and it is wise to establish a departmental policy in consultation with colleagues. When drawing up such a strategy, it would be reasonable to discuss openly with staff and the head in order to establish a budget and targets for the year. How should this be done? What factors need to be taken into account?

The departmental budget _____

As has been frequently noted in this book, the new conditions in schools brought on by the Education Reform Act (ERA) of 1988 have altered the climate in so far as the need for careful money management is concerned. It is likely that some kind of formula funding will be in operation. The head of department needs to know of this – detailed knowledge of spreadsheets is not needed, but it will be of use to consider the following:

1   The establishment of a departmental 'teaching load'. The more pupils a department teaches, and the more frequently teachers see them in a week, the more expensive it will be to equip them properly. To calculate the teaching load, it is necessary to calculate for each year the number of groups multiplied by the number of pupils in each group, and then by the number of periods taught to the group. For example:

7th year teaching load
6 groups × 30 pupils per group × 4 lessons per week = 6 × 30 × 4 = 720.

It is likely that certain age categories attract certain funding – the sixth form for example attracting a higher figure. From these figures it is possible to work out the capitation allowance with the colleague responsible. Precise allocation within the department can then be made and even a possible bargain struck if, for example, there is an extra consideration such as setting up a new language or if special needs provision is to be taken into account.

2   Consideration of the needs of the different languages in the department.

3   What are the needs of the examination classes e.g. for set books?

4   What are the needs of special groups of children, e.g. SEN?

5   What will have to be spent to make up depleted stock? Depleted sets of texts will always be there – even in a well-run department.

6   What proportion needs to be spent on expendable items such as card, glue, files, computer disks, cassettes, etc.?

7   Does the department need to contribute towards capital equipment such as a cassette recorder?

8   Is there a contingency fund for unexpected needs during the year?

And perhaps the overriding consideration:

9   What are the long-term aims of the department which may involve expenditure over a number of years? Will a change of syllabus or the introduction of a new series of course books be feasible, given other on-going items of expense?

As has so often been said it is a question of overall planning in consultation with colleagues.

Buying materials – reviewing the range and making a selection

Having established a long-term strategy and general policy, the next thing is to build up a bank of information on what is available.

1   First of all, it is important to build up an annotated collection of publishers' brochures (not forgetting to discard the last year's out-of-date editions). A 'concertina' file with lettered sections is a useful cataloguing method. The HoD should be a magpie in collecting all brochures from publishers and equipment makers.

2   If at all possible the HoD should go to exhibitions and see the materials.

3   The annual conference of the Association for Language Learning is always accompanied by the most comprehensive exhibition in the UK. Publishers often arrange workshop sessions with authors and this is a useful way of finding out about the latest products directly from the source.

4   Whenever possible, it is worthwhile talking to teachers in other schools where the books may be in use – a consumer report is invaluable.

5 The LEA adviser can also help especially if there is a resources library in the teachers' centre.

6 The approval and inspection copy service is useful to examine new publications. In the case of a new head of department, many publishers will send them a complete range of materials to look at. Publishers also employ reps who visit schools.

7 If new books are received, it is a good idea to keep a systematic record or review as in Figure 10 which will also include the opinions of your colleagues. After all, they will be using the books as well.

Title	Author	
Publisher	Date	Price
Age range		ISBN
Components		
Tapes (No.) (Quality)		
Illustrations		
Comments	Action	

Figure 10: Card index for reviewing material

8 The review section of language journals (for example of ALL) provide an excellent source of information and reviews are usually written by teachers. The *Times Educational Supplement* has reviews and twice a year a special language supplement.

Ordering stock

It is important to order sufficient stock of each title to allow for wastage. In addition it is a good idea to order for staff a selection of other titles which may stimulate good ideas. Even if a course book is not quite suitable for the school, there will still be many good ideas to pick up. So, in addition to class sets of major courses, five or six copies of other material for staff use will prove invaluable. This will be all the more important as a way of building up good practice for the implementation of the National Curriculum and the programmes of study. Such material can be placed in the staff library together with books on methodology, reports from examination boards, CILT catalogues, etc.

Keeping track of stock

This is most important and can help in the smooth running of the department. In an effort to keep wastage to a minimum, it is advisable to try to evolve a routine whenever new material arrives.

1   Is it clear who has first line responsibility for departmental stock?

2   As soon as an order arrives it should be logged in on an index card as in Figure 11. This can be a real index card or an entry on a computerised database. One 'card' per item should be used and endeavour to keep it up to date. It will be time-consuming to put the data onto a database in the first instance, but it will be quick and easy thereafter to keep it up to date and consult the card or obtain a print out if it is held on a datafile.

Title Starting French: Book 1				ISBN 0 012345 X	
Date	Additions	Reqn No.	Deleted	In stock	Initials
1/9	40	4361Q	—	40	DM

Figure 11: Card index for logging orders

3   As soon as the stock has been recorded, all material should be stamped with the official school/departmental stamp in order to identify it.

4   If there is a break-in at the school and the police/insurance company need to be involved, is it possible to give a list/description/serial number, etc. of any missing item?

5   It is essential to have a fixed time each year to take stock. A physical check is essential – and it also allows staff to check for damage and perhaps enlist pupils to do the remedial work. Sticky tape and the library transparent-covering film are excellent lifesavers.

6   It is also essential to keep a record of stock issued (date, class, staff, etc.).

7   Books should be numbered with an easy system that is consistent: e.g. 91/35 is book 35 of that title bought in 1991.

8   If the school allows it, it is advisable to adopt an approved system of monitoring damage and loss – charging, issuing receipts, etc. in accordance with school policy.

9   The HoD should try as far as possible to avoid the staff-room window sill syndrome. It is very frustrating to see the odd copies missing from a class set lying yellowing in the sun and gathering dust. The HoD should be ruthless and have a regular 'round-up' session from all the nooks and crannies in the school buildings. It is also well worthwhile leaving in the staffroom a large amnesty box, labelled 'Modern Languages' for staff to use to return copies without questions.

Audio-visual and other software

Looking after tapes, cassettes and computer software is important. A properly thought out system is vital, not only to minimise loss, but also to allow staff to make full use of the material available.

The first rule is never to use the Master copy especially of computer software, but of audio/video tapes as well.

1   Every tape and cassette should be clearly marked with a sticker to identify the contents.

2   The cassette box, etc. should carry an identifying coloured sticker (red for French, green for German, blue for A level, etc.). This will enable the item to be located and returned efficiently to the correct storage position.

3   It is worth trying to allot a particular place on the shelf for each item so that it is easy to ascertain if an item is missing.

4   If pupils have access to a loan system, it is essential to lend out a copy, NEVER the master, and to use a loans/returns book or card slotted into the place where the item has been taken from to indicate the borrower.

5   It is important to make sure that there is a security system so that at the end of each day all materials are returned and the caretaker does not find the expensive camcorder or the not so expensive, but maybe more valuable, cassette lying around.

6   The HoD should make sure that all concerned know the system.

7   When a member of staff leaves, is there a system to ensure that all school equipment and *keys* are returned?

17   Drawing up the timetable

The production of the school timetable brings to life the decisions made at many levels about school priorities and concerns. It is a complicated task, but not one so shrouded in mystery that it is impossible to understand. The head of department must seek close liaison with the timetabler and the attempt to exert some control over part of the daily diet given to pupils will entail some understanding of the process by the departmental leader. It will mean being flexible and understanding in order to make the appropriate intervention at the right time. This understanding will fall into two parts: the whole school dimension and the departmental point of view.

The school dimension

- the contribution modern languages make to the general education of all pupils (see also p. 207)
- the specialist needs of pupils
- the overall time allocation to the various interests in the school and in particular the time needed to fulfil the requirements of the National Curriculum
- cooperation with other departments, e.g. in respect of a school-wide language policy
- the number and qualifications of staff.

The departmental dimension

The needs of pupils

- the size of teaching groups, taking into consideration the age, ability and aims of each group
- the experience of a particular group with a member of staff in the previous year – was it fruitful or not?
- the need for continuity in teaching, especially with examination classes
- the desirability of a change of teacher with a view to a change of emphasis, tempo or style.

The needs of staff

- the necessity to give, as far as possible, a fair timetable to each member of staff.

The view that established members of staff automatically get the first choice of classes is not acceptable in a team situation

- the need for a policy on staff development, for example, the point of view which makes it possible for each colleague to have experience of the whole variety of classes available in the school
- the *individual* needs of staff
- the other responsibilities within the school which may demand a time allocation – for example being a year tutor or head of house – not forgetting those extra time consuming tasks which come with running a department
- new colleagues and their particular needs.

It is often at timetabling times that the various tensions in a school or department tend to arise. This is only natural and good diplomacy is called for. However, it is obvious that if the head of department is not prepared to lead from the front and accept a share in the work load which involves a range of classes of all types, both 'difficult' and 'easy', then leading is a sham. If the head of department is not able to say that he or she has experience over the whole school range, how can any real leadership be shown? The head of department who is timetabled for total involvement with the top sets has no right to demand loyalty from colleagues. Without labouring the point, it is our experience that an open sharing of the timetable process will in fact do much to defuse any problems. Before the timetable is committed to paper or the computer (see below), it is diplomatic (and not just a cosmetic exercise) to ask staff what classes they would like to be considered for. It will surprise most heads of department that their colleagues will put down a fair list and not try to stake out their own comfortable territory. If the process is open, most staff will accept that there are sometimes impossible combinations of classes and that if the first consideration is the pupils' interest, reasonableness is usually to be found. This tactic, together with a real concern for staff progress, will bring satisfaction.

The process

As is well known, it takes weeks, even months to produce a timetable. As with many other jobs which fall to the middle manager (HoD), the process must be seen as a long-term task which will begin several months before putting ideas to paper. Indeed the process really begins as the year starts with the present timetable. The making of the timetable usually has an optimistic beginning ('We'll get it right this year!'), but compromise and reality frequently temper this optimism.

The initial steps to be taken in making up a timetable

The HoD should:

1   Review the working of the existing arrangements: have they produced the desired effects in terms of pupil performance? If not, what are the obstacles

from the points of view of the pupils, the staff and the optimum use of resources? Were pupil periods unevenly distributed or bunched? Are rooms not used fully? Do staff non-contact periods fall badly?

2   Talk to the curriculum coordinator about the whole school policy and, just as importantly, about ideas coming from the department. Is the flexible learning programme to be introduced for the non A-level sixth form viable? Is the development of a second language provision calling for careful planning in year 9? and so on.

3   Discuss in the heads of department committee the overall plan being proposed. Take into account any cross-curricular working that is important and look at the time-space allocation over the whole pupil life as he or she progresses through the school. It may not be appropriate, for example, to have four lessons per week per year. Some other configuration may be correct so long as the total time span is correct in the National Curriculum context.

4   Calculate the staffing requirements in the department in terms of total staff periods to be taught against staff periods available. The staff contact ratio is a tricky topic but assuming a 40 period week, a contact time of 34 periods would be normal (85 per cent). Heads of department could expect another three noncontact periods, giving a contact ratio of about 77 per cent. It will vary and allowance may be needed for duties such as librarianship, etc. In an ideal situation the HoD would also wish to give a contact ratio of no more that 75 per cent for a probationer. If the figures do not tally, the problem should be discussed in good time with the head so that any new appointments can be made. In today's climate of falling rolls, the discussion may be different – redeployment within the school to teach other things or in an extreme case redeployment elsewhere. Above all last-minute decisions which may produce less than satisfactory results should be avoided.

5   Discuss the proposed arrangements with departmental colleagues as indicated above. Certain technical matters also need discussion:

   a) blocking the timetable allocation: teaching a group of classes at the same time to allow for flexibility of pupil grouping and cooperation between staff, team teaching, support teaching, etc.
   b) the desirability of single or double periods for different age/ability groups
   c) the spread over the week of the lesson allocation; here teachers may take into account Eric Hawkins' recommendation that there should be a policy on timetabling subjects which takes sensitive account of the unique needs of teachers who have to plant their seedlings in a 'gale of English'
   d) the optimum use of departmental rooms and equipment.

The intricacies of timetabling in a large school will demand compromises. It is here that the judgement of the head of department will come into play. This overview of the total situation and of the competing demands of the various interests in the school, will demand a wide vision and a measure of statesmanship.

Committing the ideas to paper

Although there are computer programmes which can be used to help plot the timetable, the vital qualities needed will be patience, logic, clear thinking and lots of black coffee! It is worth mentioning that using the Concept Keyboard (see Chapter 7) which is available in most schools will help in the final writing up. However, the sweat and devotion beforehand will still be considerable. It is a mistake to try and carry everything in one's head – it should be written down. The HoD should prepare beforehand the blanks which can be ruled out to fit the pattern of the school week and to show classes to be taught as well as staff availability. It is important to ascertain beforehand from the timetabler any restriction which may affect the allocation, for example, it may be that a particular teacher is not available on Mondays as they are part-time, or another colleague may be involved with games on Wednesday afternoon. At whatever stage the head of department is called in, it is useful to employ a 'visual planner' technique to plot the proposed individual allocations (initially in pencil to allow changes). This could be done as in Figure 12.

While it may not be possible for the individual head of department to affect the total layout of the periods for a particular colleague, it is useful to have a further visual check to try to ensure, for example, that the total allocation of free periods does not fall on one day with none for the rest of the week. Such a chart will also help to see the distribution of lessons from the point of view of a group of pupils (see Figure 13). It is always essential to keep a copy of the decisions and allocations as they are handed to the timetabler. The HoD may be asked to 'juggle' with allocations – so they should be sure to receive and return such changes promptly and in *writing*.

Creativity will be at a premium when dealing with clashes: will it be possible to cross timetable with (say) art, whose teachers may not object to teaching their subject in language sets? Do there have to be four periods per week – what about three one week and five the next to allow for PSE classes? These are questions the HoD will have to face *and* manage.

Above all the HoD should:

- try to be *reasonable* in all matters
- be *diplomatic* in suggestions
- be *alert* and *ingenious* in trying to solve the 'impossible'
- have *alternative ideas* ready
- try to *predict* and *anticipate* any problems that may arise because of the demands of the whole school and the department in particular.

Midtown High School

Timetable 19 _____ –19 _____   Department _____ **MOD LANGS** _____

Staff	BJ	SB	GS	RL	VO	DW	RW
Subject	F-G	F-S	F	F-S	G	F-G	F
Class U6-A	4^F	4^S	4^F	4^S	4^G	4^G	
L6^A	4^F	4^S		4^S	4^G	4^G	
L6 FLAW	–						4^F
11 opt. 1	4^F SET 4		4^F SET 3	4^F SET 2			4^F SET 1
11 opt. 4	–	4^S	4^F SET 1		4^G	4^F SET 2	
10 opt 1	4^F SET 1	4^F SET 2				4^F SET 3	
10 opt. 4	–	4^S					
YEAR 9	4^G SET 1		4^F	Allocate staff to classes to enable visual check to be made.			
YEAR 8	4^F SET 3						
YEAR 7	4^F M/A	4^F M/A	4^F M/A				
OTHER DUTIES	H.O.D.						CAREERS

Notes

Indicate staff by initials

Indicate subject by letter

In each box indicate number of periods followed by class title (e.g. set 1 or mixed ability = M/A)

Figure 12: Planner for staff allocations

The National Curriculum

The demands of the National Curriculum syllabuses mean that there is a minimum time needed to allow pupils to participate fully in the modern language programme. The minimum time in Key Stage 3 is ten per cent of the week (usually 4/40 periods). In Key Stage 4 a similar time is needed except where, in the exceptional situation of a pupil not following a GCSE course, a reduced option is available. This is allowed for in the National Curriculum where some pupils (and a very few) may opt for a minimum of two out of the four attainment targets. In this case, it may be possible to deliver the programmes of study in two lessons per week. It must be stressed that these arrangements will be the rare exception. If a second foreign language is introduced then it may be in any year in Key Stages 3 or 4. In this case,

MIDTOWN HIGH SCHOOL

Department **MOD LANGS** Timetable 199_ –199_

Staff **BJ SB GS RL VO DW RW**

Period	BJ	SB	GS	RL	VO	DW	RW			
MON 1	$U6^F$	10/4 s								
MON 2	$11/1^4F$		$11/1^3F$	$11/1^2F$		U6 g	$11/1^4F$			
MON 3	$8/3$ F	$8/4$ F	$8/1$ F	U6 S	U6 G	$8/2$ F				
MON 4	$10/1^1$ F	$10/1^2F$				$10/1^3F$				
TUES 1	$9/1$ G	U6 s					L6 F			
TUES 2	L6 F		U6 F							
TUES 3		$11/4$ s	$11/4^1$ F		$11/4$ G	$11/4^2$ F				
TUES 4		L6 s				L6 G				
WED 1	7m/A F	7m/AF		L6 G	L6 G					
WED 2						U6 G	L6 F			
WED 3	$8/3$ F	$8/4$ F								
WED 4	U6 F	10/4 s								
THURS 1		$11/4$ s		U6						
THURS 2	$11/1^4F$									
THURS 3		L6 s								
THURS 4	$9/1$ G									
FRI 1	L6 F		U6 F							
FRI 2	$10/1^1$ F	$10/1^2$ F								
FRI 3	7m/A F	7m/AF								
FRI 4										

Assuming 20-period week.
Enter class taught in box to check allocation.
Class indicated by:
YEAR/OPTION/SET
e.g. $10/1^1$=10th year option 1, set 1.
Language by letter.

Figure 13: Planner for lesson distribution

time must be found outside the core and foundation time. For some children, making exceptional progress in their foundation language, an additional five per cent time is suggested, making 15 per cent in total for the two languages. This will require organisational flexibility within the school to arrange.

Diversification

With the advent of the National Curriculum, due respect must be given to the question of diversification of first foreign language. These considerations will affect timetabling. For a more detailed discussion see Chapter 19.

18 Designing the syllabus

Schools cannot work in isolation, with no contact with the world outside. The pressures felt by all departments are considerable and have increased greatly in the last decade with the arrival of the National Curriculum. These pressures come from a variety of agencies and sections within the community. To design the syllabus for the department means taking account of all these demands – demands from parents, from industry, from other schools and educational institutions, from pupils, from staff and, not least, the demands imposed by the nature of the subject itself. It is not possible to lay down watertight rules applicable to all schools and it must be assumed that the head of department will take account of the local circumstances.

The extra dimensions teachers now have to deal with are a direct result of the Education Reform Act (ERA) in all its manifestations. We are not thinking simply of the National Curriculum but also of open enrolment, the need to provide a school development plan and many other aspects of recent reforms.

Open enrolment has meant that now all schools are in competition with their neighbours. They need to attract pupils and it is a fact that the more pupils are enrolled, the more funds they bring to the school. Formula funding is simple in concept: it may be fine for the growing school, but in times of falling rolls, it can decimate plans. Furthermore, each school now has to produce an agreed development plan. This plan sets targets, priorities and strategies for the coming year or years.

The need to develop departmental schemes of work and individual target setting, together with the necessity to elaborate plans covering such matters as pastoral programmes, have now been thrust into the limelight.

Any goal setting will only be worthwhile and achievable if the plans are jointly owned by those who have to carry them through. Thus, later in the chapter, our remarks about joint planning, agreement and ownership of the departmental programmes are of prime importance. It is in the light of the new scenario of the 1990s, that we wish this chapter to be read. It will also be appropriate to reiterate a remark made earlier in the discussion on leadership, by quoting from the *Final Report* of the National Curriculum Modern Languages Working Party:

> Successful learning is characterised by . . . teaching approaches that are consistent across the department . . . and . . . a well ordered and adaptable scheme of work, produced jointly by members of the department. It describes the agreed objectives, the progression expected for learners of all abilities and the resources and teaching methods designed to achieve it. Good schemes emphasise the need to set clear objectives both within and between lessons and contain renewable sections on specific teaching approaches (para. 10.5)

We will return to the writing of the scheme of work in some detail later, after a consideration of some of the other factors to be taken into account.

The concern of the first part of this chapter will be liaison with feeder schools and the audit of the school's needs in order to draw up the syllabus. Liaison with parents, other outside agencies, careers, etc. are dealt with elsewhere.

Liaison with feeder schools

When the study of a modern language is begun in the secondary school at the start of Key Stage 3 (year 7), liaison with feeder schools is less crucial than where there is foreign language teaching in middle or even primary schools. There are signs that the possibility of 'primary French' is being aired again when one reads in para 3.13 of the *Final Report* that such experiments are to be encouraged. What is important is the need to provide a continuity of experience for all pupils. However, even if the pupils come to the start of Key Stage 3 also beginning a new school, teachers must not think that liaison is out of place. Their pupils do not come to them as faceless blanks, ready to be moulded like clay. Pupils come to teachers with a language biography; they have all learnt some language – some only English, some two or three languages depending on their background. It is here that teachers need to find out much more by consultation and active interest *before* the pupils arrive. Whatever they have learnt in school or at home is of vital interest to teachers facing a syllabus built on the National Curriculum which by its very nature is essentially pupil centred.

There is another pivotal point in our provision; a philosophical stand on the centrality of language in the child's education. This will only be fully part of the school philosophy if there is real dialogue on the crucial nature of language provision throughout all the child's experiences. This will mean a dialogue between all teachers (since we all use language) but especially between teachers of English and teachers of foreign languages. When teachers liaise between their school and the feeder school this should be a vital topic of interest.

On a wider plane, liaison is one way of building up a picture of the new entrant to school.

However, the most important type of liaison is called for when the pupil arrives at the school having studied the language for a year or two in the previous school. Such experience must not be discounted or ignored if a healthy attitude is to be fostered. One of the major lessons to be acquired from the Burstall report on primary French[1] was that good liaison between the different sections of the system was of prime importance. This is now in sharp focus with the National Curriculum and the development of Records of Achievement. The recording of achievement is

---

[1] C Burstall *et al. Primary French in the Balance.* NFER, 1974

meant to deliver reliable information on the attainments in modern languages and also deliver records in many cross curricular areas as well. The emphasis in the National Curriculum is a developmental one which sees continuity throughout the two key stages as important. If teachers are to build positively on earlier achievement, then liaison is vital.

All sectors of the school system must work together and be regarded as interdependent in the interests of the children and their progress. Teachers in secondary schools and, in particular, the head of department, should work very closely with the neighbouring schools whose pupils will be arriving at the start of term. In the ideal situation such contacts will be both informal and formal – even extending to the idea of teaching in the other sector, with mutual exchanges of teachers for a short period.

Making formal contacts with schools

The vital reason for such formal contact is as an *exchange* of information:
- *into* receiving schools about pupil progress
- *from* receiving schools about past pupils who are now in their care.

Over the course of the school year it is a good idea to arrange a *mutual* exchange of the following material:
- syllabus and schemes of work
- examples of main text books
- examples of pupils' work.

At the time of transfer, the heads of department or their delegates should seek information on the following areas:

The achievements of pupils about to transfer
The middle school will have developed a system of *formative* and *summative* reporting and all the information should be passed on to the receiving school. Indeed, under the provisions of the ERA, there is a legal obligation to do so. A copy of the aims and objectives of the teaching together with an indication of the testing/assessment carried out should be provided as well. All the skill areas should be covered. (*Note:* A detailed consideration of recording of assessment from Chapter 20 is to be read in conjunction with this.)

Background comment about the pupils
Individual comments about the pupils that are *relevant*. For example, has the pupil been abroad? Is there a problem such as shyness in oral work? Is there a factor such as hearing impairment? Any special problems such as dyslexia or a speech defect? Are there any brothers or sisters whom the HoD already knows?

The nature of the transfer form for conveying the information will depend on the feeder-school philosophy. However, it is quite clear from the National Curriculum *Final Report* that the onus is on the school to provide reports on pupils when they change schools (and this may also be because of family removal to another area). (See para 7.15.) Since the philosophy of the NC is embodied in continuous assessment, this should not be a major problem. The chapter on assessment and reporting out on pp. 220–39 has a full discussion of this topic. Whatever the nature of the report, the receiving school should have an individual report on each pupil composed in terms of criteria referenced statements. This will mean a careful consideration of the evidence against the school's stated aims in the subject, if the reported results are used as a means of allocating pupils to teaching groups on transfer. It is also helpful if the reports carry some indication of pupil effort and attitude, since a relatively poor performance may in fact be the result of Herculean efforts!

In other words, teachers see as complete a picture as possible. And it is fruitful to try to obtain this information by means of a visit to the feeder school rather than by an exchange of letters. Talking to a colleague can reveal much that is difficult to describe in a brief report.

All that has been said so far has a crucial bearing on the development of a scheme of work – the main emphasis of this chapter. For if teachers see the curriculum from the pupils' point of view, building on what has gone before is vital – hence this section on liaison!

The two-way process

All such consultation must be seen as a two-way movement. It is immensely helpful and a sign of good relations to feed information *back* into the middle or primary schools, not least because staff in such schools can feel isolated if they are the only specialists in the school, running a one-man department for languages, and also because the public 'reward' of external examinations never comes to pupils in their immediate care.

It is particularly important, for example, that the syllabus and examination requirements for Key Stage 4 assessment are known. This topic could well form part of an agenda for meetings of teachers in linked schools. Paragraph 4.27 of the *Final Report* states:

> Progress through the levels of attainment and across the attainment targets is quite likely to be cyclic and spiral rather than linear and parallel.

The need for meetings and cooperative planning has thus been established. If well planned and relevant to the needs of the area, they will not be resisted. This type of meeting could be as a result of a local initiative or could be part of the provision made by the LEA adviser. The main aim is to ensure continuity between the Key Stages and avoidance of time-wasting overlap.

At the beginning of each school year the HoD should take back the following information:

The examination results for past pupils   It is surprising how long such pupils will be remembered.

The record of progress of the previous year's cohort What they did in the first year of their new school. Did they take up a second foreign language?

All this exchange of information will help to increase the mutual confidence and experience so that the grading will be all the more realistic and effective. It is surprising how often feeder schools will ask if their grading policy is on a level with other neighbouring schools. This task will hopefully become easier as teachers work through the more standardised assessment arrangements of the National Curriculum. It is also important that the welcoming school does its best to see what the relative assessment levels really mean. The only professional way to resolve problems is by open discussion based on mutual confidence and respect.

Making informal contact with feeder schools

Visits, exchanging teacher timetables, pupil contact, etc.
The most convenient time for personal visits to the feeder schools would seem to be in the relatively relaxed summer postexam period. Other possibilities may occur on training days when staff have noncontact time.

Mutual visits to schools
During such a visit, it is worth asking if it is possible to see some classes in action, engage in team teaching or have involvement in some other classroom activity. It is also a good idea to see, wherever possible, samples of pupil work, textbooks and other materials.

The visits must not be one-way, but it is sometimes difficult to release primary or middle school teachers who have fewer free periods. One interesting idea is to use the possibly more flexible secondary timetable to free the secondary colleague for a morning or a day in June or July getting to to know the pupils *in situ* while the opposite number is able to visit and possibly teach in the secondary school. It can be very refreshing to teach pupils outside the normal age range! Ingenuity and cooperation can help make the difficult come true.

Arranging assistant contact

Other ways of helping establish contact is via the pupils themselves or the assistant.

At certain times of the year, particularly in exam or postexam periods, the timetable of the foreign assistant shrinks. This can happen from the start of the 'oral season'. It is useful at such times to use him or her with classes in the school that do not normally benefit because this valuable resource has been restricted to examination classes during the school year. The same principle may be extended to the local middle school, where the assistant could spend an afternoon a week in June. Thus, not only do the younger pupils (and their teachers) benefit linguistically, but it will open a window to the younger learners as they meet a 'native' speaker. It is important to seek the agreement of all parties – but the initiative is rarely refused.

Involving pupils

Pupils can help as well. They often relish a return to their old school. One idea is to arrange a presentation of playlets, role-plays, songs, etc. These need not be elaborate and may be the compilation of work done in the classroom, at open day and so on, and can act as a taster for the future intake.

Most secondary schools invite new pupils to come on a preliminary visit before the September term begins. It is perfectly possible to arrange part of such a visit in the foreign language, those 'sophisticated' pupils, now a year older, acting as guides in French/German/Spanish/Urdu, etc. around the language teaching area. Inviting the new pupils to see a presentation about the school can be useful and break the ice before they move from the familiarity of the smaller school to the sometimes overwhelming size of the secondary school.

Continuity is the aim

Whatever arrangements are made, both formal and informal, the ultimate aim is to ensure as far as possible that the transition from the children's point of view is smooth and uneventful. Mutual acquaintance is but one aspect of this. Equally important is the need to ensure that the aims, objectives, methodology and approach in each sector of the system are compatible.

That is why we now approach the all important question of the scheme of work.

The scheme of work _____

> Teachers need to have clear aims, agreed methods and appropriate expectations of pupils of differing abilities. For these purposes a scheme of work is an essential tool. It defines the agreed aims and objectives for all stages and abilities, give guidance on appropriate methods and on the use of resources, and sets out the policy for assessment . . .
>
> *Curriculum Matters 8: Modern Foreign Languages to 16.* DES, 1987

In the decentralised system of education which operates in the United Kingdom, the decisions as to *what* to teach, *when* and to *whom* are largely left to the individual school and *within* the school, by delegation from the head, to the head of department in discussion with colleagues.

Even with the framework of the ERA and the National Curriculum, there is still a great deal of freedom. However, this freedom to operate is now framed within guidelines and within a new climate of *accountability*. This accountability is set out by the National Curriculum guidelines and criteria, by the monitoring procedures of HMI, the LEA inspectorate, by the powers of governing bodies and by the increased roles of parents.

However constricting this may seem, the freedom to act is still there, for the provisions of the *Final Report on Modern Languages* do not constitute in themselves a syllabus. Paragraph 17.11 of the report goes on to say:

> Teachers will need to be supported through working in well organised departments. The role of heads of department is crucial in leading curricular planning; in devising schemes of work; in establishing a policy for assessment; in supporting staff; in reviewing and developing classroom practice; and in coordinating the management of departmental resources.

In the new framework in which teachers operate, there is still freedom to manoeuvre and it places a great responsibility on those devising the departmental scheme of work. Paragraph 4.2 spells it out:

> All departments will need to review their . . . schemes of work and, if necessary, revise them to fit in with this framework.

The framework described in that paragraph has the following elements:
- profile components
- programmes of study
- opportunities, competences and strategies
- skills and processes
- statements of attainment
- areas of experience
- assessment arrangements
- cross-curricular themes and skills.

Against this background, a defined list of contents in terms of topics, vocabulary, structures and functions has not been set out. This is to be left to schools, consortia, examination groups, etc.

> **It is up to the departments in school to devise their schemes of work which will enable pupils to reach the statements of attainment.**

The Secretary of State reiterated this in May 1990 when he said:

> The statutory framework establishes principles but does not prescribe in detail what pupils should learn, nor indeed how they should be taught. The Government intends to ensure that teachers have proper discretion over what and how they teach, the proper opportunity to exercise their professional skills and judgement. So the Government's objective is and remains that the National Curriculum should leave teachers ample scope to exploit their own individual capabilities and adapt their teaching to the needs and circumstances of their pupils and their schools.

So we reiterate the situation as we find it now: teachers have freedom to operate in a framework of accountability. It is up to them to provide as rich a diet as possible for all their pupils. It is our firm belief that in devising their schemes of work, teachers should begin with skills, areas of experience, etc. and only then match up the experiences against the statements of attainment. If teachers begin with the statements of attainment, the resultant syllabus will be minimalist and impoverished.

The leadership of the head of department is perhaps most easily seen in the way in which an agreed scheme of work is drawn up. Every department is supposed to have such a document in the framework of the LEA guidelines and the school development plan:

- the HMI and LEA adviser may ask for it at short notice
- the head and governors use it as a yardstick
- the departmental colleagues need it to work with
- the new colleague wants sight of it
- the visiting student needs sight of it
- parents have a right to see it.

However, too often in the past this document was gathering dust in the head of department's cupboard!

A working document

Such a scheme, if it is to be of use (otherwise why bother?), should set out the *why*, the *what*, the *when* and the *how*:

- it should be an agreed document, reflecting the views and the experience of all the members of the departmental team; *ownership* is important
- it should reflect the ethos of the school as set out in the policy document
- it should be regularly updated and not like last year's Michelin guide useful only for its nostalgic value
- it should be precise and to the point, rather than general and vague
- it should be practical and rooted in the realm of the *possible*.

Drawing up such a document can be an arduous business, especially in a crowded term; it cannot be done in the course of a few lunchtime meetings and, if it is to be of real value, the finished document will never really be definitive and will always need revising. Here the word processor will be invaluable and we will return to this later.

What are the benefits of compiling a scheme of work collectively?

Security

It should provide a framework within which both staff and pupils can feel secure. No department is stable; staff come and go. If at least there is a definition of the aims and objectives of the team which is coherent, then there is more chance to make progress.

Planning

It will make life easier in the long term. There is nothing more wearing than having to make up lessons at a moment's notice with no real purpose: constant 'ad hocery' is the surest way to a nervous breakdown. Guidance in unison with the National Curriculum will help all involved with the school to optimise effort. The statement will also provide the criteria for judging effective teaching in an open and professional way as well as helping the reporting of pupil progress.

Publicity

A scheme of work will help staff defend more coherently the position of modern languages from the constant assault of 'disbelievers' who even in this decade are at best apathetic about language learning for all.

Induction

The helping of students, assistants, new colleagues and part-time members of the team will be facilitated and these colleagues will be seen as part of a cohesive team.

Satisfaction

It will make teachers think about what they are trying to do rather than simply reiterate last year's routine. The very exercise will involve research, questioning and problem solving – all of which can be so easily put aside in a busy year. Thinking out the rationale of the team will bring greater job satisfaction.

The ideal scheme of work will then be an *agreed* statement of policy and as such will focus the minds of individuals and ask them to listen to the ideas of others. All the issues must be openly discussed and debated in order to reach a consensus; only then will the head of department have the authority and the right to ask for loyalty from his or her colleagues. But beware – loyalty does not mean slavishly following a piece of paper and stifling initiative. On the contrary, individual teachers, by virtue of open discussion will be better able to appreciate the contribution of colleagues and evaluate their initiatives as well as their own in the context of the work of the whole department.

This document will also be a framework for expansion in another direction. The government and LEAs are now in favour of diversification of first foreign language and departmental guidelines should be available to guide the work regardless of the language taught. Chapter 19 discusses diversification at length.

Who should have access to the finished document?

- the head
- the deputies, pastoral coordinator, curriculum coordinator
- other heads of department; this is good propaganda value and sound inter-departmental policy
- assistant teachers, not forgetting part-timers and those members of staff shared with other departments; such colleagues need special help if they are to feel part of the team

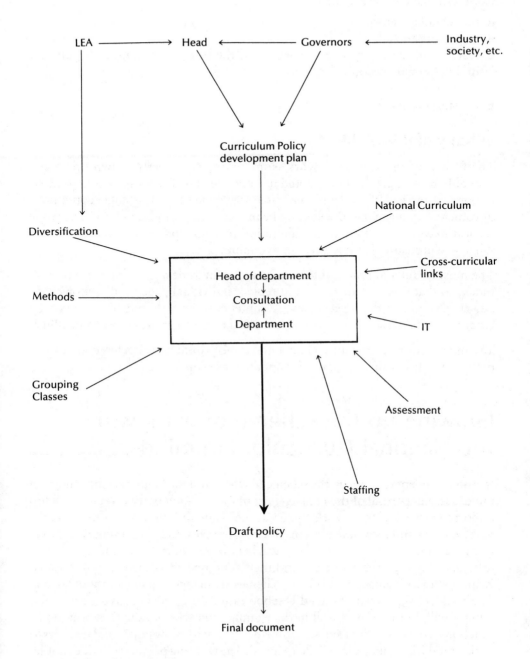

Figure 14: The scheme of work

- the assistant
- the students on teaching practice.

Copies should also be available to:

- the school governors
- inspectors and advisers
- teachers in feeder schools – especially if the foreign language is begun in a middle/primary school
- the careers staff
- the staff library.

What will it look like?

The format of the scheme of work is important. If properly drawn up, it will probably be a lengthy document and its very size may discourage reading. More important, the wealth of detail may discourage updating. The single continuous document may mean that it will never be revised, since the idea that to change one section may very well entail the alteration of whole pages, or even the whole scheme, will ensure that it is fixed for evermore.

The most useful and practical format would seem to be a *looseleaf* format, with index, so that it is easy to revise and replace individual pages and sections with newer versions as the need arises. A contents section should be followed by lettered/numbered sections in order to make it easier to grow, correct and adjust.

The use of a word processor will be found to be helpful here. Each section can be put on to disk and then retrieved for updating as wanted.

Drawing up the scheme of work with the National Curriculum in mind _____

It is only prudent to draw up the scheme of work with the National Curriculum in mind. Careful perusal of the *Final Report* of the working party reveals an all too important aspect of their work. Whereas they state that they have drawn on the best practices and recommendations drawn from the Graded Examination movement and the GCSE criteria, many teachers have noticed that there is a vital difference between the proposals and their supposed antecedents: most Graded Examinations schemes and all GCSE schemes are in fact statements about testing. The booklets issued by the Graded Test bodies and the GCSE boards describe what a pupil will do to be successful in the examination scheme: the lists of notions, functions, vocabulary lists and structures are set out to allow pupils and teachers to understand what the pupils will do to 'pass'. The working party report does not set out such a testing scheme in terms of content and examination criteria. It is in reality a document about the *process* of learning a foreign language. The teacher has to supply the content, to attach the precise linguistic and experiential contents of the lessons or series of lessons to the twin schemes of attainment targets and programmes of study. Teachers do not have a ready made syllabus to teach, they

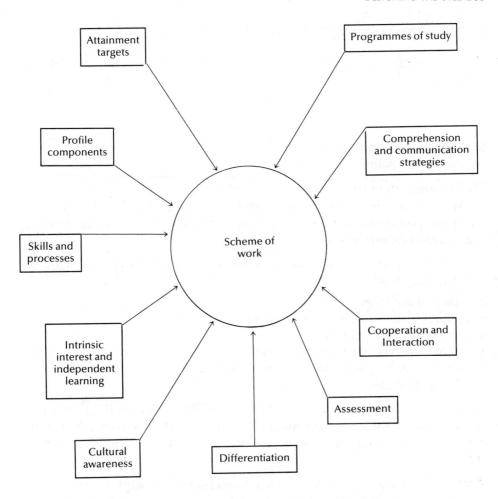

Figure 15: Drawing up the scheme of work with the National Curriculum in mind

do not have a list of structures to master, they do not have vocabulary items to learn. They *do* have a framework which gives autonomy to the department to devise an appropriate scheme of work. The professional judgement of the teacher is paramount. All this however does not preclude the provision of defined syllabuses by the school, the LEA, or the examination boards.

What are the structures in which teachers have to work?

The profile components

There are four profile components corresponding to the four attainment targets. (The opening paragraphs to each AT make excellent reading.)

1   Understanding spoken language and responding appropriately (though not necessarily orally).

2   Expressing oneself effectively in speech.

3   Understanding written language and responding appropriately (though not necessarily in writing).

4   Using written language.

Statements of attainment
Set within the attainment targets and at ten levels.

Programmes of study
These set out descriptions of linguistic content and knowledge. They are framed in terms of opportunities, competencies and strategies, as well as content expressed in eight areas of experience.

A further dimension is the list of approaches which cover the following parameters:
- skills and processes
- comprehension and communication strategies
- cooperation and interaction
- intrinsic interest and independent learning
- awareness of language and the learning process
- cultural awareness.

Added to this is the consideration of cross-curricular opportunities, defined in terms of dimensions (equal opportunities, multicultural perspectives), skills (communication, numeracy, etc.) and themes (economic awareness, health education, etc.).

With all this in mind, the task of writing a good scheme of work is an important one. We propose that there are at least two distinct areas to be considered:

1   The departmental handbook.

2   The programme of work.

The departmental handbook

This should include:

1   A statement of aims – this should be written in the context of the LEA statement of aims and the statement of the school policy.

2   An outline of the organisation of the school, and the contribution of the department to the school aims.

3   A list of the courses provided by the department and the staffing.

4   A detailed account of departmental policies.

5   A list of departmental resources, including course books, other materials and audio-visual aids in the widest sense.

An example of a departmental handbook is given below.

Midtown High School
High Street, Midtown, MD1 1DD

Section A   Aims
Section B   Courses provided by the modern language department
Section C   Departmental policies
Section D   Resources
Section E   Syllabus and scheme of work for each language

Section A   Aims

This section should contain a brief statement of the aims of the department, answering the question 'Why are languages taught in this school?'

1   Utilitarian reasons – *Communication; future needs of pupils; foundation for future study.*
2   Intellectual reasons – *Awareness of language; learning how to learn a language.*
3   Cultural reasons – *Broadening horizons; combatting insularity; civilisation.*
4   Enjoyment – *It can (and should) be enjoyable to learn a new language.*

Section B   Courses provided by the department

In this section the following questions must be addressed:

1   Which languages?
    In most schools the first foreign language will probably be French (*Though this must not be seen as inevitable*). The local conditions – LEA policy, neighbouring schools, the availability of staff, etc. will have to be taken into account (see discussion in Chapter 19). Consideration will have to be given to a policy of diversification and it is to be hoped that due consideration will be given to a second foreign language policy. Amongst the reasons to be advanced are:

    a) broadening the opportunity for the more able linguist and/or gifted pupil
    b) offering a broad curriculum

---

c) challenging the traditional place of French
d) widening linguistic horizons
e) cultural awareness
f) career requirements.

If the school teaches Community Languages, these should have parity of consideration in terms of syllabus elaboration, etc.

2 Starting age
This may not be entirely in the hands of the school, let alone the department, because of LEA policy which provides for, say, French in feeder schools, or, sadly, because of restrictions on staffing. However, if there *is* a choice, this is clearly a matter over which the head of department should come to a rational agreement. What should *not* be in dispute is the fact that *all* pupils should have the opportunity of studying a foreign language. This is in fact a requirement in the National Curriculum.

3 Length of courses
The ideal departmental policy will be that all pupils continue a study of their foundation language for all years in Key stages 3 and 4. Some provision may be needed for alternative arrangements as permitted within the National Curriculum and a policy will need to be clearly stated for the duration of the course in any second foreign language. Policy will also be needed on any sixth-form provision, A-level as well as courses of a different kind (GCSE, BTEC, CPVE, etc.)

4 Examinations
A statement should be made here indicating the various examination targets of the courses, e.g. Graded Test level; GCSE; AS; A level; BTEC; CPVE; FLAW; Institute of Linguists, etc.

5 Option courses
A policy on the various options available at different ages served by the school.

C Departmental policies

1 Teaching groups
If pupils are not taught in form groups, an outline of the departmental policy for forming teaching groups is needed.

2 Staff list
This should include the full-time members, part-time teachers, FLAs, etc. and any particular responsibilities allocated as in the section below.

3 Staff timetables

4   School year calendar
Dates of terms and holidays, dates of various staff meetings, dates of internal and external assessments and examinations, etc. to allow forward planning.

5   Differentiation of objectives
A policy must be discussed and agreed , to take account of the differing needs of pupils. A policy should be exemplified with practical ideas for use in the classroom.

6   Use of the target language in the classroom
A consistent policy is important with the encouragement of meaningful, purposeful use of the foreign language in the classroom for all communication. The target language should be seen as the medium of communication for real transactions and not just as a game to be played for 40 minutes between the 'reality' of biology or maths.

7   Assessment and record keeping
Assessment is a vital part of the work of the department and all members of staff will be called on to measure and record pupil progress at various times. The advent of the National Curriculum means that formative assessment is regarded as part of the teaching and learning styles of all schools. The head of department must ensure that an agreed policy is set up and operates. Regular monitoring of the progress of children in the classroom should be underlined by a departmentally coordinated system of monitoring and recording of pupil attainments. At certain times of the year, it will be appropriate to coordinate testing more formally in accordance with the agreed whole school policy. Such arrangements will necessitate the departmental policy being consistent with agreed management decisions. Formative and summative assessment are discussed in detail in Chapter 20 which should be referred to now.

8   Marking
This is a vital area of teaching and is seen as such by pupils. Departmental guidelines on a positive, encouraging scheme are needed. Advice will be needed for a prompt and regular marking of pupils' work and on the necessity of looking at corrections. A policy on analysing and dealing with error is worthwhile.

9   The foreign language assistant
This section should deal with the department's use of the FLA who should be treated as a member of staff. It is probable that it will merit a separate document, with suggestions and ideas (see Chapter 15).

10 Day-to-day administration
The departmental handbook should contain an outline of the duties

allocated to the various members of staff as well as information which will allow the smooth running of the affairs of the department. A suggested list of areas requiring attention is given below. Each item is potentially able to be devolved to a colleague. The staff list section above may be annotated with a suitable indication of their duties.

a) helping new staff in school
b) the assistant
c) minuting of meetings
d) stock, requisitions
e) rooms, displays
f) foreign links, penfriends, visits, exchanges
g) links with other schools, feeder schools, HE/FE, etc.
h) particular year groups
i) examinations, internal and external entries
j) record keeping
k) audio-visual aids, maintenance, storage, security, booking out
l) reprographics, home-made materials, production and filing/ storage
m) the library
n) links with other departments
o) cross-curricular elements
p) stationery.

11 Discipline

A short comment for the guidance of colleagues on matters such as classroom environment and atmosphere, pupil behaviour and sanctions, policy on punishment and referral to other staff.

Section D   Resources

Detailed lists of resources are not required, but an outline should be given. It is also important to give some indication of the allocation of materials to the various year and class groups to ensure a fair distribution and to avoid frustrating repetition of use. It may be useful also to append on loose-leaf sheets teacher comments and accounts of the use of materials – hardware and software – especially for the benefit of new colleagues.

Section E   Syllabus and scheme of work for each language

The National Curriculum report suggests that the nature of the programmes offered to pupils will be cyclic and spiral rather than linear and parallel. This has important consequences for the writing of the scheme of work and implies a planned visiting and revisiting of the topics chosen as the vehicle for the working out of the programmes of study. It goes without saying that, where more than one language is taught in school, a common approach is imperative, with variations only appearing because of the intrinsic differences in the languages themselves.

1 Objectives
  Specific objectives should be set for each stage of the course. These language specific objectives should be stated in 'can-do' terms. The simple heading, for example, 'object pronouns', is not explicit enough. The balance of the four skills should be kept in mind as well as mixed skill approaches.

  Progression in terms of grammar and vocabulary will also need to be taken into account.

  This section is the most difficult and complex to write and will reflect genuine language use in the classroom. A communicative syllabus, however, needs to take into account factors other than structures and vocabulary lists, since the ability to make grammatically correct sentences is not the only ability needed to communicate. An indication of communicative strategies is useful here. A full discussion of a scheme of work and programme of study is to be found elsewhere in this chapter.

2 Methodology
  Guidance must be given to staff on methodology. At the same time, the document must not restrict individual initiative or enterprise. There will be no 'right way', and this is why discussion must be open so that ideas may be generated and used with confidence in an agreed framework.

Checklist for devising the departmental handbook

Does your finished product contain the following details?
- Departmental staff list
- Departmental and staff timetables
- Details of language suite
- List of hardware/software and the location
- Booking details and procedures for repair/servicing
- Arrangements for use of books and consumables
- Reprographic system
- Capitation arrangements
- Description and location of materials
- Teaching group organisation
- Activities such as clubs, visits, etc.
- Departmental aims and objectives in line with LEA/school policy
- Departmental development plan
- Cross-curricular work guidelines
- Policies on display
- Policies on management of classroom and guidelines on methods
- Policies on discipline
- Policy on assessment
- Guidelines on record keeping

- ☐ Guidelines on assessment of skills such as collaboration, initiative and other personal skills
- ☐ Policies on marking/homework/attitude to error, etc.

Criteria for:
- ☐ Assistants
- ☐ Use of target language
- ☐ Communicative activities
- ☐ Differentiation
- ☐ Special needs
- ☐ Information Technology.

For each language:
- ☐ Guidance on use of materials/course books, etc.
- ☐ Details of programmes of study in terms of:
  - Areas of experience
  - Activities
  - Skills and processes
  - Statements and levels of attainment
  - Topic
  - Cross-curricular elements
- ☐ External examination policy.

The programme of work

A full account of the scheme of work for all languages taught needs to be written in yearly chapters, spelling out carefully the programmes to be followed by pupils and addressed with the following parameters in mind:

- profile components
- attainment targets
- statements of the levels of attainment
- approaches and activities
- areas of experience
- topics and tasks
- cross-curricular dimensions, skills and themes,

leading to references to the standard attainment tasks (SATS).

Since teachers are dealing with a modern language, there will be a clear need to plan all activities with clear and precise reference to vocabulary and grammatical structure.

Postscript

The National Curriculum Working Party has produced a document which, as we have said above, is a document describing a process. It is not a defined syllabus. However it is important to note that for the purposes of assessing attainment, particulary at Key Stage 4, there will already be agreed syllabuses written in terms

Areas of experience A – Everyday experiences
                     B – Personal life
                     C – World around us
                     D – World of communication

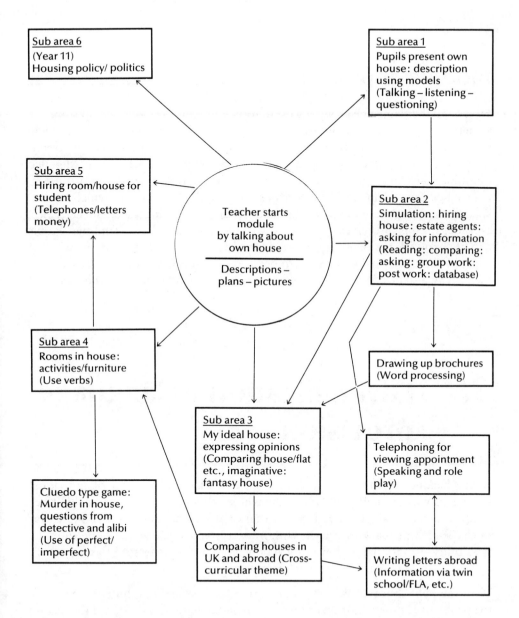

Figure 16: Topic-web 'Housing'

of defined contents and probably elaborated by the examination boards since the GCSE is the means of 'reporting out' to the world outside the classroom. It will therefore be necessary to consult the appropriate documentation when it appears in order to see that there is a match between the departmental ideas and those of whatever defined syllabus is adopted. In essence, that is no different to the case when the GCSE was first elaborated.

An example of planning by the topic-web/ module approach

First of all there must be an agreed list of topic functions, notions and appropriate structures to be covered in the given year. These may be from the main textbook in use in the school (in the order to be decided by colleagues) or based on materials developed by the staff. Having decided on the main areas of a topic, detailed planning can take place. By considering skills, language and opportunities, colleagues can 'brainstorm' ideas grouped around the topic and which lead to specific learning activities. At the same time as arriving at these activities, consideration is also given to learning styles and assessment possibilities. Pupils can be involved, for example, in the order in which areas are taught, by bringing some of their personal experience to bear on the situation while cross-curricular themes can also be opened up. (See Figure 16, p.213 for an example of a topic-web.)

19 Diversification of language provision

It has become a necessity for schools to consider the position of individual languages within the framework of the whole school provision. Ironically it has become a national priority, if not a national policy, to consider the so far unchallenged primacy of French within the system, while at the same time the possibility of national and even local concerted action is lessened as the implications of local management are felt in schools.

With the publication of the National Curriculum list of 19 permitted languages, the problem of diversification of first foreign language and the place of the second language has been brought into sharper focus. Much valuable research has been conducted at the University of Oxford Department of Education, under the direction of David Phillips and his team. The first publication *The Second Foreign Language* (Phillips and Stencel) was in 1983 and since then a stream of research reports on diversification under the research programme OXPROD (Oxford

Project on Diversification of First Foreign Language Teaching) has produced interesting documentary evidence for considerations (see Bibliography for details.)

The DES recognise the need for diversification programmes. In *Curriculum Matters 8: Modern Foreign Languages to 16* they state:

> . . . There is a need for people fluent in a range of languages, particularly those of our European trading partners . . . greater diversification in schools is desirable.

The diversification of the first foreign language in schools will be considered first. The programme for diversification must not be taken lightly for there are huge implications for time, staffing and resources. These implications are NOT insurmountable but need careful planning and above all discussion with the senior management team. It is not a case of proposing all the answers here but simply of posing questions which can only be answered in the light of precise local circumstances.

National and/or local development plans

As was mentioned in the preamble to this chapter, if there is a local LEA or regional plan in this domain, then the HoD should find out about it before embarking on a change. At the very least, they should ascertain what other local schools do. If this is not possible because of the competition embodied in the LMS system then they should take account of the local parents and their attitudes. Advice from the governors and the school adviser is also essential.

Attitudes

There will be as many attitudes as there are staff and parents. It is essential that, at the very least, the HoD's colleagues are positive, since their long-held ideas may be challenged and their timetable time may also be altered if the HoD spreads their provision into two or more languages. Changing the status quo is often a difficult thing to achieve. However the OXPROD work seems to indicate that where diversification has been properly launched with good PR, attitudes were positive from pupils, staff and parents.

Worries

Worries may be expressed on several fronts:

Money and capitation; teacher supply and continuity of staffing; continuity for pupils if they have started French in a middle or primary school; lack of materials; lack of continuity post-16; parental opposition; timetable problems in the school; lack of expertise in the teacher's second language; lack of INSET opportunities; the need for the first time to make arrangements for the teaching of French as a *second* language – a fact that may mean a realignment of materials and methodology.

Perceived advantages

The school is different and more attractive to would-be pupils; there is more choice; it takes away some of the pressure for the survival of second languages; it allows staff to use languages they have qualifications in; there are more opportunities for pupils in the post-1992 scene.

When the debate has been publicised and a decision made in principle, then the various timetable models can be explored. Some of the variations are as follows:

1 A new language is chosen as the first language (e.g. Italian) and French is offered as the second foreign language. Problems may arise with setting in a large school unless there is a good pool of Italianists. There may also be objections from parents who see French as the 'natural choice' for first foreign language.

2 Two languages are given equal priority in the entry year. This in many schools is an attractive model provided there is staffing provision. It gives greater prominence to a new language without disadvantaging too much the traditional French. It will entail some restrictions on setting if the school considers it a priority but in a six-form-entry school that problem is not too serious. Consideration needs to be given to the allocation of pupils to the languages in the entry year. Probably the best way is 'negative selling', that is, writing to parents asking for any objections to a particular language, but otherwise simply splitting the year group into two equal divisions (ability and social).

3 *A wave model*   In this case the entry language in one year is, say, French, and in the following year the entry language is, say, Spanish. This eases setting problems but has two major problems – transfers in, when a pupil from another school arrives with the 'wrong' language for that year, and staffing problems which occur if the French or Spanish is in years 1/3/5 or years 2/4 which will result in a shift of demand for a particular language teaching facility each complete timetabled academic year. There must, in this case, be a supply of good dual linguists in the department.

4 *Two-language model*   Pupils start two languages in year 7, and then decide at a later date their main National Curriculum language.

Having decided on the possibilities offered by the various models, it will then be important to project the staffing and resource implications for the model proposed for the school. This is best done in a diagrammatic form, year by year, until the full programme is realised.

In the exercise, take account of the staffing teaching load, the language qualifications, the number of lessons per class, the setting/grouping arrangements, the point where a second language is introduced for those wishing to take up such an option. A similar exercise for resources should also be carried out. It will then be easier to present the case to the school management.

Forward planning is essential in all timetabling and management strategies. When talking to the senior management team, HoDs are likely to get a better reception if they present a development plan that is well documented. Below is a suggested layout for considering new developments.

This is a guide to presenting a case to the senior management for the development of modern language teaching in a 'Languages for All' policy. The figures presented below must of course be changed to suit the school but are a guide to an effective presentation of the case. (The working assumes a 'Language for All' policy is already in operation in years 7/8 so the figures are working on years 9 and above.)

Present Situation (year X 199–)

9th year:	5 sets French × 4 periods × 35 mins = 20 periods per week 3 sets German × 4 periods × 35 mins = 12 periods per week
TOTAL =	32 periods per week
10th year:	4 sets French × 4 periods × 35 mins = 16 periods per week 2 sets German × 4 periods × 35 mins = 8 periods per week
TOTAL =	24 periods per week
11th year:	3 sets French × 4 periods × 35 mins = 12 periods per week 1 set German × 4 periods × 35 mins = 4 periods per week
TOTAL =	16 periods per week
L6: U6:	1 set French × 8 periods × 35 mins = 8 periods per week 1 set French × 8 periods × 35 mins = 8 periods per week
TOTAL =	16 periods per week
TOTAL = Staffing equivalent:	88 periods 2.6 staff

Projections (year X + 1 199–)

9th year:	5 sets French × 4 periods × 35 mins = 20 periods per week 3 sets German × 4 periods × 35 mins = 12 periods per week
TOTAL =	32 periods per week
10th year:	5 sets French × 4 periods × 35 mins = 20 periods per week 2 sets German × 4 periods × 35 mins = 8 periods per week
TOTAL =	28 periods per week
11th year:	4 sets French × 4 periods × 35 mins = 16 periods per week 2 sets German × 4 periods × 35 mins = 8 periods per week
TOTAL =	24 periods per week (continued)

217

L6:	1 set French × 8 periods × 35 mins = 8 periods per week
	1 set German × 8 periods × 35 mins = 8 periods per week
U6:	1 set French × 8 periods × 35 mins = 8 periods per week
TOTAL =	24 periods per week
TOTAL =	108 periods
Staffing equivalent:	3.2 staff

A further projection should be made for year $X + 2$ and so on as part of the departmental development plan – though we have not provided this material here. It is our experience that such forward planning is appreciated by senior management.

Assumptions are that four periods per week are allocated to cover fully the GCSE and National Curriculum requirements. Staff load is approximately 34/40 periods per week.

In the case of staff, it may be that a language expertise audit will reveal under-utilised talents. It may be possible to use peripatetic staff or join in a consortium arrangement; new appointments will need to be made with future requirements in mind.

A similar exercise could be done with regard to capitation. Projections and future planning would help strengthen the case for funding. Projections on the present amount allocated to each pupil can be made though we would suggest a strong case could be made for extra help to re-equip the department for a 'Languages for All' policy. Again, forward planning to phase in changes and new materials would be appropriate (bearing in mind that there will be a slightly reduced demand for the original dominant language – a fact that will release resources). There is also a case to be made for capital/one-off investment as a pump-priming gesture, for example, to purchase hardware such as tape recorders and external speakers, as well as software such as tapes. In an LMS situation this may not be any more difficult than beforehand. If the school is a TVEI school, there will be some monies available for enhancement of the curriculum

Copies of such a document should ideally be seen by the head and senior management team prior to a full discussion at the appropriate committee. In some schools the curriculum committee of the governors likes to be involved.

The place of the second foreign language is also a difficult problem. The original advice for the National Curriculum was that the second language be introduced in year 10. This has caused consternation for those concerned. It seems that that advice has been somewhat loosened in later publications and schools are now freer to experiment. The real problem is the balance between the need to provide an adequate broad diet for all pupils and the demand for some specialisation; each school will need to sort out its own priorities. One way is to consider the whole of Key Stages 3 and 4 as a totality where the 10 per cent time allocation is able to be varied in any one year within the whole school curriculum and where some dual linguists may opt for combined humanities, for example, in order to free time; or there may be trading off of timetable space between languages. If there is a solid programme of diversification, then it is also likely to have a significant impact and consequence on the demand and availability of the second foreign language.

No single solution is available, but strenuous efforts should be made to offer as wide a choice as possible.

Finally, in those schools where there is a sixth form, then that age group must be considered in the overall planning, by providing *ab initio* courses, courses leading to qualifications other than the traditional A level and so on. As has been the case with many of the management issues raised in this book, overall planning of the whole school policy offers many solutions to problems. Considering only the lower school or the sixth form in isolation creates problems and also disadvantages the pupils.

Community Languages

In the equation of languages in a school it may be that there is a demand for community languages. Certainly there is a vast wealth of language experience in British communities (184 are spoken by pupils in London schools) and depending on the situation of the school, serious consideration must be given to the provision of classes in languages such as Urdu, Gujarati, Chinese and Hebrew. This is also a political and social question. However there are several points to be noted:

1   Community language teachers are often not language specialists and will need training (in school and by the training agencies such as universities, colleges, LEA, etc.).

2   These colleagues may very well be peripatetic and should as far as possible be integrated into the full-time department; help in particular must be extended in methodology, use of equipment, access to resources, etc. so that they can be integrated into the life of the department.

3   Careful research will be needed to provide adequately for the varied linguistic experience brought into school by those children who use the language at home (in whatever form) and those who wish to acquire it as a 'foreign' language.

20 Assessment

Assessment and recording of achievement are both *essential* parts of the teaching process and as such it is vital that all members of staff understand what is involved.

Now that we work within the guidelines of the National Curriculum, there are several new departures from what has been the traditional practice of past decades.

It must be stated that the principles embodied in the National Curriculum guidelines in respect of assessment will necessitate a close inspection of the teaching and learning styles teachers employ in their everyday work. Although this is a separate chapter for very good reasons, it must be read in conjunction with other areas of this book which deal with classroom management, pupil and teacher relationships, teaching and learning styles and so on. The assessment instruments should be devised with existing good classroom practice in mind and with an emphasis on flexibility which will provide feedback for the benefit of both teacher and pupil. This process will be referred to in great detail in the coming pages.

Aims

Assessment has several aims which may be summarised below:

Measuring attainment

Given that one of the main aims of the teacher is to teach a body of knowledge, then assessment, testing and examinations are used to measure how far this has been achieved. The care with which the test has been drawn up will affect the accuracy of the measure. Poorly composed tests will confuse the interpretation of the results.

Feedback

It is vital for teacher and pupil to be able to review progress (or lack of it). Parents also want to see the strengths and weaknesses of pupils. The ability for pupils to see where they have done well, as much as to realise where they have gone wrong, and for teachers to evaluate the effectiveness of their teaching *and* do something about it, can be helped by the proper use of evaluation and tests.

Tests can also help with prediction. Whether we like it or not tests will be used to predict the next stage or the suitability of the pupil to proceed further.

Motivation

The 'stick-and-carrot' effect of testing should not be underestimated. Language learning is a long-term task and pupils starting out on the long road to mastery of a

220

Teacher   Pupil

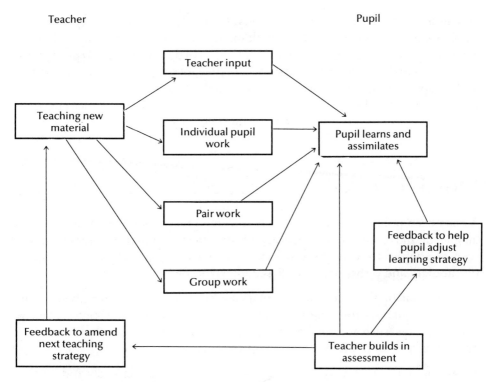

Figure 17: Importance of feedback

new language need recognition as one element in motivation. Teachers must not overestimate the effect of examinations themselves, but pupils are more likely to succeed when clear standards of attainment have been set. It is important that the standards set are within the capability of the pupils and this is one of the notable features of the Graded Examinations movement.

The concern here is not with the setting, marking and use of external examinations such as GCSE and A level, but rather with the practicalities of testing and assessment within the school.

In recent years there has been a build up in teacher expertise as a result of several discernable influences:

- topic-based courses, which reflect communicative concerns rather than purely structural/linguistic matters
- communicative courses which demand communication of messages rather than concentrate on total, native-speaker accuracy
- criteria-based schemes as opposed to norm-referencing
- continuous assessment schemes – including a course work element rather than the traditional 'sudden death' examinations
- task assessment where the assessment of a whole integrated task is of prime importance rather than the testing of exercises.

221

However, the *Final Report* of the National Curriculum Working Party lays more emphasis on structure and pattern building for very good reasons – not least of which is the admission that one of the weaknesses of the GCSE was the production of transactional language which in some cases did not enhance the survival chances of the pupil when thrown in at the deep end in the country of the target language. However, in spite of this, there will always be a place for informal, quick checks of the mechanics of the language and these must not be neglected.

Quick checks

As has been pointed out the language learning process is a long affair and the diagnostic and motivational functions of testing what is taught are important. Any such testing must involve both the mechanical mastery of the various elements (vocabulary and verbs, etc.) as well as understanding.

It should not be that the teacher's marking burden is always increased by the frequent use of tests, for there are many occasions when quick marking in class by various means (such as exchanging papers, true or false/multiple-choice answers, providing keys for pupils to use) are appropriate.

What is important, however, is that pupils take the process seriously and see that the teacher also considers it to be worthwhile. If it is indicated that something will be tested, then it must be tested and not forgotten. Learning homeworks in particular must be tested or else the temptation to spend the evening watching television will overcome most pupils. Equally tests must only be given with prior warning – surprises only breed hostility and cries of 'not fair' from the pupils.

Vocabulary

This provides the building blocks of the edifice and should be sampled regularly, but not to the exclusion of using these elements in real exchanges. As each stage, topic or unit is completed, the teacher should test quickly 'both ways' – English to foreign language and foreign language to English. Pupils can mark their own or each other's work. It is important to review any difficulties and retest if necessary. If writing is not part of the course, then the teacher can test by pictures, odd-man-out or other multiple choice strategies.

Grammar or structures

This should be tested as the teacher proceeds, even in courses where formal grammar is not the linchpin as before. Tests can range from forms of tenses to particular usage. Again, it is important to be to the point and precise. But the teacher should not think that the ability to analyse grammar will enable a pupil to become fluent – it is simply a *stage* on the way.

Comprehension

This can require different sorts of skills – intensive and extensive, detailed and cursory. Both should be sampled. It can be done orally at the beginning of the lesson, after a homework or by means of written tests of varying levels of difficulty. However, the teacher should make sure the pupils know beforehand that they are to be tested and that they are being asked to read or listen either for the fine details *or* simply for the 'gist'. The sampling at this level should be done in English since comprehension should not be confused with composition at this level of testing.

Writing

Perhaps the easiest of the skills to test, but the teacher should beware of using it if the tuition has been largely aural/oral.

Oral competence

This is difficult to measure in a large class when time is at a premium. There are several ways, however, of lightening the burden and still sampling on a regular basis. The real key to this problem lies in the teaching and learning styles adopted by the teacher (see Chapter 2 and the discussion on group work) and in the situations created where the teacher is able to focus on an individual and/or a small group of pupils. Pupils must be clear about what the teacher's strategy is and if they are put in a situation where they can perform as naturally as possible then the task will be easier. A great majority of pupils are less afraid if they 'perform' in small groups rather than to a whole class.

Strategies for oral testing

Using the assistant

He or she must be told what to look for and what standards to expect. If possible a checklist could be devised. Using the assistant as part of a group work strategy within the normal classroom rather than sending a group out to another room is a useful tactic.

'Target' lessons

During a series of lessons a group of five to six pupils is observed with more detail than usual. They are graded say on a five-point scale (A–E) and thus the whole class can be observed over a short period of time without too much interruption. This method is particularly suited to topic work where pupils may be engaged on a *carousel* of activities within the topic area.

'Target' weeks

Oral work is particularly noticed and thus a picture is built up over the year of the pupil profile.

Statutory obligations

The assessment policy of the National Curriculum is twofold: a combination of external tests – Standard Assessment Tasks (SATs) – and teacher assessment.

The purpose of the SATs is to monitor and moderate teachers' own continuous assessment so as to ensure comparability of standards. They are to be administered by the teacher in the course of the final months of each Key Stage, but the real burden of the continuous teacher testing must clearly be integrated in the teaching and learning process if it is to serve its formative purpose.

It cannot be overstated that the assessment process must not be a bolt-on addition – for it will then be neither manageable nor supportive. Formative assessment must be devised to support good classroom practice.

At the end of each Key Stage, the SATs will arrive in school from the agency appointed to devise them and they will reflect the teaching practices embodied in the National Curriculum programmes.

The concern here is with the two pillars of teacher assessment – the *formative* and *summative* processes. The following sections should be read in conjunction with the section on reporting (pp. 235–9).

What then are the guiding principles for the departmental scheme of formative assessment?

Formative assessment

Planning and assessment go hand in hand

As each topic, module or task is planned as part of the scheme of work, there should also be a consideration of the precise way in which the teacher and pupils will know that they have mastered the targets set.

The publication of a planning document will form part of the departmental recording system and do many other things as well. The pupil version will serve to help in the following ways:

1   The start of each module or stage will contain a description of the aims of the unit: the linguistic considerations as well as the communicative aims. These

must be couched in active, positive 'can do' terms that the pupil will understand.

2   It will form a planning schedule for staff and pupils.

3   It will allow some degree of autonomous learning management.

4   It will allow a greater degree of differentiation in the classroom.

5   It will allow greater feedback.

6   It will be a document that will show parents what, as well as how, the pupils are doing.

7   If the pupil is involved in the assessment process, this will be a positive encouragement. All schemes which have this document built in, report an increase in pupil motivation. This can only be a good thing.

8   Other skills such as organisation and attitudes can also be built in and thus form part of a record of achievement. Figure 18 shows a sample page from such a document.

Checklist for departmental review of assessment procedures (formative)

☐ Is there a clear statement of knowledge/skills/understanding to be acquired available for each course/module/teaching unit?
☐ Are expectations and learning objectives clear to pupils?
☐ Are pupils aware of the assessment criteria?
☐ Are pupils involved in the assessment?
☐ Is the assessment used formatively to identify strengths and weaknesses and to enable future work to be planned?
☐ Is the emphasis on achievement?
☐ Are standards consistent across the department?

Recording the language skills and the problem of communicative competence.

What is required by the National Curriculum?

1   Pupils must be assessed over a range of tests and tasks to match them with the attainment targets.

2   Evidence will be required to support the assessment.

Name of pupil_____ Form_____

Unit module: Ordering a snack

Unit aims

1 At the end of this unit you will be able to order something to eat and drink in a café.

2 You will be familiar with the vocabulary for these items and use certain verbs.

3 You will be able to reply to the waiter.

4 You will be able to handle sums of money.

Unit module: Ordering a snack   ## Progress Chart

Now I can:	well	quite well	with hesitation
Read a simple menu			
Ask for something to eat/drink			
Use expressions such as *'je voudrais'*, *'Avez-vous?'*			
Understand the reply			
Ask 'How much?'			
Tender the money and ask if 'service included'			

I can remember the following words:

I can use the following expressions:

Signature of pupil_____ Date_____

Signature of teacher_____

Figure 18: Pupil version of the planning document

What sort of evidence will the teacher need to keep?

For work that results in hard copy there will be few problems. The teacher should keep exercise books or other examples of pupils' work – but only sufficient as is necessary and until the evidence is replaced as work progresses. In essence this is not much different from the process the teacher has been engaged in beforehand – only he or she must be more systematic.

In the case of assessment for those areas of the syllabus with no tangible outcome such as oral work, then there is a more difficult problem. In this case there must be agreed criteria to work to with simple checklists as guides. As a starter it will be helpful to inspect the attainment targets of the National Curriculum and to home in on one group of pupils at a time during the lessons spent on the module in question. This again has implications for the way the teacher arranges the teaching and learning situations (see Chapter 2, particularly pp. 34–42).

Keeping records for formative assessment

Keeping adequate records will probably mean being much more systematic in maintaining mark books than was previously the case. If, as is likely, the departmental work is arranged in topics or modules, then a separate page or section should be allocated to each topic. Pupil names are listed in the left column as normal, and the mark columns are in sections:

1   Columns separated for each skill area ('Listening', 'Speaking', 'Reading' and 'Writing'). These are completed according to predetermined criteria, settled by the department at the planning stage and possibly noted on the back of the formative record sheet. Each skill should have, say, four levels of competence/ levels of achievement. The tasks in each skill area correspond to the skills in the topic as described in the scheme of work.

2   Columns for more conventional recording of items such as verb tests. These can use the historical convention of marks out of 10.

3   Columns, if so desired for other assessment, such as aspects of oral work (intonation, pronunciation) or study skills (organisation, participation).

Most schools now have access to desktop publishing and the departmental mark-books can be easily produced on such systems so that they look attractive and easy to use (see Figure 19). It is unlikely that commercially produced books will be appropriate for the system. All this will have repercussions on the style of reporting out to pupils and parents on progress. This is dealt with later on pp. 235–9.

Summative assessment _____

This document is probably the one that will go out to parents at the end of the school year or whatever interval is required by the whole school policy. It makes sound sense to see that the setting up of the summative document is done hand in hand with the formative scheme – otherwise there will be tremendous headaches in transferring the information.

If the work involves topic areas/modules, as has been suggested, then the summative document will need to contain (at least in précis form) the elements of

	Listening			Speaking			Reading			Writing			Year 8 Module 3
	Date and topics			Date and topics			Date and topics			Date and topics			
D. Adams	1	1	2	2	3	1	3	3	4	–	1	3	
M. Brown	2	3	3		3	4	3	3	3	2	2	3	
M. Carter	2	2	2	2	2	3	3	3	4	2	2	2	
P. Davies	1	1	1	1	1	1	1	1	2	1	1	1	
M. Evans	2	3	4	4	4	4	3	4	4	2	3	4	
J. Fear	1	3	3	1	4	4	3	3	2	2	2	2	
P. Goodge													
M. Hill													
P. Jenkins													
T. Lilley													
D. Morris													
D. Oxford													
C. Price													
K. Russell													
A. Smalley													
J. Timmis													
V. Unwin													
P. Williams													
M. Young													

Figure 19: Possible layout of markbook for 'Topic/Module' approach

Language tests Description and maximum score							A → E				
Vocab. (1)	Verb test	Perfect tense ex.	Use of adjective				Pronunciation	Fluency	Accuracy	Intonation	Year 8 Module 3
20	20	20	20								
16	18	14	19				A	A	B	C	
17	14	13	20				C	B	C	C	
13	16	14	13				B	B	B	B	
9	6	8	4				E	D	E	D	
15	13	17	19				C	B	A	B	
14	16	17	10				B	C	B	A	
					New page for each module						

the recording of several formative documents *plus* sections for reporting other matters via teachers' and pupils' comments. A built-in contribution to the record of achievement may also be necessary. Within the National Curriculum, it may be necessary to 'report out' in such documents (at the end of a year, say) the level of attainment reached.

Above all the teacher should consult the senior management team at school and the LEA guidelines (if any) before deciding on the final format.

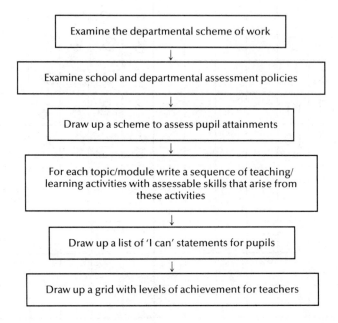

Figure 20: The stages involved in drawing up a departmental formative assessment policy

Catering for pupils of different abilities: differentiation by activity or differentiation by outcome?

Teaching in mixed-ability groups means that there will be problems of motivation and assessment. If all pupils are given a single test or battery of tests, then the teacher must decide if the learning situations are differentiated by *task design* or by *task outcome*. It is easier to set a single task/test and differentiate by the outcome – but that can demotivate pupils who are not able to reach the higher outcomes. It is harder to devise a variety of tasks/tests differentiated in design. If the departmental team can afford the manpower and time to set a battery of tasks and tests designed for different levels of ability, then the time consuming task will make the area of judgement easier to work through.

Formal testing

Some schools may have a system of formal examinations at various times of the year and, if this is the case, then departmental teams will have the task of devising schemes that work. An understanding of the basic ideas is therefore important.

Devising tests

What is said in this section is also relevant to the devising of other sorts of tests, and should be seen as a guide to post-16 testing.

Over the past few years a lot of discussion and argument has been generated over the 'backwash' effect of examinations and testing on the teaching of modern languages. This is particularly so at external examination level, when the syllabus and the methodology of the school have been increasingly dominated by the need to get pupils over the examination hurdle. The passing of examinations is seen by many – pupils, teachers and parents – as the reason for embarking on a course of study. The syllabus has been seen to be examination-driven, crowding out many other desirable aims. There is now, however, an awareness that this approach is restricting, that syllabus design is the first priority and that test design must follow and not dictate it.

It is considered important that tests should endeavour to simulate as closely as possible the normal language situations which have been anticipated in the course of designing the syllabus. This should increase both *reliability* and *validity*.

What do we mean by *reliability* and *validity*?

Reliability
A test is said to be *reliable* if it produces a consistent result from one occasion to the next for the same group or pupil, irrespective of marker.

Validity
Tests and examinations have both content and predictive validity. *Content validity* will mean that the test will sample the appropriate content in question; *predictive validity* will mean it will predict a future event, that is, in this case, the ability of the pupil to cope in 'real' language situations.

It is not often possible to apply statistical measures of reliability to a single school, but by building up a file of tests over a number of years, refined by use, then it is possible to improve reliability. Validity can be improved by careful and systematic production of tests and by the help of a grid or checklist as in Figure 21.

Settings	Topics	Personal Identification	Family	House/home	Geography	Travel	Food/drink	Money	Free time
Home									
Home town									
Transport									
Restaurant/café									
Place of entertainment									
School									

Figure 21: Grid for producing valid tests

Devising tests: Dos and Don'ts

Dos

1　Be clear from the beginning *when* you are going to test: *plan ahead*.

2　Draw up a list or table of what is to be tested. Draw from the syllabus and make sure that the sampling in the test covers the range of topics, situations and structures encountered in the teaching syllabus. Test *only* what has been taught and avoid overlap.

3　Decide on the skills to be tested.

4　Decide on the length of the test according to the time available, the age and the ability of the pupils. This is one of the most difficult of all balancing acts: too little time increases pressures; too much time is wasteful and can produce discipline problems.

5　Decide on the marking strategy at the same time as devising the test.

6　Decide *who* will mark the test. Try to ensure that there is a fair distribution of the burden and of consistency in marking the test or the section. It is a good idea for as many teachers as possible who teach a particular group to be involved in the marking and assessing for one can learn a lot about the pupils when going through the often monotonous pile of scripts.

7　Attach great importance to precise rubrics and instructions.

8　Devise tests which search out what pupils *know* rather than what they don't know.

9　Use the target language as far as possible as the testing 'vehicle'.

Don'ts

1   Don't wait until the last minute to set the papers. Haste is not conducive to good policy.

2   Don't draw up the paper and then fit the teaching to the test.

3   Don't use 'trick' questions.

4   Don't introduce unfamiliar routines to the class for the first time in a test.

5   Don't set the pupil against the clock. Be realistic on the length of paper and the number of elements to be attempted.

When the papers have been set, it is a good idea to pass them on to colleagues for their comments. This is particularly important when the resultant examination is to be taken by a number of groups taught by different teachers. This openness is important – secrecy should play no part in testing as the teacher is not aiming to destabilise the staff.

A checklist for reviewing an examination

- □ Are all the questions set within the syllabus?
- □ Does the test adequately sample the syllabus?
- □ Is there any overlap in the material?
- □ Does the test allow the pupils to demonstrate their abilities?
- □ Are the instructions clear?
- □ Is the visual material clear?
- □ Is any recorded material clear?
- □ Is the French, German, Spanish, etc. correct?
- □ Can the paper be completed in the time allowed?

What should be tested?

It is reasonable to assume that the teacher will want to test all four skills and, if it is appropriate, to test in a mixed-skill mode. This is a real-life situation and can be achieved to a greater or lesser degree if strategies reflect real-life outcomes. There will always be some mixed-skill element in testing: when the teacher sets a listening test, for example, the stimulus material will be in the target language and this can to some extent contaminate the results if they also expect the answer in the target language. This should not worry the teacher unduly, for this is true of real communication and they can do their best to reduce the contamination by careful question construction. The teacher should not attempt, however, to make the question so devious that it resembles an IQ test.

A second broad consideration in determining test types will be the need to reflect the general philosophy of the syllabus: if teachers accept that the main aim of the teaching is communicative competence, then it must follow that their tests have realistic communication as their hallmark and should be authentic and useful beyond the classroom. Having said all this, it has to be admitted that examinations are not 'realistic', that they impose restrictions of time and format if they are to fulfil their role as measuring instruments. But the balance must be in favour of realism and the examples below reflect this assumption.

If the teacher accepts that one communicates to achieve something, to change something or to express an opinion, then the strategies open out – even though the main vehicle used may be pen and paper.

Test strategies: a few suggestions

Listening skill
Listen and do
- filling in forms
- filling in symbols on, say, a weather map
- completing an itinerary on a map from an announcement
- matching pictures to an oral stimulus
- following instructions (e.g. tracing a route on a map)
- completing a picture
- doing a puzzle
- filling in a grid
- identifying a photograph in a police identity-parade scenario.

Listen and react
- listening to a railway announcement: what does the pupil do next?
- listening to news bulletins and matching up headlines
- listening to a story – what happens next?
- listening to a telephone conversation and relaying the meaning to a third person
- making a précis.

Reading skill
- comprehending notices and signs
- extracting relevant points from authentic material
- matching written work to pictures
- putting sentences in order
- reading material and answering a questionnaire.

Written skill
- writing postcards on the basis of similar stimulus material
- leaving messages as a result of stimulus ideas

- writing letters formal/informal
- describing pictures
- writing description based on other visuals, e.g. picture of accident
- filling in forms
- writing list of advantages/disadvantages of various activities proposed.

Speaking
- role play (structured and open ended)
- reporting to third party, 'interpreting'.

Marking policy

It is a good idea to mark papers and discuss a sample with a colleague in order to make sure of the standards being set.

In order to improve the reliability of the examination, it is important to devise a scheme which will allow consistent standards to be applied over the whole range of pupils. It is therefore suggested that a member of staff be responsible for a section of the examination so that the criteria will be assimilated all the quicker.

The criteria to be applied will depend on the test but, as has been mentioned frequently in this chapter, there will be a need for a scheme that is positive in rewarding the communicative aspects. At certain times it may be necessary to employ a negative scheme – taking off marks for errors – but that will be in specifically designed testing.

Reporting the results

This is a vital area for a departmental/school policy and the design of the reporting out system is extremely important as it affects all kinds of decisions. It is fully discussed in the next section.

Keeping records

Pupil records

Good record keeping is vital in a well-run department for the benefit of pupils, parents and staff. The concern here is with the recording of pupil progress. Other areas requiring monitoring – the syllabus provision, staff, stock levels, etc. – are dealt with in other chapters.

First of all there is a discussion of the rationale and this is followed by a brief consideration of computer aids to record keeping.

The most important start is a clear assessment policy which will provide:

- evidence for consideration
- information that is useful
- feedback to those concerned.

Much of this is dealt with in the section on assessment (pp. 220–2). Any such policy must be in line with the policy of the school in general and this is particularly important at those times in the school year when departments come into direct contact with the world outside via reports. There are also times when the department is in contact (and even in competition) with other departments, for example, when pupils are required to make choices as to future study patterns. Is the department consistent with, say, the geography department? Did Wayne Brown choose geography because of the A grades which the German department rarely gives? Children do make that sort of judgement – and it can lead to disappointment. Within the department, staff are compared by pupils. Do all the departmental team use the same assessment standards? If not, then promotion/demotion are problematical. These are some of the organisational consequences of 'reporting out'.

But nowadays reports are seen in another light – as summative documents encompassing a whole range of skills, knowledge, attitudes and dimensions which have formed part of the school's programme.

As a result of recent legislation, teachers must be provided with a clearly stated assessment programme, which will provide correct information to all those who have a legitimate need to know – pupils, parents, colleagues, careers staff and certain outside agencies such as higher and further education institutions and prospective employers.

A Word of Warning

All data kept on computer files is open to inspection by those who have a right to know – parents and guardians and pupils over the age of 16 (for their own information only). It is therefore important to be accurate and to consult with the senior management of the school if there is anything stored in files that may be controversial. Information held on paper does not fall within the scope of the Data Protection Act.

Of course, the general school policy on reports and assessment affects the nature of departmental record keeping and the head of department should see that deadlines are met. This will involve planning, cooperation and well-advertised dates for action. As well as end-of-term and end-of-year examinations which result in reports, the department will certainly be involved in some form of continuous (formative) assessment of pupil progress and in addition will probably involve pupils in the reporting process. Appropriate testing and monitoring, if carried out in a positive manner, which reflect the aims and objectives of the course, can be a valuable aid to teaching and learning, providing opportunities for remedial action as necessary at the various stages in the course.

The process begins with the design stage of the course. What is to be taught, and how is it to be tested and assessed? How is the record to be made? How are activities, skills and dimensions beyond the narrower linguistic skills to be incorporated? How often should the teacher report out? These questions need to be addressed at the very outset of the planning.

If teaching within the National Curriculum, then teaching and assessing go hand in hand. If the school demands an end-of-year report, then consideration will need to be given to incorporating the formative process with such a summative document.

Discussion will be needed on the format. It is unlikely that the old style report sheet, with a single line for comment on each subject, will be adequate.

Assuming that the department works in modules, then each module will require a review sheet which reflects what has been taught. These review sheets should be so designed as to fit into a final or summative document.

These review sheets should contain the following elements:

- school name
- language
- pupil name
- date of review
- teacher name
- tutor group of pupil
- module name/title/reference (e.g. 8/2 = year 8 module 2)
- skills assessed and levels attained
- pupil comment
- teacher comment
- other assessed areas
- signature and, if appropriate, space for parents' comment.

The back of each sheet could contain explanations for the levels of attainment.

This design is only an example and the exact format will depend on the processes that have been gone through in the course of designing the teaching materials, the learning styles, the assessment package and the formative documents.

If the school has a computer-based management system, then it is perfectly possible to plug into the system to store and retrieve information using a spreadsheet system, and desktop publishing to design the final outcomes.

As well as the statements of attainment that report on the linguistic achievements of the pupils there will also be a space for teacher comments. In this space, some schools see a chance to use computer-generated statements drawn from a 'bank' kept on disk. This can be extremely impersonal and it is preferable that staff write in their own comments in this section.

General points about reports

1   It is important to watch how the report is presented. Parents scrutinise them closely and do make comments on handwriting and spelling. If a report looks as though it could be made up at the chemist, neither headteacher nor parent is happy.

2   The teacher should think carefully before making any comment that could be misunderstood, such as 'This is quite good progress for a girl of Jane's ability'. Does this mean that the girl's ability was already so high that the teacher could not imagine further progress possible . . . or is she beyond the pale?

3   At all costs avoid the funny remark of the 'he is trying . . . very' kind.

4   It is wise avoiding being too technical. For example, 'In spoken French, her uvular "r" has improved greatly, but her dentals still need attention'.

5   A record of past comments should be kept so that it is possible to comment on progress since the previous report.

6   A school report is not the place to make criticism of the school. For example, 'It is a pity she has not been allowed to start a second language this term'.

7   The teacher should ensure that the remarks are fair and reflect the whole period a report is supposed to cover. It is all too easy to be influenced by one extra piece of good or bad work.

8   Parents often seek out staff on parents' evenings to ask for clarification of a comment. It is important to be prepared to substantiate remarks put in a report made two months or more beforehand.

9   It is a mistake to make firm predictions about expected progress and especially about the possible outcome of public examinations.

It is also possible that there will be a space for pupils to comment on their progress. This may be guided by appropriate spaces on such areas as self-confidence and willingness to speak, or a box may be used for comments written with or without the help of the teacher.

Records of Achievement

The DES Statement of Policy (July 1984) paved the way for a new style of reporting – Records of Achievement. To reach this aim it is now necessary to cover a pupil's progress and activities across the whole educational programme of the school, both in the classroom and outside . . . and possibly activities outside the school as well.

Records of Achievement are seen as a vital part of the assessment process by the writers of the *Final Report* for languages in the National Curriculum (para. 7.23). Language teachers should be aware of this development and it is suggested that this will be the vehicle for reporting on the skills and attitudes of pupils as well as on the cross-curricular dimension.

Plan of action

1 Plan as a department – medium/short term. (Work on units/modules with assessment activities and clearly identified learning targets.)

2 Agree assessment criteria/methods of assessment.

3 Agree method of involving the pupils. (Sharing learning targets / Teacher-pupil dialogue / Self-assessment.)

4 Agree common approaches for building up formative/summative records. (Marking policy/use of formative record sheets/types of teacher records.)

5 Decide on use/frequency of National Curriculum grid.

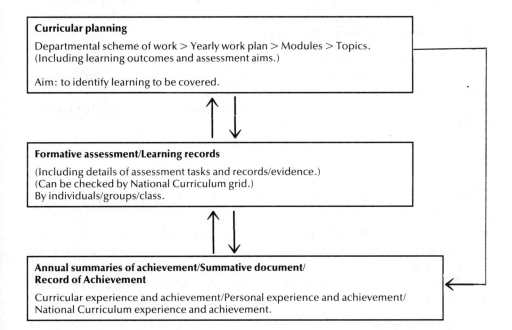

Curricular planning

Departmental scheme of work > Yearly work plan > Modules > Topics.
(Including learning outcomes and assessment aims.)

Aim: to identify learning to be covered.

Formative assessment/Learning records

(Including details of assessment tasks and records/evidence.)
(Can be checked by National Curriculum grid.)
By individuals/groups/class.

**Annual summaries of achievement/Summative document/
Record of Achievement**

Curricular experience and achievement/Personal experience and achievement/
National Curriculum experience and achievement.

Figure 22: Procedure for assessment

21 Languages and special needs

The range of pupils with special needs is very wide. At any one time the numbers of pupils with special needs may be up to 20 per cent of the population and many of these are in main stream schools. In principle *all* pupils should have the right of access to a modern language and it is not envisaged in the National Curriculum that pupils with special needs should be excluded.

What will be needed is a sympathetic approach with a whole school policy and probably some extra resourcing to enable such pupils to gain from the undoubted benefits of learning a language other than their own. The use of information technology to support such work will be particularly helpful as well as some of the techniques used in primary school teaching.

Many departments are convinced of the value of languages for all, but the fear expressed by some colleagues, faced with pupils who have not in the past had such opportunities open to them, is understandable. However, there is no genetic reason why pupils in this country should be less gifted than others in the language-learning business.

Possible aims for special needs pupils

- to develop general language skills through new learning experiences and success
- to increase social skills by providing new avenues for communication and interaction
- to increase awareness of other peoples and cultures by offering new horizons
- to provide pupils with at least the basic linguistic tools in the target language.

The individual school may decide that there are more precise linguistic aims worth pursuing, depending on the abilities of the pupils concerned.

Difficulties

- retention of any learned material
- difficulty in articulating in the 'productive' skills
- length of courses
- need for rewards quickly and frequently

- lack of self-motivation and self-esteem
- behaviour
- teacher attitudes
- parental expectations.

The school will need to address these problems and allocate appropriate resources to the pupils. It is suggested that the latter two difficulties (attitudes and expectations) are the main ones. If some headway can be made in these two respects then some of the other perceived difficulties may be more easily solved.

Policy planning

In framing a policy for languages and special needs in mainstream as well as special schools, consideration will need to be given to the following:

1   Smaller teaching groups.

2   Allocation of support staff within the classroom.

3   Cooperative planning with support staff so that they have an active role within and outside the classroom; team teaching strategies.

4   Careful use of audio-visual and computer aids.

5   Careful appraisal of worksheets and other presentations.

Smaller teaching groups

These can be allocated by the use of staff across a year group, by the use of support staff, by the introduction of nonteaching assistants (NTAs), by the use of assistants (FLAs) and even sixth-formers and parents.

Allocation of support staff

Support staff should be used sparingly outside the classroom for withdrawal groups. Their most valuable use is within the normal classroom. This is to avoid creating 'sink groups' who have even more limited access to the curriculum, for they never catch up if constantly withdrawn.

Cooperative planning and team teaching

If a specialist language teacher is available then that is a bonus. However, even nonspecialists can be most useful if the preplanning is positive. They can help in a variety of ways:

- supervising a group on the computer
- hearing a pupil read
- explaining the task in hand if not understood the first time
- helping a group on a cassette recorder
- preparing display material
- being attached to someone with behavioural problems
- helping with role play.

Audio-visual and computer aids

Proper use of hardware can enhance the learning situation. For example, a listening corner with a cassette recorder and headsets will enable a listening group (or pupil) to work at a tape at an individual speed and for short periods of time without involving the whole class in a lockstep approach to activities. As with all planning with SEN groups, there will need to be greater attention to individualisation of the tasks, in other words, differentiation. However, it is the experience of many staff who have gone down this road (with considerable success), that methodology developed with the special needs child in mind is equally effective with other groups. This is an important spin-off for departments who invest time and resources to this area of the school.

The judicious use of video recordings can help reinforce paralinguistic elements such as gesture and facial expression to help comprehension. Computers can be a most positive motivating force. Pupils can work at their own speed and with word-processing packages such as 'Folio', they are able to produce very acceptable final versions without too much frustration. Recently modern language teachers have discovered the concept keyboard which is in widespread use in primary education (see p. 90). Details are available from NCET (see address list in Part Four) and your IT specialist or adviser in your area can also help.

Proper use of worksheets and similar material

Special attention should be paid to layout which should not be cluttered. Care is needed in printing such material to make it accessible and attractive. Words should be in both upper and lower case (they are easier to recognise), and in single columns (two-column layout is apparently confusing). It should be clear which words belong to which pictures and also the sequence on the page should be clear and not flit from one part of the page to another. Instructions should be in the active voice as opposed to the passive.

A final word: most LEAs have special needs advisers and it will pay to ask for their help via training days and/or TVEI money.

Giving recognition

Pupils respond to positive praise and this is especially so in special needs classes or groups. It will be essential to have a plan to build on success within the class, within the school and through reporting out. Even such rewards as house stars and the like are attractive. It is essential to recognise and to reward what is probably the most difficult aspect of teaching such children – retention of material from one lesson to another. It will be helpful (as in primary schools) to have lots of prompts around the room. These can be gradually withdrawn when appropriate. Such aids as number cards on walls, a perpetual calendar, vocabulary/picture cards, colour coded cards; all are positive features of good primary classrooms. If possible, it is well worthwhile arranging a visit to a primary school which is noted for its language development work where the ideas gleaned will be very useful. The teacher can ask the primary adviser to arrange such a visit or even request INSET in school or on an LEA basis to explore this area.

Using the target language

This may appear impossible to many, yet a lot of schools do use the foreign language in such situations with remarkable success. Expecting pupils at least to understand instructions in the language is possible (even if they answer in English).

Making it enjoyable

If possible, the teacher should make activities reflect pupils' interests with games and such-like. TV games, board games and bingo come to mind. It is also important to make things practical by doing rather than simply answering. Chaos is sometimes the result but well-ordered chaos is better than silence and lack of progress.

Planning

Above all lessons and the sequence of lessons should be planned on modules that are responsive to the pupils' needs and capabilities. Work via modules is more flexible and allows short-term objectives that can be seen and understood by the pupils themselves.

The environment

Attention must be paid to the particular needs of the individual. This is always true, but more so in the case of special needs children. The room should be arranged so that pupils can move around from group to group; those with hearing or visual impairment must be near the blackboard or speech source; those with reading problems need access to other aids to understanding and so on.

What can be taught?

It will be important that the department brings together its ideas. Below is a short list of *possible* topic areas and exploitation that have proved helpful in the elaboration of schemes of work for special needs pupils. It is *not* an exhaustive list but is based on commonly used areas of experience.

Topic areas suitable

- greetings
- introducing oneself to friends
- identifying people; saying who they are
- quantity – numbers
- saying and asking where pupils live (town and country; house and flat, etc.)
- days of the week; dates
- describing one's family
- describing relationships (brothers, sisters, parents, etc.)
- asking questions
- colours
- likes/dislikes
- weather
- leisure activities
- directions (getting to a place)
- telling the time
- food (going to a café/restaurant)
- shops and shopping
- money
- buying simple things such as food, ices, postcards, etc.
- clothes and describing people.

Ideas for exploitation

NB   Ideas listed under one topic area may very well be suitable for exploitation in other areas.

Greetings

Beginning each lesson with ritual of saying 'hello', etc. in target language (TL).

Filling in speech bubbles in cartoons illustrating greeting session in various situations.

Spelling names in TL – teaching TL alphabet. Spelling bees. Letters and numbers game like TV game 'Countdown'. Pupils bring photo of themselves when young, others guess who it is and ask in TL.

Making flash cards of real people cut out from magazines. Pupils ask who they are.

Using pictures and matching with jumbled names.

Word search cards with names (of pupils and even famous people). When pupils have found them, they spell out names.

Using puppets.

Pupils given name badges when they can say their name in TL in reply to questions (other rewards in other topics can be worked out).

Chain games: pupils greet each other in random order in class, those who do not answer are 'out'.

Numbers
Bingo game (NB This idea can be used as picture bingo with any other vocabulary/ topic area.)

Basic 'sums'.

Reading from telephone books.

Car number plates and numbers of *départements* in France.

Postcodes.

Random numbers put on board – calling them out in any order – pupils circle them on blackboard (can be team game).

Mileage charts of distances between towns. Birthday charts for dates. Reading from digital clocks.

Dice games e.g. simple snakes and ladders where pupils count dice number thrown and places moved.

Numbers/figures to be matched with jumbled spellings of those numbers.

Designing children's counting book e.g. drawing numbers one to ten in figures and words with appropriate number of objects. Can be coloured and later used in colour work.

Price lists. Shopping till-roll.

Dot pictures such as one finds in children's games books. Teacher/pupil reads out the correct sequence of numbers to enable others to complete the picture – winner has to say what it is in TL ('*C'est une maison*'/'*Das ist ein Haus*', etc.).

What is it?
I-Spy game. Pupils have cards of well-known objects and others guess. '*C'est un. . .?*'/'*Es ist ein(e) . . .?*' '*Oui, c'est un. . .*'/'*Ja, das ist ein(e) . . .*' or '*Non, ce n'est pas un. . .*'/'*Nein, das ist kein(e) . . .*'

Pictures with jumbled definitions.

Kim's game.

Word labels all round the room.

Where you live

Flashcards of houses/flats. 'I live in/at . . .'/'*Ich wohne in . . .*'/'*Ich wohne . . .*' plus jumbled names/maps.

Maze game: people joined to names of places/types of dwelling with maze lines. Pupils follow, say, copy. (NB this idea can be used with other topic areas).

Using estate agent's photos to talk about where they live.

Personal identity

Making identity cards of famous people/pop stars.

Days of Week

Calendar in room.

Date always on headings of written work.

Make simple perpetual calendar.

House and home

Drawing house and labelling.

Jeu des sept erreurs. Drawings with differences. Put furniture in rooms and label. Then furniture in wrong rooms.

Members of family

Family trees.

Carte d'Identité.

Time

Wooden cut-out clock with moving hands.

Simple bus/train timetables.

Clock drawings.

Asking and telling time. Jumbled sentences with clock times to match. Bingo with clock times instead of numbers – pupils and/or teacher acting as caller.

Colours

Colouring in pictures after teacher dictates what to do in TL. ('*La voiture est rouge*'/'*Das Auto ist rot*'/'*El coche es rojo.*')

Weather

Weather map with symbols (like TV).

Jumbled sentences for weather descriptions.

Leisure

Asking what pupils like – filling in opinion-poll chart.

Directions

Town-map work. Pupils follow and give directions. Drawing on map.

Maze game '*Je vais à*'/'*Ich fahre nach*'/'*Voy a* . . .' Lines join people and places. '*Je cherche*'/'*Ich Suche*'/'*Busco* . . .' '*Il est à côté de*'/'*Es ist neben*'/'*Esta al lado de* . . .' '*à gauche de*'/'*links*'/'*a la izquierda* . . .' from map and diagram.

Practice *in situ* Who is sitting where? Next to, etc.

Money
Adding up. Using shop bills and café bills.

Items with price tags, e.g. cut from mail order catalogue.

Clothes
Describing people (and pictures from catalogues.) 'Wanted' posters (*On cherche*). Recognising people from spoken descriptions about series of pictures.

Labelling clothes line.

Making up/drawing 'monsters' from descriptions given by teacher or another pupil in target language (e.g. 'Draw a tall man with a red painted hat, trousers – one leg is red, the other green, two pink eyes', etc.).

Café
Practising very basic role plays/scenes in café and shops.

Quantity practice by cards (three types: a) asking words e.g. '*Je voudrais*'/'*donnez-moi*'; b) quantity words, e.g. '*une bouteille de*', '*une tranche de*', '*un kilo de*'; c) items, e.g. '*poires*', '*vin*').

Basic signs
Using pictures of signs in the street, in shops, etc. – mix and match signs (English and target language).

General Ideas
Bingo: rooms, weather, money, furniture, food (all via picture bingo).

Jigsaw words. Pieces with words on – matched to make sentences.

Word searches.

Picture crosswords.

True/false games.

Happy Families-type games.

Simon says ('*Jacques a dit*') games.

'Rain-blot' techniques. Pupils complete, for example, a postcard where some words are obscured by blots. This technique can be used in many circumstances.

Cloze test activities.

Odd-men-out lists of words.

> Above all it will be the teacher with a sense of humour, personality and a realistic idea of aims and expectations who will win through.

In 1989, HMI reported[1] on provisions for pupils with special educational needs in ordinary schools and they came up with the following points:

1 There is a need for a whole school policy.

2 Most successful experiences occur in schools where the SEN pupil is in a mainstream class with SEN support.

3 There is a need for differentiation of aims and objectives.

4 There is a need for joint training and agreement on mutual roles and support.

5 The tasks must be matched to pupils' learning needs.

6 Experience-based learning is to be preferred with a wide range of media and practical activities.

7 Good work can be expected if the pupil understands the nature of the task, what the end product is and how to reach it.

8 Good work is often seen in oral skills.

9 The range of resources must allow for a suitable match in content, readability and conceptual needs.

10 Good monitoring and recording of progress is needed to keep track of pupil progress.

In essence, many of these ideas apply to all classes. It will also be useful to refer to the chapter on behaviour and discipline (Chapter 6) as well as to the discussion on group work (pp. 34–41).

---

[1] *A Survey of Pupils with Special Needs in Ordinary Schools 1988–89.* DES, 1989

22 How to survive administration

Departmental meetings _____

For the department to run successfully, regular consultation is vital. It is to be hoped that informal consultation will take place in the staffroom and that such discussion will be lively and informed. It is also necessary to have a structure for staff meetings to make sure that all the staff are involved in the decision-making process, and that clear lines of communication are established from the department in all directions. It is well known that long rambling meetings 'after hours' are not liked and therefore it is important to see that all such meetings are businesslike and worthwhile. In order to to allow more time to discuss matters of real importance, it is a good idea to to deal with routine administrative details by circular and then mention them at the departmental meeting.

Good management is a skill that is vital in the complexities of today's schools. However, management does *not* mean carrying out a prescribed task in a prescribed way – it is a matter of strategies:

1 Setting aims and objectives.

2 Planning *how* a goal is to be reached.

3 Organising all resources (people, time and materials) so that the goals are achieved.

4 Controlling the process.

5 Setting organisational standards.

A meeting will be effective if it justifies the time spent in it and if the outcome can be acted upon to the benefit of all.

Meetings have several purposes:
● to take decisions
● to collect views to enable informed decisions to be made
● to brief people
● to exchange information
● to generate ideas (brainstorm)
● to investigate a problem.

It is important to be aware of these matters in order to be a good chairman and to conduct the meeting in a positive way. It will certainly earn the gratitude of staff at the end of a long day.

Running the meeting

The HoD should:

1   Have no more meetings than are necessary – but not too few either!

2   Publish the dates well in advance and ensure that those who need to be there are invited. (It may be relevant for the head or a deputy to be present for some or all of the meeting as a feeling of mutual understanding may be developed).

3   Publish a researched agenda.

4   Appoint someone to take the minutes (perhaps on a rota).

5   Circulate the minutes to the senior management as well as to members of the department.

6   Follow up all suggestions and ideas and report on progress.

7   Occasionally use the meeting for INSET. If the HoD knows a colleague in the school (or elsewhere) who has a particular expertise or has a relevant research interest, this could be the place to share the experience.

Administration

Very few heads of department receive training in the day-to-day management of paperwork and the mountain is growing higher everyday. As the National Curriculum becomes established, it is all the more important to be well organised. Much frustration can be avoided by attention to detail and the setting up of a routine. But one must not let setting up systems take over from the real task of running a team.

Now that many schools have computer management-systems, it will be worthwhile using any available software to streamline daily routines. Simple needs will be for word processing, databases and specialised systems (if easily available) for sorting marks, etc. Even a basic knowledge of word processing can speed up the production of minutes and agendas by saving a master template on disk and editing in dates and names for each occasion. Stock control can be helped by a simple computer card-like database, set lists can be produced by a filing system and, once produced, can be re-sorted for use in new set combinations another year. It is worth discussing such procedures with the computer coordinator or information technology centre if the LEA supports one.

A beginner's guide to systems would be as follows:

Checklist

- □ Have an 'in' tray and a 'pending' tray.
- □ Deal with matters as soon as possible and in strict order of priority.
- □ Keep 'file' copies of all important documents, marked with a coloured sticker stating 'File Copy'.
- □ Have separate files (real or computer – and if on disk with a backup copy) for the various areas of responsibility
  - a) entries, exam syllabuses, set-book lists, results, circulars from exam boards
  - b) internal assessments and examinations
  - c) schemes of work
  - d) stock and requisitions
  - e) pupil records
  - f) staff records and references
  - g) school policy documents
  - h) publishers' brochures
  - i) careers documents and HE/FE course materials and publicity
  - j) departmental minutes, agendas, etc.
- □ Make sure that all members of staff have copies of relevant documents.
- □ Discard materials that are out of date and be ruthless at least once a year.
- □ Specify action needed on departmental and other matters and ensure that staff know what they are to do. On a circulation list to be attached to documents two sections should be added: Action (specified), by whom (specified) and by when (specified).
- □ Tidy up each week – there's nothing like a tidy desk!
- □ File all documents as soon as possible to avoid loss.
- □ Have an agreed system for filing tapes and worksheets that is simple and understandable to all. If the HoD is the only person with the key (to filing cabinets as well as the key to the system) it won't work. It is important to make sure that the Number two also understands the system, and has access to it.

Delegation

The head of department cannot be expected to do everything in the complex organisation of today's schools – nor is it advisable to try. It would be particularly short-sighted in terms of administrative efficiency and also from the point of view of one of the most important roles of the head of department – that of assuring staff development.

Delegation of responsibility should lead to greater staff involvement and is good for individual morale even if the financial rewards are not so freely available as before. It is also wrong to assume that colleagues will always be with the school

251

and the HoD must look to their career development. As a middle manager, the head of department is a personnel manager as well. Nor must one assume that the head of department will be in the post for ever and it is therefore professionally prudent to plan for continuity. One of the worst scenarios will be when the 'key' person leaves, with those left only able to stumble along.

Delegation must therefore be seen as a healthy process and not as a threat to the head of department's position. But any tasks delegated must be *real* tasks and not merely thought up for the sake of it. Furthermore, it is a good idea to redefine and reallocate responsibilities from time to time: staff will then have a chance to taste a variety of experiences, both routine and clerical as well as creative. This mixture is important; simply dealing out routine tasks to others (however important) may be counterproductive if the HoD keeps all the more enjoyable jobs.

Particular schools will provide areas of personal initiative, for example, on a split site school, a second-in-charge may have day-to-day responsibility for a section of the buildings. When language staff have several languages to teach, particular responsibility for one of the languages may be devolved onto a particular teacher within the overall framework of the departmental strategy, with the final responsibility of the head of department answerable up the management structure to the head.

The following task list may help the HoD in formulating an individual plan:

In connection with particular year groups
- liaison with feeder schools
- examinations for a section/year group of the school
- arrangements for option-choice and guidance
- 'setting'

In connection with departmental resources
- care and maintenance of audio-visual aids
- stock and requisitions; review and inspection copies
- production, storage, filing , etc. of home-made materials
- displays in the language area and beyond

In connection with administration
- external examination entries
- oral/practical examination arrangements
- agendas and minutes
- oversight of assessment/records of achievement

General
- visits, exchanges, penfriends, bids for funding to bodies such as *Lingua*
- The language club
- careers information

- library; suggestions for books, the staff library
- students working in the department.

Delegation will only lighten the administrative load if properly planned. Too often we hear the complaint 'I could have done it better myself', when all that was needed was proper discussion beforehand.

The departmental diary

An invaluable tool for efficiency will be the academic year diary. At the first opportunity, the important deadlines of the school year should be entered. (Highlighter pens of various colours are a good idea.) Events to include are:

- external examination dates, including entry dates, deadlines for course work submissions, etc.
- internal assessment dates
- pupil report dates
- parent/teacher consultations
- requisitions
- major staff and departmental meetings
- university and college open days
- sports days
- holidays (not just to anticipate the relief from pressure, but because holidays do vary from year to year and thus affect the cycle of work to be done. Easter is the most difficult break to predict and can come in the middle of final examination preparation.).

Even if all the ideas suggested in this chapter are put into practice, things may still go wrong on occasions. Help *within* school will probably be largely administrative, but help in terms of subject expertise is also required and can usually be found without much difficulty.

What to do if things go wrong

Within the school, it is helpful to be honest and open with the senior management team, discussing problems as they arise in an atmosphere of trust. If there is a need to go beyond the school, there are several avenues to explore and individuals who can help in different ways.

The language adviser/advisory teacher

The roles may vary from area to area, but there are a number of functions which they fulfil. Giving advice is of prime importance and so it is important to make friends with the advisers in the area: both the subject specialist and the general adviser assigned to the school. In most authorities there is an information bulletin sent to all schools giving information about the services offered and courses available. There is sometimes a language-specific information bulletin.

The adviser can help in four main ways:

1 By individual visits to schools to discuss particular problems and ideas.

2 By organising courses and workshops on topics of interest. Attendance at such meetings is always valuable, not only for the topics and ideas discussed but also for the opportunity afforded to meet colleagues from other establishments.

3 By providing help in the classroom for the development of particular ideas and strategies.

4 By being the link between individual schools and any other agencies which may be able to help solve the problem.

The teachers' centre

Most authorities maintain a teachers' centre within the LEA area, and facilities will probably include a library, resources area (films, videos, tapes, cassettes, computer software, etc.), exhibition area, reprographic facilities and perhaps a recording studio. But above all it provides rooms for meetings. The personnel will have the job of keeping teachers informed on a variety of matters and their collective expertise can be used most profitably.

The examination boards

Questions about external examinations can be addressed to the various boards – they all keep research and development units and produce various publications of interest as well as their various examiners' reports. See address section.

Information services of foreign countries

A lot of use can be made of these services and a list can be found in Part Four. There are many countries in the other parts of the world, Eastern Europe and beyond, who speak the language being studied. For example, some 45 countries belong to the French-speaking world which is known as *Francophonie* and all welcome enquiries. It is important to remember that language teaching should not be confined to the 'traditional' European countries.

Three invaluable organisations for the teacher are the Association for Language Learning (ALL), the Centre for Information on Language Teaching and Research (CILT) and the Central Bureau for Educational Visits and Exchanges (CBEVE). For further details see Chapter 27.

PART THREE

Beyond the school

23 School links, penfriends and exchanges

Links

There are many ways of organising a school link and one of the most useful and effective ways is to build a scheme into the local town twinning arrangement. Anyone who is unsure about twinning arrangements or who is considering trying to persuade local councillors to investigate possibilities should first obtain details on procedure from:

The Joint Twinning Committee, 65 Davies Street, London, W1Y 2AA.

This body was set up by the local authority associations, the British Council and the Central Bureau for Educational Visits and Exchanges. The secretariat publishes a twice yearly *Twinning News,* which is distributed free to local authorities. It contains ideas based on reports of successful local twin-town events and also lists towns in many countries seeking to establish links with a British town.

The CBEVE also distributes a very useful publication at least twice a year – *Schools Unit News.* This carries reports on projects, links and materials, as well as guidelines for links and exchanges. A most useful appendix is the list of individual schools in other countries seeking UK links. For details contact the CBEVE (address and telephone number in Part Four).

Penfriends

Once a link with a school is established, it is then the stimulating task of someone in the modern language department to organise the development of correspondence between pupils. The failure rate is high for many reasons, but the successes make the enterprise worthwhile and no one ever loses by it. Nevertheless it does take active staff participation to ensure even a moderate rate of success for a penfriend scheme. The staff themselves need good correspondents on both sides to pass on messages that X has not yet replied to Y's letter this term. It could be just too much in a busy term, but with encouragement and an active teacher it is worthwhile. It does help if the teacher gives encouragement especially when the pupil asks 'What shall I write about?'

Some schools have found that the scheme works better if it is done as a class activity or group effort with the teacher taking the initiative. With this sort of scheme no individual pupil is heavily committed because it is only in the later stages that links between individuals begin. Initially it is often a letter contributed to by the whole class that goes off to the foreign school with a small parcel of photos and other *realia*. After a while the teacher can exchange tapes of interviews, talks about school events, maybe talks from the radio and other news items, adverts, pop songs and so on. Nowadays even a video can be sent, though one needs to be aware that the French and English video systems are not totally compatible and recordings turn out in black and white only. From this point anything becomes possible, and individual links arise naturally from the class link. Both links can continue side by side and the whole process can be even more exciting if exchange visits are made (see later). Barry Jones has described some fascinating exchanges of parcels between schools – swapping rubbish even – which give a valuable insight into the everyday life of pupils. (See Barry Jones (ed.) *Using Authentic Resources in Teaching French*.)

Electronic penfriends

Electronic mail (Email) enables people to communicate across frontiers by using communications software on a computer linked to a telephone by a modem. Information can then be sent to an electronic mailbox to be read at the convenience of the recipient.

By working through a word processor, saving the work to disk and sending it at off-peak times, communication is easy. To use Email, you need to subscribe to the Campus 2000 system and it offers vast possibilities to access authentic material.

The importance of Email is such that it is recognised by its inclusion in the National Curriculum for IT and clearly this requirement could be fulfilled by the modern language curriculum.

More imaginative projects are possible with Email and there are ideas being tested such as the production of international 'newspapers' and such like.

Exchanges

Once a good link is established, the teacher can think seriously about an extension to include a pupil-to-pupil (home-to-home) exchange. A private scheme between two schools means that everything can be tailor-made to suit local conditions. Sometimes such a scheme is run on a larger scale involving a number of schools on both sides. There are several advantages in this – cheaper fares, simpler arrangements and more likelihood of pairing off every pupil who wishes to take part. The disadvantage can be that it is more impersonal, but this is soon overcome as pupils are put into contact with each other. In any case the establishment of an exchange scheme should be seen as a landmark and an enriching experience for all concerned.

Who goes?

Not every pupil is ready to take part in an exchange at the same time. Before there can be any hope of success, teachers should look carefully at the applicants and decide whether their language has reached 'survival' level and whether they are sufficiently mature to cope with a separation from home for a two- or three- week period. Experience has shown that the most vulnerable are girls under the age of 15 who are quiet, even withdrawn at home and amongst friends. They often show very little curiosity about their surroundings in the foreign home. Teachers who feel that they have a pupil who falls into this category should beware of thinking that a fortnight away is just what is needed. It could be a very miserable two weeks for all concerned. The trouble is that once back home this kind of pupil tends to lay the blame for the failure at anyone's door and this can have a disastrous effect on other exchanges. Far better then, to suggest that the pupil waits another year until a suitable partner can be found. An exchange which confirms prejudices, strengthens insularity and undermines self-confidence does far more harm than good.

Preparation for an exchange

For an exchange to stand a chance of success, some careful preparation of the participants is needed. Such an exercise falls into three categories:

1   Fostering the right attitude.

2   Providing the necessary survival language.

3   Familiarising the pupil with the region to be visited.

The right attitude

All pupils are bound to have some misgivings about going to live with an unknown family and it is sensible to recognise this even with the supposed sophistication of today's teenagers. It is a good thing to stress that it is a short visit and that it is exciting. The most important single quality the teacher should stress is curiosity. It will in fact help if all participants are given a list of things to find out. It will give them something to talk about in the early days when relationships are being established. The list can cover every aspect of daily life – how much a *baguette* costs, what time the TV news is on, how much it costs to post a letter, what the family cat or dog is called. One tried method is a list of questions in the target language which can be discussed by visitor and host.

It is also reasonable to point out to pupils that they can occasionally feel homesick. It is normal and will pass and they can expect their partner to have a similar experience in Britain.

Finally, it is most important that pupils go abroad with the right attitude to foreign customs and manners, i.e. they are not better or worse but different. Unless this is clearly put the teacher runs the risk of strengthening prejudices and of undoing anything good that might otherwise come of the exchange.

Survival language

We do not suggest here that extra lessons will be called for, especially as such communicative language is now the stock in trade of all courses. But the teacher does need to ensure that all exchangees have the minimum *bagage linguistique* to handle the most basic situations. The foreign assistant can be of immense use here. Without this basic provision, the pupil runs the risk of being considered uncouth, ill-mannered and uncooperative and that is when the trouble starts. The simplest way is to equip every pupil with a basic word list containing all the appropriate conversational lubricants: 'I don't understand'; 'What do you mean?'; 'Will you say that again please'; 'I am not well'; 'I enjoyed the visit to . . .'. In addition attention should be given to body language – the importance of shaking hands, kissing – and to the ordinary polite phrases such as saying good morning and goodnight to everyone.

Knowing the region to be visited

It would be wonderful if a detailed regional study could be undertaken by every-one. It is not always possible but some fruitful cross-curricular work could be undertaken. At least organise a display of maps, photographs and *realia* from the area prior to the visit.

Charges for school visits

Since the introduction in the 1988 Education Reform Act of new regulations for charging, it is vital that teachers update themselves on the regulations for school visits and the need to monitor parental contributions. As the position is in a state of flux, with the regulations not entirely clear, it is wise to seek advice. Full details of the latest position are available from the LEAs or the Central Bureau.

24 How to organise a foreign visit

If the teacher is to bring the learning of a foreign language alive, then it must be obvious that the visit abroad is essential and as such will be part of the work of the modern language department. Such trips can be very varied, ranging from the one-day 'Boulogne Flyer' to the exchange visit lasting several weeks. All have their own merits and the attractions of the exchange have been fully developed in Chapter 23.

The shorter visits have attractions for the younger pupil, particularly as a taster to complement the work done in the confines of the classroom. On the other hand, it is better to reserve the extended exchange for the more mature youngster who is better able to cope with longer periods from home both from the point of view of the personality as well as linguistic maturity.

These days it is possible to participate in all kinds of visits – ranging from the traditional week away to specialised visits for the school football teams and other groups. But all have one thing in common – the need for meticulous planning before departure. Taking a group abroad is a great privilege as well as an enormous responsibility from the educational, organisational and legal points of view and should not be undertaken lightly and particularly should not be the sole responsibility of the first-year teacher.

A particular problem is charging and it is imperative to obtain the latest guidelines. If a reputable school-tours firm is used, they will certainly have the relevant information. It is also wise to seek advice on this matter when writing the invitations to participate as the terminology used can affect the legal position in respect of charging for activities deemed to take place in school time. If in doubt, the latest professional opinion should be sought.

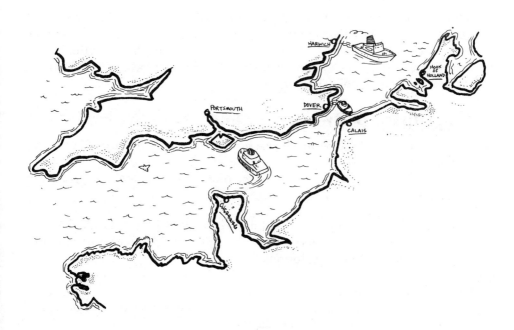

Planning

The following are the major steps in planning a school visit abroad.

The first steps

Teachers should:

1   Obtain the permission of the head and governors *and* if necessary of the LEA.

2   Ask their colleagues to join them. It is important to make sure there is correct ratio of men:women for the party. It is worth checking on the staff:pupil ratio required – it may differ for different sorts of activities or the age of the children. For visits abroad it will be a minimum of at least two staff for up to 20 pupils and one teacher for every ten thereafter, subject to having a member of staff of each sex if it is a mixed party.

3   Scrutinise carefully the brochures sent by the tour operator and read the small print.

4   Choose carefully the centre and the dates. Is the museum the teacher wishes to visit open at that time? Is the activity specified available for the period required? Has the teacher an indication of the quality of accommodation on offer? Are basic rules such as fire precautions in force?

5   Obtain a quotation **in writing**, making sure that they know what the quoted price includes and what is extra. Is insurance included? Are the excursions extra? What meals are included? Is packed lunch available if required? How many 'free' staff places are included? Does the price include travel from school or another starting point, such as a port?

Making up the party

1   The teacher should decide which year groups are eligible to participate. There are arguments for keeping the age groups to two year groups, making for greater homogeneity of interest. On the other hand, a wider age group can make the party easier to handle.

2   It is important to let all eligible pupils have a letter setting out the details – place, dates and cost. Parents should be invited to reply by means of a tear-off slip which has the following formula:

I wish my son/daughter .... of
form .... to be considered for the school visit
to Germany during the Easter holidays 199 .
Signed..   Date...

Teachers are thus not obliged to accept all applicants if they or other staff feel that it is not appropriate. Full and precise details of the purposes of the visit should be available to parents before they commit themselves by sending any money. In particular, there should be clear guidelines on the behaviour expected, the nature of the supervision and details on such problem areas as free time.

Choosing the members of the party

To some extent this depends on the nature of the visit and the purpose. It is important to consult as widely as possible. Excluding children is very difficult and not to be done lightly but if there are likely to be problems for whatever reason it is wise to consult the head. Remember that if there are problems abroad, it is the teacher who eventually has to sort them out. It may be wise to exclude any pupil whose behaviour in school gives rise to concern.

It is essential to have a reserve list in addition to the list of selected pupils, particularly if there is a minimum number stipulated by the tour company. Once the selection has been made, write to all the families with the following details:

Information checklist

- ☐ Departure date and time
- ☐ Return date and time
- ☐ Total cost and details of what the cost covers
- ☐ Request for a deposit (and if it is non-returnable, say so)
- ☐ Dates when further payments should be made and where to; dates for final payment
- ☐ Undertaking that parents know that participation is voluntary and that payment is by contribution
- ☐ Tear-off acceptance/medical slip on the following lines:

I agree to my son/daughter..........................taking part in the school visit to Germany from............to............ . I also agree to make full payment by .... I declare that there is no known medical condition to prevent full participation in all activities. (Any relevant medical information must be disclosed prior to acceptance.)

Signed .... Date...

This does not mean that one should exclude a pupil with a known medical condition, but rather that the parents should inform the group leader.

Managing the finances _____

The teacher should consult the head or the bursar to ascertain if there are special arrangements in force in the LEA concerning the financial aspects of running school visits. It may be that the place for such funds is an account within the normal accounting system of the school funds. If not then the teacher should:

1   Open a bank account called the 'X School German Visit Account' (for example), making sure that there are at least two signatories. Some banks may allow the account to be a deposit account thereby earning interest which can go towards the expenses.

2   Make arrangements for the participants to pay by instalments but be careful to make it known that money will be accepted only on fixed days and in a fixed place. Money should not be accepted casually on the corridor and certainly not without making an entry in the cash book and in the pupil's payment book. It is all too easy to get into a mess without simple rules like that.

3   Insist that final payment is made at least ten days before the final payment is due to be made to the tour operator.

4   Quote a price slightly above the actual cost for emergencies and the unused part can be refunded at the end of the holiday. Any interest from a deposit account can also serve in this way.

5   Make arrangements for pocket money. This is a difficult question but the age of the participants may well decide the question. It is certainly wise to stipulate the maximum amount a pupil can take and to suggest in what form it can be taken (notes, travellers cheques). For younger groups it is possibly better for the teacher to dole out the money in daily instalments to prevent the all too frequent case of the pupil who, not realising the value of the strange looking coins, spends it all within three hours of landing on foreign soil. Perhaps an agreement might be made at the previsit parents' meeting.

Preparation for the holiday

Although a holiday, the visit should be a holiday with a difference. The aim will be educational, but not restricting. Parents (and pupils!) will want to get good value for money and so good preparation is called for. It is an idea to hold regular meetings according to the nature of the adventure. Various facets of the visit should be explored in a way which stresses the holiday aspect as well as the educational value of the tour. If the group is going to Berlin for example, then there could be some input about the historical, geographical and political significance of the city. This will vary according to the composition of the group. Help should also be given with the linguistic aspects of the holiday – and the pupils made aware of at least the basic survival language.

It is also a good idea to have some sort of workbook or project for the pupils. Some tour operators provide such material but it is better in the end for teachers to use their own imagination and suit the material to the group's aims. A prize at the end is a good incentive!

It is important to involve the pupils in the preparations by asking them to write to the tourist offices for maps and guide books, brochures and information, and/or by mounting an exhibition in school about the area to be visited, using posters, maps, slides, etc. (The geography department may be able to help.)

Just before going, the teacher should have a meeting for parents and pupils to explain the final details such as the amount of luggage required, labels, the need for packed lunches for the journey, etc. Parents should be given an opportunity to ask questions and it is important to engage their cooperation on the topic of behaviour.

The teacher could also prepare a tour brochure for all the participants. It should contain at least the following information:

Checklist

- ☐ List of participants
- ☐ Map of the journey and sketch map of the area to be visited
- ☐ Address of the hotel, centre or hostel
- ☐ Telephone numbers with international dialling codes
- ☐ Details of itinerary
- ☐ Daily programme of excursions and events
- ☐ Basic rules of behaviour, meal times, bed times, etc.
- ☐ Basic expressions in the target language for directions, shopping, etc.
- ☐ Comparisons of distances and money values
- ☐ Appropriate details of history, geography and culture according to the nature of the holiday and the ages of the pupils
- ☐ The holiday quiz and project.

Finally, the teacher should leave with parents and also the school details such as addresses and telephone numbers for emergency contacts.

Official forms and documentation

Passports
If a collective passport is decided upon, early application is necessary to the passport office appropriate to where the teacher lives. Applications should be made as soon as the final lists are drawn up. In particular, early application is necessary if the party contains pupils whose parents were not born in the United Kingdom. The complicated procedures are explained on the application forms and

these must be followed precisely. In case of difficulties, advice should be obtained as soon as possible from the passport office. Foreign nationals and those of other Commonwealth countries cannot be included in a collective passport unless they also have United Kingdom citizenship. It is known that it takes at least four to five weeks to process documents and so it is advisable to make the arrangements early. Full details about the latest position in respect of passports can be obtained from: The Passport Office, Clive House, 70 Petty France, London SW1H 9HD.

If pupils are to have individual passports, it is essential to make sure that they obtain them in good time. The teacher should have a physical check that they have them on departure and at various times in the course of the holiday. Some countries accept visitors' passports – again this should be checked carefully as they are cheaper.

Insurance

It is vital that the party is adequately insured, in particular if it is liable to be taking part in dangerous activities such as skiing. Insurance will usually be arranged by the tour firm. Even so, it is worth reading the small print carefully. If teachers are in charge of this aspect of the visit, they should make sure that they are covered for accident, illness, injury, third-party liability and loss of luggage. The local office of the national insurance companies will supply details and there are special rates for parties. Alternatively the LEA may have a master policy where it has been able to negotiate special rates. Whatever the case, the teacher should *never* go away without adequate insurance. In the case of skiing and such like activities where the danger is greater, the insurance should cover all eventualities.

Sickness insurance

Now that the UK is part of the European Community, it is advisable to contact the local office of the Department of Social Security to obtain a European claim form (E111). This should be obtained for each family and filled in by the person paying social insurance in the family (usually a parent); this enables medical treatment costs abroad to be refunded.

Credentials

It is a good idea to obtain from the school a statement from the head, on official notepaper, saying that you are a bona fide school party. By showing this to officials it is possible to obtain free entry or reduced fees when visiting museums, etc. Make sure that it is written in the target language.

The journey

1 The pupils should be put into groups of no more than ten, in the charge of a member of staff. When checking in at ports and stations it will simplify matters and spotting the missing pupil will be easier.

2 Each teacher should be provided with a register, divided into groups. It is essential to take regular roll calls. It is all too easy to lose someone!

3 When using trains and boats, the teacher should decide firmly on a place and time for meeting before the party breaks up.

At the centre

The teacher should:

1 Make sure that ALL members of the party know the fire drill, the emergency exits, etc.

2 Explain the routine and programme for each day.

3 Never leave the pupils unattended in the hotel or on walks. This is especially important in the evenings. A staff rota and some activities for pupils should be arranged.

4 Insist that pupils do not wander around on their own, especially after dark. The teacher is responsible!

Returning home

The teacher should:

1 Warn pupils about going through customs. Duty free goods are not allowed for pupils under 17.

2 Arrange a parents' evening to show slides and finished projects.

3 Take steps to see that all accounts are audited and wound up.

A do-it-yourself trip abroad

Today a large number of schools have their own minibus and it is perfectly possible to arrange a school holiday abroad using the school's own transport. This is particularly convenient when taking the football team on a 'European Tour' or when taking the upper-sixth French class to Paris or for a week to the twin school. The preparations will more or less mirror those in this chapter but, in addition, there will be some important matters to deal with in connection with the vehicle and the drivers. Overall it must be realised that there are restrictions on driver age and experience and the rules are those applying to foreign coach travel.

1 It is advisable (and for longer distances essential) to have two drivers.

2 Correct insurance should be obtained for the vehicle (the Green Card).

3 Written permission should be obtained from the vehicle's legal owner to take the vehicle abroad.

4 From the motoring organisations, insurance should be taken out to cover breakdown, vehicle repatriation, etc. This is usually negotiated in a package according to the size of the vehicle.

5 It is important to make sure that the teacher takes the documentation, e.g. the log book.

6 The teacher should check up on the permitted hours of driving and the tachograph regulations (the motoring organisations have full details). For travel abroad a waybill will also be needed. Details can be obtained from the local traffic commissioners or the LEA.

7 The sea crossing should be booked in good time. There are often special terms for minibuses.

8 The journey should be planned with plenty of spare time. The drivers should not be taxed with the risk of accidents.

By taking on this responsibility, especially with small groups where a full coach load is not possible, the teacher can save money, though there is extra work involved.

Special note about safety _____

In recent years there has been a great debate about the safety of pupils taking part in school activities such as visits abroad. It is absolutely essential that safety considerations are paramount in the teacher's planning. The following points should help:

Common factors in accidents

- lack of control
- lack of discipline
- lack of self-discipline
- lack of common sense
- lack of reasonable behaviour.

Parents must be told of the standards the teacher expects and if they cannot agree with you, then there should be no question of accepting such a pupil.

Staffing ratio

This must take into account the needs of staff (e.g. that at some time a 'breather' for individuals is allowable – a cup of coffee for all staff at the same time can mean unsupervised pupils). Also vital is a staff ratio that is adequate to enable teachers to be *in loco parentis*. The longer the duration of the visit the more staff will be needed to provide adequate supervision. At the parents' meeting before the trip is finalised, there must be a proper explanation of the activities that the pupils will engage in – there should be no surprises such that risks are undertaken without parental knowledge. If skiing and such activities form part of the holiday, the staff should at least have the minimum qualifications demanded by the LEA.

Foreign laws

The teacher should beware that foreign laws are different and can cause problems. This is especially so in the case of minibus driving and other activities which may give rise to third party or public liability claims.

Help can be obtained from the professional unions. All unions issue advice to members and some unions have issued booklets to help.

Checklist for planning

- ☐ Has the activity a clear educational purpose?
- ☐ Is the activity suited to the age, aptitude and experience of the pupils?
- ☐ Is the planning and preparation satisfactory?
- ☐ If the visit involves an outside agency and/or premises, are they of an acceptable standard?
- ☐ Are the staff numbers adequate? Are they suitably qualified?
- ☐ Is there adequate supervision for the whole duration of the visit?
- ☐ Has adequate insurance cover been taken out?
- ☐ Have adequate procedures, including channels of communication in case of emergency, been set up?
- ☐ Is full approval given?
- ☐ Has parental consent been obtained?
- ☐ Is the LEA fully in agreement?

25 Cooperating with parents

Parent power is increasing and will continue to do so. That is a good thing for, if parents and staff can work together more closely, the children they are interested in can do nothing but benefit.

It goes without saying that parents are the original VIPs of this world. Without them there would be no schools and hence no teachers. In short, teachers need them around and should welcome their close cooperation and involvement. And, let it be understood, even if teachers do not want parents around they are going to get them for, on the new governing bodies of schools, parents have much more than the token presence that they used to have. Indeed, with the increased powers and responsibilities of governing bodies there will be a great deal of outside influence on the curriculum that is offered in schools.

Language teachers need to give some thought to this, for not every parent is convinced of the value of language learning in spite of the higher profile it enjoys in this decade. Too many, in fact, are living proof of the lack of success of earlier generations of teachers now perhaps writing out their verb conjugations on the great blackboard in the sky. To many parents still, the aims, objectives and methods of today's teaching are a mystery. Teachers will still have to convince such parents that modern languages as a school subject has a clear and attainable aim. Many parents will have to be convinced that four or more periods per week spent learning a foreign language is a worthwhile occupation when most people abroad speak English.

The sorts of arguments that teachers will need have already been referred to in Chapter 11. Here suggestions are made for strategy which, in the first place, will ensure that the teacher does a professional job and which, in addition, will convince parents of the validity of modern language teachers' claims that they have a great deal to offer children in their special subject. In other words, it is vital to have parental backing, especially as a modern language is now a compulsory part of the National Curriculum arrangements. If the parents support what the teacher does there is a very good chance of success. The following points will contribute to the understanding between parents and language teachers.

1   It is important to stress at all times to pupils that teachers and parents work together to help them as much as they can. It will, therefore, pay teachers not to play into the hand of pupils who from time immemorial have enjoyed exaggerating school teachers' eccentricities with the consequent alienation of parental sympathies.

2   The need to involve parents when the department is on show has already been emphasised (Chapter 14). Open days and open evenings are the ideal time to

demonstrate the value and the success of the work of the department in as lively and as relevant a way as possible.

3 On parents' evenings when they attend to discuss their children's progress, it is important to convince them of the department's efficiency. Teachers should make sure they have up-to-date mark books and notes on pupils who are having particular difficulties.

They should also avoid slip-ups such as talking about a pupil to the wrong parents. They should check if there are two with similar surnames. A check beforehand with the form tutor about particular circumstances will avoid embarrassing remarks.

It is vital to let the parents see that the teacher really knows the child well. Parental confidence increases enormously.

4 When it is necessary to complain about a child (for bad work or un-cooperative behaviour) it is good practice to make sure that the parent is sympathetic to the teacher by, first of all, speaking of the child's good qualities (there will always be some!). They may then go on 'However . . .' When such criticism is necessary, then it is important that the teacher has some kind of remedy to propose, some positive help which will need parental backing. Most parents will cooperate.

5 It is important to avoid making open accusations against a pupil. If there is suspicion of truancy a naïve comment about absence may well bring out the truth almost by accident. Parent and teacher can then cooperate to the child's good. In this respect, the teacher must have evidence to back up any statement. If there is a detailed record of attendance, it is easier to check.

6 Discussions between parents and teachers are professional duties that, on occasions, verge on the confidential. Teachers should show parents that they can have confidence in the teacher and that there is no danger of the child being discussed with another parent. This can easily happen if a parent starts to complain about the influence of X in the same form. Teachers must make it quite clear that they do not discuss other people's children, nor do they talk about their own affairs and still less about colleagues on the staff.

7 If, in the course of a five-minute interview on a parents' evening, a substantial issue emerges, for example, an accusation of incompetence or worse, the teacher should rapidly bring the conversation to a close and insist on an interview being arranged for a later date at which some senior colleague can be present. It is unprofessional and time-consuming to get into an argument at what is essentially a public session.

8 Parents will occasionally criticise school policy. Teachers should bear in mind

that this is not the time to seek allies, and that the best thing to do is to state what the school policy is and advise the parent to approach the head or deputy head or parent-governor if he or she wishes to make an issue of the matter.

9   Most teachers want to see parents going home satisfied at the end of an evening, but they must beware of making promises that they cannot keep if the circumstances change. So they should say 'I hope she will get a grade A or B in her GCSE next year' and not 'I will see that she gets a grade A'.

10 Even if children are weak at languages, the teacher must avoid giving the impression that they are some kind of pariah. In fact it is a good thing to find out which areas of the curriculum are the ones they do best in, for the teacher who begins 'I wish I could say that her German is as good as . . .' has already obtained a sympathetic hearing.

11 Even on ordinary parents' evenings, it is a good idea to put out some evidence of the department's work – a few posters, examples of pupils' work, adverts for the next exchange or evidence of the last trip abroad. All can make a positive impression.

12 For meetings with new or prospective parents, this display will be very important, together with a short handout on the work and aims of the department. Good advertising is always positive.

13 For open evenings and parents' evenings, it is occasionally possible to run a ten-minute beginners' class or taster lesson, in Spanish or German. Letting the parents see the teacher in action is to convince them of the quality of the contribution that modern languages can make to the well-being of their child.

14 In the past, teachers have failed to make enough of parental expertise, an area that all teachers would do well to explore. Teachers of languages would be particularly well advised to seize the opportunity of inviting a parent to describe his or her experiences in the world of work here and abroad, especially if languages are involved.

26   Careers for linguists

The creation of the European Community has opened the door to modern languages, especially in the world of commerce and industry. The completion of the Channel Tunnel is of almost equal importance and so, while the teacher cannot offer a wide choice of careers for the pure linguist, in almost every case, skill in foreign languages can be seen to be an adjunct, highly desirable perhaps, but still an ancillary skill to the one that earns our living. In other words, teachers should be telling their pupils that if they wish to use their languages in a career they must at some time acquire other marketable skills as well.

A second important point that teachers should make plain at school level is that, when it comes to the lesser known languages, there are increasingly more and more openings, especially as the European Community expands and as contacts with the Middle and Far East grow. So there is likely to be a bigger demand for Greek, Arabic, Chinese and Japanese. These ideas should be presented to sixth-formers before they fill out their UCCA and PCAS forms. The great advantage is that these more 'exotic' languages are often available in *ab initio* courses in higher education, alongside starter courses in French, German, Italian, Dutch and so on. Teachers should also ensure, as the National Curriculum recommends, that language courses in school equip pupils with the linguistic tools to enable them to acquire new languages later in life as the need arises.

Career possibilities

This is just a selection. Teachers should be encouraged to liaise with careers staff in order to give an up-to-date picture to pupils.

Translating

There are very few such posts in firms. Most translators work through agencies who normally expect translations to be done into the mother tongue. To stand a chance, one needs a range of languages, at least one 'exotic' language and a good knowledge of certain specialisations – the textile industry, medicine, the law or commercial practice. In other words, most translation work is technical and translators need to understand what they are talking about. Translating literary work is much more limited and much of it is done freelance. Publishers often have their contacts and seldom buy a translation from an unknown source.

Employment for translators is to be found in international organisations (United Nations, EC, etc.) and in the civil service. In commerce there are possibilities for linguists with high-level office skills, for example, a postgraduate diploma. Such people tend to become personal assistants who can use their languages as they are needed, very often in a social setting rather than in a more technical area.

Interpreting

Much of what was said above applies to interpreting – except that there are even fewer openings. Conference interpreting is a highly skilled job and few are required. Other organisations which are dependent on staff being able to translate usually require staff to undertake many duties, for example, air hostesses, airport staff, travel agents, couriers and hotel staff.

Teaching

Nowadays entrants to the profession are advised to have at least two languages that they are able to teach to a high level. As the National Curriculum comes onto stream in schools, there will be a growing demand for language teachers. This is one job where skill as a linguist is the main qualification though teachers will need to point out to pupils that, if they consider this profession, other personal qualities are needed to be successful. One other possibility for the language graduate is to take an additional TEFL qualification and seek a teaching post abroad. As the regulations for a post-1992 Europe take effect, there is likely to be growing competition for language specialists.

Commerce and trade

The so-called bilingual secretary has been referred to above. Skills in foreign keyboard skills are essential as well as good interpersonal and telephone skills.

Language graduates are taken in by firms dependent on exports but such graduates are not necessarily taken on to sell products abroad. They may be placed on a managerial course within the company. Much selling abroad is carried out by agents resident in the country concerned. They are often native speakers. Many more openings are now available as commerce becomes more international and firms such as accountants and investment and insurance companies have strong links abroad and may require linguistic skills of their employees.

Broadcasting

There are external and monitoring services. The actual broadcasting in the foreign language is almost always done by the native speaker in the language sections. In addition to the linguistic knowledge, candidates have to be able to show familiarity with the social and political institutions of the country concerned and have a good microphone voice.

Monitoring requires first-rate comprehension ability of at least one language, good English, ability to condense and basic office skills. There is a test for applicants involving translating, listening and general knowledge. The monitoring service is at Caversham Park, Reading.

Travel agents, couriers, tourism

Again, much local work is carried on by native speakers in the country. Nevertheless, there is a small demand for representatives to negotiate terms with foreign hotels and so on. Couriers, in the main, are in contact with the English customer. Airports have information staff, and cabin staff (male and female) are needed by most airlines. The languages needed will be relevant to the routes they fly. Airlines tend to recruit from their own native speakers. Hotels need receptionists who speak several languages but again languages are an ancillary skill. Some chains are international and so there are possibilities for work abroad. The telephone services recruit some language speakers for their international service.

Librarianship

For this career, the linguist will need to take appropriate postgraduate qualifications in librarianship. An alternative route offered by some polytechnics is to follow a BA course in librarianship and a language may be offered as part of the course. There are public libraries (probably little scope to employ linguists), academic libraries where the librarian may become a subject specialist and scientific and technical libraries where knowledge of a science is paramount.

International banking and financial services

There are increased openings here, but the linguist must be prepared to undergo additional training. Some financial institutions will sponsor hand-picked candidates through university but it is the mathematicians who are likely to be chosen for such sponsorship. Personal qualities count for a great deal. With the increasing influence of the EC, British banks are operating more positively abroad and foreign banks can be seen in British cities. It is certain that this trend will increase in the future.

Manufacturing and service industries

It is a sad fact that as a nation the British are generally quite slow to realise the advantage of fluency in foreign languages in employees. However, even if companies are not prepared to pay a bonus for language fluency, there is some evidence that things are changing. Gradually, even in a world of technological change and easy communications via FAX machines and satellites, the human contact promoted when the telephonist can answer a call in another language is seen as an advantage. Perhaps for the ordinary worker, the ability to strike up warm relationships with a foreign client or potential trading partner is just as important as fluency in a specialised and technical sphere. Perhaps this social and interpersonal dimension should be positively stressed.

Helping the student in the new Europe

It is now increasingly common to see foreign and multinational firms in the annual recruiting markets held at British universities. The theory at least is that all professional qualifications are valid in all member states within the EC. But the best way in is to seize opportunities with multinational companies for whom the barriers are coming down. Language may still cause problems, but many companies are taking this on themselves with training for languages on in-house courses. The EC directive means that each country must recognise the professional qualifications of other member states, but it does not guarantee employment. Nor will it be easy for the professional operating in the foreign country to attract clients easily. Cultural difficulties are sometimes to blame for this nonacceptance.

If the student has had language-learning experience at school, it will be easier to adapt to new needs as careers take shape, and many centres of further and higher education work with commercial companies to provide crash courses as the companies need them.

For further information contact:

CILT, Regent's College, Inner Circle, Regent's Park, London, NW1 4NS;

Institute of Linguists, 24a Highbury Grove, London, N5 2EA.

Other useful contacts include:

Civil Service Commission, Alençon Link, Basingstoke, Hants, RG21 1JB;

The Recruitment Unit, The European Commission, 200 Rue de la Loi, Brussels, 1049, Belgium;

The European Staffing Unit, Cabinet Office, Horse Guards Road, London SW1 3AL;

The UK Committee for the College of Europe, King's College, London, Strand, London, WC2R 2LS.

Gathering careers material

What can the department do to provide appropriate information to pupils and parents? It is as usual a good idea to involve all staff but to delegate particular responsibility to a colleague to coordinate the departmental effort in this direction. Below are some ideas which can be put into operation without too much difficulty.

1   As is often necessary in teaching – the teacher should *be a magpie!*

2   From newspapers, trade journals, magazines and handouts, it is worth collecting advertisements for jobs which directly or indirectly call for foreign language skills. These can be filed for staff or pupil use or mounted in a display for the classroom or for careers meetings.

3   The teacher should collect advertising literature of all sorts, even from the most unlikely places, with examples of foreign languages at work – Marks and Spencer labels, French sweet wrappings, foreign catalogues, advertisements from international editions of newspapers. (For example, there are weekly international job adverts in some English newspapers.) This can

indicate to pupils that high-street companies which are familiar to them have vital links and partners abroad.

As many brochures as possible should be collected from English/foreign tourist offices with bilingual/trilingual presentations. These can now be seen in many provincial towns and lesser known tourist areas as visitors venture out from the magnet of London. Languages can thus be seen as useful not only abroad but also on home territory

4 Past pupils should be invited to come back to school and talk about their experiences at work if they have any use for their languages in both white- and blue-collar posts.

5 The help of personnel departments of local companies should be enlisted. Not only should the teacher find out about openings for their students but also about the needs of industry in respect of languages and their training schedules. A two-way contribution to the debate can be beneficial.

6 Teachers should gather as many brochures and prospectuses as they can from all agencies involved in postschool education – universities, colleges, polytechnics, government training agencies, etc., including the Civil Service and national bodies such as the Post Office.

7 Outside speakers should be encouraged to address pupils and parents. Particularly important will be representatives from future training and education providers, as regulations and subject combinations are constantly being updated.

8 It is important to attend careers meetings/conventions whenever possible.

9   It is a good idea to adopt a local company – especially one with contacts abroad. Some schools are setting up work-experience courses abroad (for sixth-formers) in conjunction with local firms and these can be extremely positive. The Teacher Placement Service can help give staff experience in local industry and thus widen their horizons. There is now some emphasis placed on language links by this service.

10 The teacher could arrange a European evening or week in school and invite the local chamber of commerce to contribute.

Study after school

SCHML (the Standing Committee of Heads of Modern Languages in Polytechnics and other colleges) publishes a comprehensive guide to language courses and courses with a language element. It is a book which should be in every school library (see Bibliography).

It is as well to remember that many HE/FE courses in a wide range of subjects now feature an element of integral study abroad (via the ERASMUS scheme). This often can lead to a dual qualification (a degree/diploma in the UK and a foreign country), a fact which places the student in a good position for the new Europe.

27   What can the specialist organisations do for you?

There are a considerable number of organisations and bodies which provide help of various sorts for modern language teachers. They are certainly too numerous to deal with in detail in a volume of this size. There is a list of such organisations in Part Four. This section is therefore selective and not inclusive. We have attempted to outline some of the services provided by the best known bodies. If the answer to any query is not within the scope of these bodies, they will certainly help you to find the answer somewhere.

Some of the organisations mentioned are voluntary, in the best tradition of the British education service, others are official or semi-official. All are experts in some way or other. The order of appearance implies no hierarchy or favour – it is simply a choice made by the authors.

The subject-teaching associations

The Association for Language Learning

This Association came into being on 1 January 1990 as a result of the decision of the founding associations to merge and so form a united voice for language teachers and language learning.

The Association was formed by the amalgamation of all the former language associations, MLA, BALT, ATSP, ATI, ATR and ADULT. This new body brings together all the language interests in the country to enable them to speak with one voice. Members include teachers of modern languages in schools, colleges, polytechnics and universities as well as anyone else interested in languages in and beyond the education system.

The strength of the Association lies in its branches which provide a lively forum for members as well as a variety of activities for teachers and their pupils.

There is an on-going publishing programme. The main contact for members is the series of journals:

The Language Learning Journal A journal of general interest to language teachers. It is published twice a year in March and September and is a lively platform for methodology and linguistic as well as cultural interests.

There are, in addition, a series of language specific journals, also published twice a year (June and December): *Francophonie*; *German Teaching*; *Vida Hispanica*; *Tuttitalia*; *Rusistika*; and *Dutch Crossing*.

Full membership details are available from the Head Office, 16 Regent Place, Rugby, CV21 2PN. Tel. 0788-546443; FAX 0788-544149.

The annual course conference and exhibition bring together all that is best in language books, hardware and computers, as well as holding several days of talks, presentations, workshops and discussions. The conference is open to members only, so it is well worth joining in order to benefit. The exhibition is open to all and is always an eye-opener.

In addition to this main association which is open to teachers to join, there are other bodies, councils and congresses which do not accept individual members, but which are very important. They usually have representatives from specialised areas of interest and bring together views, opinions and ideas from a wide cross-section of the language world. These include:

Council of Subject-Teaching Associations (CoSTA); National Council for Modern Languages in Higher and Further Education (NCML); Standing Conference of Heads of Modern Languages in Polytechnics and other Colleges (SCHML); Fédération Internationale des Professeurs de Français (FIPF); Fédération Internationale des Professeurs de Langues Vivantes (FIPLV); Internationaler Deutschlehrerverband (IDV).

Other organisations in the United Kingdom of the utmost importance are:

The Central Bureau for Educational Visits and Exchanges (CBEVE)

The CBEVE has offices in London, Edinburgh and Belfast. It is a national agency responsible for the development of educational travel and exchanges with other countries and is under the auspices of various education departments in the British Isles. It operates schemes for pupils and young people and also some specifically for teachers and administrators.

For pupils and young people in general, it organises penfriends, home-to-home exchanges, work abroad, children's holiday camps abroad, language camps and twinning.

For teachers and administrators, it organises post to post exchanges from between three weeks to one year, short courses abroad, intensive study bursaries, reciprocal study visits and specialised study visits.

The third service run by the CBEVE is the Foreign Assistant Scheme. For state schools this is administered locally by the LEA in conjunction with the Bureau.

In addition there are various publications on all aspects of visits, exchanges and work abroad. Some of these are published annually and a full list can be obtained direct from the Bureau (see address section in Part Four). The CBEVE has also recently become responsible for the UK office of the 'Lingua' scheme for enhancing language work in the European Community.

Centre for Information on Language Teaching (CILT)

The centre aims to collect and coordinate information on all aspects of modern language teaching and also to disseminate this information to individuals and organisations in the United Kingdom. The centre publishes a vast range of lists, catalogues and digests on all aspects of teaching and learning. It maintains a library which has a unique collection of over 25 000 titles and in addition is a repository of well over 1000 samples of language courses. A most useful service is research, sometimes in cooperation with other bodies into particular areas of need and the convening of conferences in various parts of the country. It is possible to be on a mailing list (see 'Organisations Useful to the Language Teacher' in Part Four for address).

National Association of Language Advisers (NALA)

This association represents inspectors, advisers and advisory teachers in the United Kingdom. It serves to develop the expertise of its members and initiates research of interest in particular to language teaching in schools. It publishes guides and pamphlets and is active in collecting views of language teachers and presenting these to government and other decision-making bodies.

PART FOUR

Reference section

Acronyms

As in many fields, the language teaching world uses many acronyms. The following list gives all the common ones plus some of the lesser known examples.

AAPF	Assocation Allemande des Professeurs de Français
AATF	American Association of Teachers of French
ABH	Association of Hispanists of Great Britain and Ireland
ACE	Advisory Centre for Education
ACL	Association for Computer Assisted Learning
AEPE	Asociacion Europa de Profesores de Espanol
AFLS	Association of French Language Studies
AFMTLA	Australian Federation of Modern Language Teachers' Associations
AILA	Assocation Internationale de Linguistique Appliquée
ALL	Association for Language Learning
APEDAC	Association Pédagogique Européenne pour la Diffusion de l'Actualité
APLV	Association des Professeurs de Langues Vivantes
AS	Advanced Supplementary Level
ASM & CF	Association for the Study of Modern and Contemporary France
AT	Attainment Targets
AUPF	Association of University Professors of French and Heads of French Departments
BAAL	British Association for Applied Linguistics
BASIC	Beginners' All-Purpose Symbolic Instruction Code
BELC	Bureau pour l'Enseignement de la Langue et de la Civilisation Françaises
BERA	British Educational Research Association
BIS	British Italian Society
BOTB	British Overseas Trade Board
BUAS	British Universities' Association of Slavists
CAL	Computer Assisted Learning
CALL	Computer Assisted Language Learning
CATE	Council for the Accreditation of Teacher Education
CBEVE	Central Bureau for Educational Visits and Exchanges
CD-ROM	Compact Disc Read-Only Memory
CIEP	Centre International d'Études Pédagogiques de Sèvres
CILT	Centre for Information on Language Teaching
CIREEL	Centre d'Information et de Recherche pour l'Enseignement et l'Emploi des Langues
CNAA	Council for National Academic Awards
CNDP	Centre National de Documentation Pédagogique
COMAC	Comité d'Accueil
CPVE	Certificate for Pre-Vocational Education
CUTG	Conference of University Teachers of German in Great Britain and Ireland
DES	Department of Education and Science
DES	Diplome d'Études Supérieures
DEUG	Diplôme d'Études Universitaires Générales

DTI	Department of Training and Industry
EAT	European Association of Teachers
EC	European Community
ECU	European Currency Unit
EFVA	Educational Foundation for Visual Aids
ERA	Education Reform Act
ERASMUS	European Community Action Scheme for the Mobility of University Students
ESP	English for Special Purposes
ETA	Esperanto Teachers' Association
FIOCES	Fédération Internationale des Organisations Correspondances et d'Echanges Scolaires
FIPF	Fédération Internationale des Professeurs de Langues Vivantes
FLA	Foreign Language Assistant
FLAW	Foreign Languages at Work
FLIC	Foreign Languages for Industry and Commerce
GCSE	General Certificate of Secondary Education
GOML	Graded Objectives in Modern Languages
GREX	Graded Examinations
GTTR	Graduate Teacher Training Registry
HMI	Her Majesty's Inspectors
IATEFL	International Association of Teachers of English as a Foreign Language
IDV	Internationaler Deutschlehrerverband
INSET	In-Service Training
IoL	Institute of Linguists
IPA	International Phonetic Association
IPTS	Institut für Praxis und Theorie der Schule
ISBN	International Standard Book Number
IT	Information Technology
KS	Key Stage (in National Curriculum)
LEA	Local Education Authority
LMDU	Language Materials Development Unit (York)
MHRA	Modern Humanities Research Association
MLANI	Modern Language Association of Northern Ireland
NALA	National Association of Language Advisers
NAME	National Association for Multicultural Education
NATE	National Association for the Teaching of English
NCC	National Curriculum Council
NCET	National Council for Educational Technology
NCLE	National Congress on Languages in Education
NCML	National Council for Languages in Higher and Further Education
NCMTT	National Council for Mother Tongue Teaching
NFER	National Foundation for Educational Research
NPRA	Northern Partnership for Records of Achievement
OFINES	Oficina Internacional de Informacion y Observacion del Espanol
OMLAC	Oxfordshire Modern Language Achievement Certificate
OXPROD	Oxford Project on Diversification of First Foreign Language Teaching
PoS	Programmes of Study
PAD	Pädagogischer Austauschdienst
PGCE	Postgraduate Certificate in Education

284

QTS	Qualified Teacher Status
SALT	Scottish Association for Language Teaching
SBPF	Société Belge des Professeurs de Français
SCHML	Standing Conference for Heads of Modern Languages in Polytechnics and Other Colleges
SEAC	Schools Examinations and Assessment Council
SFS	Society for French Studies
SIS	Society for Italian Studies
SODEC	Service d'Orientation et de Documentation pour l'Enseignement de la Civilisation
SUFLRA	Scottish Universities French Language Research Association
TESOL	Teaching of English as a Second Language
TTNS	The Times Network System
TVEI	Technical and Vocational Education Initiative
UCCA	Universities Central Council on Admissions
UKCEE	United Kingdom Centre for European Education

Examination boards

Name/Address	Examination level
Associated Examining Board, Stag Hill House, Guildford, Surrey, GU2 5XJ	A; AS; GCSE
Cambridge University Local Examinations Syndicate, Syndicate Buildings, 1 Hills Road, Cambridge, CB1 2EU	A; AS; GCSE
East Anglian Examinations Board, The Lindens, Lexden Road, Colchester, Essex, CO3 3RL	GCSE
East Midlands Regional Examinations Board, Robins Wood House, Robins Wood Road, Nottingham, NG8 3NR	GCSE
Joint Matriculation Board, Manchester, M15 6EU	A; AS; GCSE
London Regional Examining Board, Lyon House, 104 Wandsworth High Street, London, SW18 4LF	GCSE
North West Regional Examinations Board, Orbit House, Albert Street, Eccles, Manchester, M30 0WL	GCSE
Northern Regional Examinations Board, Wheatfield Road, Westerhope, Newcastle upon Tyne, NE5 5JZ	GCSE

Oxford and Cambridge Schools Examinations Board,
Elsfield Way, Oxford, OX2 8EP
Brook House, 10 Trumpington Street, Cambridge   A: AS: GCSE

Southern Universities Joint Board,
Cotham Road, Cotham,
Bristol, BS6 6DD   GCSE

University of London Schools Examinations Board,
32 Russell Square,
London, WC1B 5DN   A; AS; GCSE

University of Oxford Delegacy of Local Examinations,
Ewart House, Ewart Place,
Banbury Road, Summertown,
Oxford, OX2 7BZ   A; AS; GCSE

Welsh Joint Education Committee,
245 Western Avenue,
Cardiff, CF5 2YX   A; AS; GCSE

West Midlands Examination Board,
Norfolk House, Smallbrook, Queensway,
Birmingham, B5 4NJ   GCSE

Yorkshire and Humberside Regional Examinations Board,
31/33 Springfield Avenue,
Harrogate, HG1 2HW   GCSE

The GCSE Boards are working in five groups as follows:

1 London and East Anglian Group: LEAG

2 Midland Examining Group: MEG

3 Northern Examining and Assessment Board: NEAB

4 Southern Examining Group: SEG

5 Welsh Joint Examinations Committee.

Other language examinations are held under the auspices of:

Business and Technical Education Council, BTEC, Central House, Upper Woburn Place, London, WC1H 0HH

City and Guilds of London Institute, 326 City Road, London, EC1V 2PT

London Chamber of Commerce Examinations Board, Marlowe House, Station Road, Sidcup, Kent, DA15 7BJ

RSA Exam Board, 8 John Adam Street, London WC2N 6EZ

The Institute of Linguists, 24a Highbury Grove, London N5 2EA

Organisations useful to the language teacher

Alliance Française (England and Wales)
Queensbury Place
London, SW7 2DN

Alliance Française (Ireland)
1 Kildare Street
Dublin, 2

Alliance Française (Scotland)
1 Lillybank Gardens
Glasgow, G12 8RZ

Anglo-German Association
2 Henrietta Street
London, WC2E 8PS

Anglo-Austrian Society
46 Queen Anne's Gate
London, SW1H 9AU

Anglo-Swiss Society
16 Montague Place
London, W1H 2BQ

Association for Language Learning
16 Regent Place
Rugby, CV21 2PN

Austrian Embassy
18 Belgrave Mews West
London, SW1X 8HU

Austrian Institute
28 Rutland Gate
London, SW7 1PQ

Austrian National Tourist Office
30 George Street
London, W1R 9FA

Belgian Embassy
103 Eaton Square
London, SW1 9AB

Belgium National Tourist Office
38 Dover Street
London, W1X 3RB

British-Italian Society
Kensington Palace Barracks,
Kensington Church Street
London, W8 4ET

British Association for Applied Linguistics
Department of Education
The University of Southampton
Southampton, SO9 5NH

British Overseas Trade Board
1 Victoria Street
London, SW1H 0ET

Bureau pour l'Enseignement de la Langue et
de la Civilisation Françaises (Le Français
dans le Monde)
9 Rue Lhomond, Paris 75005
France

Central Bureau for Educational Visits and
Exchanges (England and Wales)
Seymour Mews House, Seymour Mews,
Wigmore Street
London, W1H 9PE

Central Bureau for Educational Visits and
Exchanges (Scotland)
3 Bruntsfield Crescent
Edinburgh, EH10 4HD

Central Bureau for Educational Visits and
Exchanges (N. Ireland)
16 Malone Road
Belfast, BT9 5BN

Centre de Documentation Pédagogique
29 Rue d'Ulm
75230 Paris
Cedex 05

Centre for Information on Language
Teaching (CILT)
Regent's College,
Inner Circle, Regent's Park
London, NW1 4NS

City and Guilds of London Institute
326 City Road
London, EC1V 2PT

Commission of the European Communities
200 Rue de la Loi
1049, Brussels

Commission of the European Communities
(UK office)
8 Storey's Gate
London, SW1P 3AT

Council of Europe
67006, Strasbourg

Council of Europe
Documentation Centre for Education in
Europe, BP 431 R6, F-67006
Strasbourg, Cedex

Department of Education and Science
Sanctuary Buildings, Great Smith Street
London, SW1P 3BT

Department of Education and Science
Publications Centre
Canons Park, Honeypot Lane, Stanmore
Middx, HA7 4PT

**Department of Education for Northern
Ireland**
Rathgael House, Balloo Road
Bangor, Co. Down, BT19 2PR

Educational Foundation for Visual Aids
PO Box 566, 25 High Street
Maidenhead
Berks, SL6 1NP

European Association of Teachers
20 Brookfield, Highgate West Hill,
London, N6 6AS

European Parliament (UK Information
Office)
2 Queen Anne's Gate
London, SW1H 9AA

Federal German Republic Embassy
23 Belgrave Square
London, SW1X 8PZ

**Fédération Internationale des Professeurs
de Langues Vivantes**
Seestrasse 247
CH-8038, Zurich, Switzerland

Food and Wine from France
41 Piccadilly
London, W1V 9AJ

French Cultural Delegation
188 Oxford Road
Manchester, M13 9GP

French Embassy
58 Knightsbridge
London, SW1X 7JT

French Government Tourist Office
178 Piccadilly
London, W1V 0AL

French Railways
179 Piccadilly
London, W1V 0BA

German Food Centre Ltd
44–6 Knightsbridge
London, SW1X 7JN

German Language Centre
Hatfield Polytechnic
PO Box 109, Hatfield
Herts, AL10 9AB

German Tourist Office
61 Conduit Street
London, W1R 0EN

Goethe Institut (Glasgow)
3 Park Circus
Glasgow, G3 6AX

Goethe Institut (London)
50 Princes Gate
London, SW7 2PH

Goethe Institut (Manchester)
Ridgefield House
14 John Dalton Street
Manchester, M2 6JR

Goethe Institut (York)
Kings Manor, Exhibition Square
York, YO1 2EP

Graduate Teacher Training Registry
PO Box 239
Cheltenham, Glos, GL50 3SL

Great Britain-USSR Society
14 Grosvenor Place
London, SW1X 7HW

Hispanic and Luso-Brazilian Council
Canning House
2 Belgrave Square
London, SW1X 8JP

Institut Français d'Ecosse
13 Randolph Crescent
Edinburgh, EH3 7TT

Institut Français du Royaume Uni
17 Queensbury Place
London, SW7 2DT

Institute of Linguists
24a Highbury Grove
London, N5 2EA

Inter-Nationes Audiovisuelle Medien
Kennedyallee 91–303, D5300 Bonn 2
Germany

International Baccalaureate Office
18 Woburn Square
London, WC1H 0NS

Internationale Deutschlehrerverband
c/o Professor Karl Hyldgaard-Jenson
Eriksfaltsgaten 16a, S-214 Malmø
Sweden

Italian Embassy
14 Three Kings Yard
Davies Street
London, W1Y 2EH

Italian Institute
39 Belgrave Square
London, SW1X 8NX

Italian State Tourist Office
201 Regent Street
London, W1R 8AY

Lingua
c/o Central Bureau,
Seymour Mews House, Seymour Mews
London, W1H 9PE

Luxembourg Embassy
27 Wilton Crescent
London, SW1X 8SD

Luxembourg Tourist Office
26–7 Piccadilly
London, W1V 9PA

National Association for Language Advisers
c/o Association for Language Learning
16 Regent Place
Rugby, CV21 2PN

National Association for Teachers in Further and Higher Education
(Languages Section)
Hamilton House, Mabledon Place
London, WC1H 9HB

National Council for Educational Technology (NCET)
Sir William Lyons Road, Science Park
University of Warwick, Coventry,
CV4 7EZ

National Council for Mother Tongue Teaching
5 Musgrave Crescent
London, SW6 4PT

National Curriculum Council
Albion Wharf
25 Skeldergate
York, Y01 2XL

National Foundation for Educational Research
The Mere, Upton Park
Slough, SL1 2DQ

Portuguese Embassy
11 Belgrave Square
London, SW1X 8PP

Quebec Government –
Agent General in London
59 Pall Mall
London, SW1Y 5JH

Royal Society of Arts
Examinations Board
Progress House, Westwood Way
Coventry, CV4 8HS

Russian Embassy
18 Kensington Palace Gardens
London, W8 4QX

School Examinations and Assessment Council
Newcombe House, 45 Notting Hill Gate
London, W11 3JB

School Journey Association
  48 Cavendish Road, Clapham
  London, SW12 0DH

Scottish Education Department
  New St Andrews House
  St James Centre
  Edinburgh, EH1 3SY

Service d'Orientation et de Documentation
  pour l'Enseignement de la Civilisation
  (SODEC)
  Centre d'Etudes Pédagogiques
  1 Avenue Léon Journault
  Sèvres, 92310, France

Spanish Embassy
  24 Belgrave Square
  London, SW1X 8QA

Spanish Embassy Education Office
  20 Peele Street
  London, W8 7PD

Spanish Institute
  102 Eaton Square
  London, SW1 9AN

Spanish Tourist Office
  57–8, St James Street
  London, SW1A 1LD

Swiss Embassy
  16–18 Montague Place
  London, W1H 2BQ

Swiss Tourist Office
  Swiss Centre
  1 New Coventry Street
  London, W1V 3HG

The British Council
  10 Spring Gardens
  London, SW1A 2BN

United Kingdom Centre for European
  Education
  Seymour Mews House, Seymour Mews
  London, W1H 9PE

Welsh Office (DES)
  Cathays Park
  Cardiff, CF1 3NQ

Bibliography

Adams D *What Can I Do With a Foreign Language?* Association for Language Learning, 1989

Ahmad K *et al. Computers, Language Learning and Language Teaching.* Cambridge, 1985

Baer E *Teaching Languages: Ideas and Guidance for Teaching Languages with Adults.* BBC, 1976

Barley A *Making the Most of Audio.* CILT, 1990

Barnes D *From Communication to Curriculum.* Penguin Books, 1976

Barnes D *et al. Language, the Learner and the School.* Penguin Books, 1969

Beattie N *How to Pass A Level or AS Level in Modern Languages.* Association for Language Learning, 1988

Bird E (ed.) *Minority Community Languages in School.* CILT/NCLE, 1984

Bird E and Dennison M *Teaching GCSE Modern languages.* Hodder and Stoughton, 1987

Brown E (ed.) *Learning Languages with Technology.* NCET, 1988

Brumfitt C J and Johnson K (eds.) *The Communicative Approach to Modern Language Teaching.* Oxford University Press, 1979

Buckby M *et al. Graded Objectives and Tests for Modern Languages: An Evaluation.* University of York, 1981

Burstall C *Primary French in the Balance.* NFER, 1974

Central Bureau for Educational Visits and Exchanges *Study Holidays* (16th edn). CBEVE, 1988

CILT *Information Lists* (published on over 100 topics). Contact CILT for information

Crawshaw B E *et al. Jouez le Jeu.* John Murray, 1985

Crystal D *The Cambridge Encyclopedia of Language.* Cambridge University Press, 1989

Dakin D *The Language Laboratory and Language Learning.* Longman, 1973

Davidson J M C (ed.) *Issues in Language Education.* CILT/NCLE, 1981

Davis G and Higgins J J *Using Computers in Language Learning: A Teachers' Guide.* CILT, 1985

Davis P and Rinvolucri M *Dictation – New Methods, New Possibilities.* Cambridge University Press, 1988

DES *Modern Languages in the Comprehensive School.* HMI Matters for Discussion, 1977

DES *Departmental Organisation in Secondary Schools.* Welsh Office, 1984

DES *Modern Foreign Languages to 16.* HMSO, 1987

DES *The Education Reform Act.* HMSO, 1988

DES *Modern Languages in the School Curriculum: A Statement of Policy.* HMSO, 1988

DES *Long Courses.* Teachers' Branch, DES, London, annually

DES *Short Courses.* Teachers' Branch, DES, London, annually

Dickson, P and Lee B *Diversification of Foreign Languages in Schools.* NFER, 1990

Everard K B and Morris G *Effective School Management.* Harper Education, 1985

Filmer-Sankey C *A Study of Second-year Pupils' Attitudes Towards French, German and Spanish.* OXPROD (Oxford Univ. Dept. of Education), 1991

Fontier G and Le Cunff M *Guide de l'Assistant de Français.* Longman, 1975

Frémy D and Frémy M *Quid.* Robert Lafont, annually

Gathercole I *Autonomy in Language Learning* (Conference Papers). CILT, 1990

Gill P and Holly E *The German Assistants' Handbook.* Association for Language Learning, 1985

Green P (ed.)*The Language Laboratory in School*. Oliver and Boyd, 1975
Green P (ed.) *York Papers in Language Teaching*. University of York, 1985
Grellet F *Developing Reading Skills*. Cambridge University Press, 1981
Hadley E (ed.) *Teaching Practice and the Probationary Year*. Edward Arnold, 1982
Hall G *Records of Achievement: Issues and Practice*. Kogan Page, 1989
Halliwell S *Yes – But will they Behave?* CILT, 1991
Halliwell S and Jones B *On Target. Teaching in the Target Language*. CILT, 1991
Hantrais L *Using Languages in a Career*. Aston Modern Languages Club, 1985
Harding D H *The New Patterns of Language Teaching*. Longmans, 1967
Hares R J *Teaching French*. Hodder and Stoughton, 1979
Hawkins E W *Awareness of Language: An Introduction*. Cambridge University Press, 1984
Hawkins E W *Modern Languages in the Curriculum* (revised ed.). Cambridge University Press, 1987
Hewer S *Making the Most of IT Skills*. CILT, 1990
Hill B *Making the Most of Video*. CILT, 1990
Hill B *Making the Most of Satellites and Interactive Video*. CILT, 1991
HMI *A Survey of Pupils with Special Needs in Ordinary Schools 1988–89*. DES, 1989
Holmes B *Communication Reactivated*. CILT, 1991
Jesperson J O *How to Teach a Foreign Language* (first published 1901). Allen and Unwin, 1980
Johnstone *Communicative Interaction – A Guide for Language Teachers*. CILT, 1989
Jones B (ed.) *Using Authentic Resources in Teaching French*. CILT, 1984
Jones C and Fortescue S *Using Computers in the Language Classroom*. Longman, 1987
Jones K *Simulations in Language Teaching*. Cambridge, 1982
Kershook L *Schemes of Work*. CILT, 1990
King A *Degrees of Fluency* (Sixth-formers' guide to language degree courses). CILT, 1990
King L *Graded Objectives and TVEI*. CILT, 1989
Krashen S D *Principles and Practice in Second Language Acquisition*. Pergamon, 1982
Krashen S D and Terrell T *The Natural Approach: Language Acquisition in the Classroom*. Pergamon, 1983
Lee B and Dickson P *Assessment in Action*. NFER, 1989
Lee W R *Language Teaching Games and Contests* (2nd edn). Oxford University Press, 1982
Little D *et al. Learning Foreign Languages From Authentic Texts: Theory and Practice*. CILT, 1989
Littlewood W T *Communicative Language Teaching: An Introduction*. Oxford University Press, 1981
Littlewood W T *Language Teaching Methodology*. B.H. Blackwell, 1989
Lloyd-Jones R *How to Produce Better Worksheets*. Hutchinson, 1985
Lonergan J *Making the Most of Your Video Camera*. CILT, 1990
Lunt H M (ed.) *Communication Skills in Modern Languages*. CILT, 1982
Maley A and Duff A *Drama Techniques in Language Learning*. Cambridge University Press, 1982
Maley A, Duff A and Grellet F *The Mind's Eye*. Cambridge, 1981
Marland M *The Craft of the Classroom*. Heinemann, 1975
Marland M *Head of Department*. Heinemann, 1975
Marland M and Hill S *Departmental Management*. Heinemann, 1981
Matson M *DTP Seeds*. 4 Mation, 1990
McArthur T *A Foundation Course for Language Teachers*. Cambridge University Press,

1983

Mermet G *Francoscopie*. Larousse, 1985

Mitchell R *Communicative Language Teaching in Practice*. CILT, 1988

Morgan J and Rinovolucri M *Once Upon a Time: Using Stories in the Language Classroom*. Cambridge University Press, 1989

Morris D *The Head of Department: A Guide to Good Practice*. Association For Language Learning, 1984

Moys A *et al. Modern Language Examinations at 16+: a Critical Analysis*. CILT, 1980

Muckle J (ed.) *Russian in Schools*. Association of Teachers of Russian, 1982

Munby J *Communicative Syllabus Design*. Cambridge University Press, 1978

National Association of Language Advisers *Using the Foreign Language Assistant*. NALA/ALL, 1988, new edn, 1991

NCET *Guide to Logging on to Teletel*. NCET/MESU, 1988

Nunan D *Understanding Language Classrooms*. Prentice-Hall, 1989

Nuttall C *Teaching Reading Skills in a Foreign Language*. Heinemann, 1982

Oudet S *Guide to Correspondence in French*. Stanley Thornes, 1984

Page B and Hewett D *Languages Step by Step. Graded Objectives in the UK*. CILT, 1987

Partington J and Luker P *Teaching Modern Languages: A Teaching Skills Workbook*. Macmillan, 1984

Peck A *Language Teachers at Work*. Prentice-Hall, 1988

Perren G E (ed.) *The Space Between: English and Foreign Languages in School*. CILT, 1975

Phillips D (ed.) *Languages in Schools: From Complacency to Conviction*. CILT, 1987

Phillips D *Which Language? Diversification and the National Curriculum*. Hodder and Stoughton, 1989

Phillips D and Stencel V *The Second Foreign Language*. Hodder and Stoughton, 1983

Phillips D *et al. Occasional Papers on Diversification of First Foreign Language*. Univ. of Oxford Dept. of Education, 1988

Picken C (ed.) *The Translator's Handbook* (2nd edn). ASLIB. The Association for Information Management, 1989

Powell B *Boys, Girls and Languages in Schools*. CILT, 1986

Rees F *Languages for a Change: Diversifying Modern Language Provision in Schools*. NFER-Nelson, 1989

Rendall H *Making the Most of Micro-Computers*. CILT, 1991

Richards G (ed.) *Teaching Modern Languages*. Croom Helm, 1983

Rinvolucri M *Grammar Games*. Cambridge University Press, 1984

Rivers W *Teaching French*. Stanley Thornes, 1988

Rivers W *Teaching Spanish*. Stanley Thornes, 1988

Rivers W *et al. Teaching German*. Stanley Thornes, 1988

Rowlands D *Group Work in Modern Languages*. University of York, 1979

Sanderson D *Modern Language Teachers in Action. A Report on Classroom Practice*. University of York, 1982

SCHML *A Guide to Courses with Languages*. SCHML, annually

Sidwell D (ed.) *Teaching Languages to Adults*. CILT, 1984

Sinclair I *Desktop Publishing on a Shoestring*. BSP Professional Books, 1988

Smalley A *A Probationary Language Teacher's Handbook*. Association for Language Learning, 1990

Smith D G (ed.) *Teaching Languages in Today's Schools*. CILT, 1981

Stenhouse L *An Introduction to Curriculum Research and Development*. Heinemann,

1976

Stevick E *Teaching and Learning Languages*. Cambridge University Press, 1982

Swarbrick A *Reading for Pleasure in a Foreign Language*. CILT, 1990

Swatridge C *Sixth Sense: Studying Beyond GCSE*. Stanley Thornes, 1987

Thoroughgood J *Recording Progress*. CILT, 1990

The Training Agency (TVEI) *Educational Technology in Modern Language Teaching*. The Training Agency (TVEI), 1990

Trim J L M *Minority Community Languages in Schools*. CILT/NCLE, 1980

Ur P *Discussions that Work*. Cambridge University Press, 1981

Ur P *Teaching Listening Comprehension*. Cambridge University Press, 1984

Various *Educational Authorities Directory and Annual*. School Government Publishing Co. Ltd, annually

Various *Education Year Book*. Longman, annually

Walker R and Addleman C *A Guide to Classroom Observation*. Methuen, 1975

Weiss F *Jeux et Activités Communicatives*. Hachette, 1983

Widdowson H G *Teaching Language as Communication*. Oxford University Press, 1978

Wilcox G *Dial Search*. 1990

Wright A *1000 Pictures for Teachers to Copy*. Collins, 1984

Wright A, Betteridge D and Buckby M *Games for Language Learning*. Cambridge University Press 1984

Wringe C *The Effective Teaching of Modern Languages*. Longman, 1989

Index